The Pagan Temptation

by
THOMAS MOLNAR

WILLIAM B. EERDMANS PUBLISHING COMPANY
GRAND RAPIDS, MICHIGAN

Uxori dilectissimae

Copyright © 1987 by Wm. B. Eerdmans Publishing Co.
255 Jefferson Ave. S.E., Grand Rapids, Mich. 49503

All rights reserved

Printed in the United States of America

Library of Congress Cataloging-in-Publication Data

Molnar, Thomas Steven.
    The pagan temptation.
    1. Christianity and culture. 2. Civilization,
Christian. 3. Myth. 4. Symbolism. 5. Paganism.
6. Occult sciences — Religious aspects — Christianity.
    7. Civilization, Modern — 1950-   . I. Title.
    BR115.C8M64   1987   261.2   87-8898

ISBN 0-8028-0261-1

Contents

	Introduction	1
1	The Pagan-Christian Conflict	5
2	The Pagan Revival	51
3	The Christian Desacralization	80
4	Neopaganism	110
5	The New Occult	146
6	From Christianity to Paganism	170
7	The Desacralization of Christianity	185
	Index of Names	197

*To the Memory
of my Mother*

Introduction

Many serious thinkers and scholars would not register dissent if confronted with the statement that the Western world has entered a period of grave crisis, possibly even decay. Hesitation and doubt about such a diagnosis begin only when it is added that Christianity might share this fate. Christianity—the Christian religion, church, and civilization—has not only been an organic part of the West for two thousand years; it has also shaped the West to a far greater extent than has any other intellectual movement, institution, or network of symbols. Moreover, Christianity qua religion and church has a divine guarantor; it is, unlike many other creeds in human history that have declined and vanished, supposed to end only with the end of humanity. For this reason, many are reluctant to concede that Christianity is endangered. Others, on the other hand, regard the decline of Christianity as a fait accompli. And some go even further, seeing the restoration of the West as dependent upon a radical dechristianization in which Christianity will be replaced by some ideology (e.g., Marxism or secular humanism) or by repaganization.

The proponents of the latter view, whom we will call the neopagans, while not having the political importance of Marxists or secular humanists, present an attractive alternative for those who are hostile to, or tired of, Christianity. Their analysis, like those of other ideologies, possesses a partial truth, a certain coherence, and a perspective based on a historical interpretation that is not easy to refute. Though this analysis does not constitute a compelling argument, its elements deserve careful consideration, and, what is more, agreement on a number of points.

Christianity, the neopagans argue, has become a rationalistic religion and has consequently deanimated and desacralized the cosmos. But it did not stop there; it even turned its rational quest against itself. In the process Christianity discredited the element of the sacred and the myth elements on which religion—any religion—relies to give believers a coherent worldview and symbology. While Christian civilization allowed the arts to flourish and granted the freedom for knowledge and science to thrive (precisely because it had eliminated the daemons from the material universe), it undermined religiosity: it concentrated the sacred in a distant God and left to the human world nothing but the profane. If God jealously claims all that is good and perfect and saintly, nothing remains to this world; nature, legend, art, and the political community all become desacralized, easy prey to ideology.

This, in a nutshell, is the neopagan argument, which I will examine in greater detail on the following pages and will accord the justice it deserves. Not only neopaganism but also the "new occult" is of essential interest to a cultured elite; and I shall devote attention to the latter and its growing popularity as well. The two, usually appearing in combination to challenge the Christian worldview, are today much more than a fashion; they present themselves as constitutive elements of a civilization to be based on a post-Christian worldview.

It seems indeed that a new civilization is emerging in today's spiritual vacuum, described earlier as decadence. Christianity is not only a prodigious edifice claiming to represent the totality of human aspirations; it has also been a guarantor of equilibrium for society, counterbalancing the horizontal interactions of people and community with a vertical interaction with God. Yet this equilibrium at times seems to be decaying, and the experience of our contemporaries with Christianity has been a baffling and confusing one including the desacralization of the liturgy, the removal of cultic symbols, the jettisoning of a fixed, awe-inspiring language, and a general demythologization of Christ and of the origins of Christianity.

To many believers and to interested bystanders these things seem, not parts of a salutary reform, but a servile imitation of modern utilitarian, materialist, and pleasure-seeking society. While the center of Christian worship, the celebration of the Lord's Supper, is deserted by disappointed believers, religious leaders the world over address themselves less to the soul-trying problem of salvation than to political reform, the energy crisis, worker participation in management, and other issues for which they lack competence, and in so doing they discredit their redemptive mission to mankind.

This is indeed desacralization. Yet even though I later make the point that the "pagan temptation" is never very far from a civilization organized by the Christian religion (indeed, this is my very thesis), this does not mean surrender to the pagan and the occult. This is because the neopagan analysis, sophisticated and subtle as it is, makes one decisive error: it regards the Christian religion as spent and exhausted, trapped in the supposed contradiction between an omnipotent and perfect God and powerless, pitiable humanity. It ignores the magnificent tension that this contradiction creates in human souls, a tension infinitely more precious than what paganism and the occult promise: deified humanity with a cooled-off soul, no longer touched by God. The neopagan analysis selects from Christianity only those elements serving its purpose; and its attack, like those of other ideologies, is only partially successful. Christian truth remains vast and powerful enough to confound it.

CHAPTER 1

The Pagan-Christian Conflict

THE CONFLICT

It is difficult to imagine today the novelty that the emergence of the religion of Jesus Christ represented at the high noon of Hellenistic-Roman civilization. In the beginning, Christianity was regarded merely as one of the many Eastern cults that had been penetrating Rome and other imperial cities since the third century B.C. against which the decrees of the Republic and later imperial governments proved ineffective. All things considered, the generalization that Christianity was just another sect or an offshoot of Judaism served its cause because Rome was not really hostile to Eastern religions. Roman religious imagination was too narrow to weigh what was at stake, and the government thought that by establishing a pantheon in which the deities of all subject peoples were gathered, both the peoples and their gods might be neutralized and Roman dominion over them consolidated.

It has been the assumption not only of the Romans but of many political authorities throughout history that if the gods of the conquered could be removed from their native soil and sanctuaries and transferred to the conquerors' capital, they would lose their efficacy and their protective power over their original worshipers. Remember Pompey's fury and disbelief when, stepping into the sacred chamber of Jerusalem's synagogue and expecting to find there an idol—a donkey head, as the malicious had suggested—he found nothing. Yahweh, a spiritual being, was not a divinity that the gross imagination of the Romans could assimilate, either in their system of belief or in their pantheon. In the case of Jesus they could at least focus on a "crucified mendicant prophet" as the fountainhead of the new cult; yet they still suspected that at their secret ceremonies the Christians worshiped a strange and repulsive idol.

In Roman eyes, Christianity was to share the fate of Judaism—it was considered a mere subclass of a despised and troublesome tribal faith. Yet the new religion arrived with credentials that gradually lifted it from classification with Judaism and established it as a rival not only of the Eastern sects but also of three other competitors: the myriad cults of the Mediterranean shores, the philosophies that originated in Hellas,[1] and the Roman state religion.

The literature dealing with the success of Christianity is, of course, extensive, and the theories attempting to explain it range from the economic to the spiritual. Yet—and this may be surprising—very little has been written about a related phenomenon that ought to have struck many historians and other scholars: the spiritual and intellectual devastation that the victory of the new religion brought to the entire Mediterranean basin, a devastation in two clearly discernible areas, the *mass cult* and *elite culture*.

Let us be more specific about these occurrences, the significance of which is hardly measurable. Any movement invading a new territory—whether it be an armed invasion, a more lasting territorial conquest, or the triumphant penetration of art, literature, and speculation—tends to abolish, displace, neutralize, or convert to its own uses the many beliefs, symbols, attitudes, and myths it encounters. But Christianity found before its conquering religious fervor the greatest civilization ever elaborated—stretching from Brittany and Gaul to the Middle East and including large parts of Africa and, through Alexander's conquests, Iran and India. This empire was not only geographically but also historically imposing; the civilization that we call Hellenic, later Hellenistic, then Ro-

---

1. By "Hellas" one should understand the following areas, not only politically, but also in regard to the origin and spread of the Hellenic speculative systems: Ionia (the west coast of Asia Minor), continental Greece, Magna Graecia (southern Italy), and Sicily, as well as the islands west of Cyprus to Sicily.

The Pagan-Christian Conflict 7

man looked back at the time of Christianity's emergence to a history of about a millennium and a half, if we take into account recognizable origins and influences. The vastness of the area and the length of its duration are such that we can select only the main lines of influence to show the essential features of the mass cult and elite culture with which Christianity had to cope and finally overcome, either by assimilation or by suppression.

The dynamism that the Christian religion displayed from its beginning does not mean that it remained free from pagan admixture. In fact, its partial roots in the regional myths and cults—without which it would have been a wholly alien import and perhaps would have been rejected—may be reckoned as a strength of the new religion. The extraordinary potency and universality of the Orphic myth,[2] for example, made it possible for early Christian artists to represent Christ as sharing certain features with Orpheus. The various cults of the Mother Goddess—Demeter in Hellas, Isis in Egypt, and Ashtarte in the Middle East—certainly helped to foster the acceptance of the veneration of the virgin Mary as the mother of God.[3] Paul, too, when trying to clarify the mystery of Christ, had recourse to comparisons not only with such great and universally known mysteries as those celebrated at Eleusis but also with the local cults he found during his journey through Asia Minor.

But generally the church clashed with the pagan cults, myths, and mysteries. Their resulting suppression had incalculable consequences, unapparent at the time but becoming evident in certain subsequent periods. The myths and cults that we mistakenly call ancient or archaic, and often primitive, irrational, and unscientific, cannot truly be considered dead relics of a past age. Since the nineteenth century, a variety of scholarly disciplines has been revealing the universality and universal validity of these myths, and in recent decades scholars have concluded that the permanent

---

2. The myths about the descent into Hades of a mortal man or a semi-divine hero on a rescue mission or to learn a dreadful secret include not only Orpheus's descent in search of Eurydice, but also the imitation travels through the underworld of both Odysseus and Dante.

3. See note 10 to Chapter 3, which makes the point that this veneration also represented a threat to doctrinal purity.

human psychocultural and spiritual substratum is invariably articulated in such myths.

In later chapters we shall see that as a consequence of its conquest, Christianity has lost imagination and cultural vision that roughly parallels the gains it made in other respects—a loss not only because of the suppression of the sacred symbols with which people had lived, but also because of the form of that suppression: Christian doctrine demythologized human imagination and the soul's harmony with nature and the cosmos.[4] Even though it replaced them with an impressive system of its own, combining religion, philosophy, and universal vision, it also prepared the way for an exclusively rationalist explanation of the mysteries of humanity and nature. This rational system built on Christian foundations resulted in the drying up of the souls of modern people—deprived of the support that myth and mystery once provided, they were left to their own narrowly rationalist devices, which made them extremely vulnerable in the face of psychological and cultural upheavals.

Archaic or ancient people were able to personify the forces around and inside them, and thus to integrate themselves with a vast world in which they were not necessarily the privileged focus and in which they had to fight hard, psychologically and through their cults, in order to win peace. Their position in the world was far from exalted; in fact, it was the lowest rank in the cosmic and divine hierarchy. But at least they *knew* that they occupied a definite position. It was precisely this that made the world intelligible from their point of view and that made the human condition stable; it confirmed the daily experience of having to maneuver among potentially hostile forces.

Christianity, however, dedaemonized the cosmos: it denied the existence of the supernatural daemons between the gods and humans and left a vast rift between the realms of the human and the divine. Humanity thus lost its moorings in a cosmic hierarchy, and the cosmos ceased to be an orderly and compact totality. In dissolving the popular pagan worldview, Christianity disoriented the world's inhabitants. Indeed, it did something more radical. By eliminating from the cosmos the elements that once both frightened and reassured people, by laying the foundations for the scien-

4. See below, Chapters 3 and 7.

tific worldview, Christianity prepared the way for a desacralized universe and, ultimately, a dehumanized one. The danger was evident: if the Christian religion should at any time show doctrinal or cultural weakness, or if rationalism should gain the speculative upper hand, humans would have lost their spiritual home. And in such a case they would have only one recourse—a return to their earlier mythical worldview.[5]

Let us examine first how the arrival of Christianity affected the mass cults in the Roman world, as well as in some other areas as the triumphant religion penetrated into Africa, South America, and Asia.

The new religion, and the cosmology, ethics, and rational propositions inseparable from it, appeared in a world in which myths and cults formed a vast substratum of extrarational explanations of the place of humanity and the gods in the universe and of their mutual relationship. There are dozens of broad themes common to these universal myths, and beyond these there are many hundreds of local variations.[6] Here we can offer only a few examples; yet those given are illustrative of pre-Christian forms of thought and symbolization.

1. The myth of death and rebirth recounted, for example, in the Eleusian mystery in which Persephone is taken by force to the underworld by Pluto. According to popular interpretation, this myth exemplified the life of the seed from sowing time to harvest, yet a rich imagination made it symbolic of many processes of maturation, including the spiritual.

2. The mother's mourning of her son's death and her rejoicing at his resurrection. Related to the previous form (as Demeter despaired over the loss of Persephone), this has examples in the myth

---

5. Further on, I show that the historical content of the Christian beginnings—the story of Jesus as told in the Gospels—is an inadequate substitute for the pagan myth. (It was factual, not subject to embellishments by poets and mystagogues, and it was attackable by rationalist exegetes.)

6. The vast literature pertaining to this subject has been developed in the works of a number of modern scholars: Mircea Eliade, Otto Kern, Walter Wili, Paul Schmitt, Walter Otto, Carl Kerényi, Erwin Rhode, Hans Leisegang, Henri-Charles Puech, Henry Corbin, Gerardus van der Leeuw, and many others.

of Isis's mourning of Osiris, in the myth of Ashtarte's grief over the death of Adonis, and, naturally, in the Christian Mater Dolorosa.

3. The hero who fights the forces of chaos until he establishes order and becomes ruler. Illustrations include the Mesopotamian Gilgamesh epic and the war of Zeus against the Titans whom he strikes down with celestial fire. This myth form often pictures the combat as involving a sea monster,[7] which represents chaos, and symbolizes carving out an orderly, ultimately humanized land from the surrounding disorder.

4. The foundation myth illustrating the notion and experience of the community's beginning through ritual events that are henceforth deeply engraved in the collective memory. Examples include Romulus's slaying of his brother Remus, who defied him and crossed the wall of Rome, still only a furrow, and also Cain's slaying of Abel, which symbolized the transition from a pastoral to an agricultural form of life and the establishment of stable settlements. Strength is lent to these myths by the periodic reenactment of the foundation rite, which imprints on the citizens' minds the importance and sacred character of the community.

5. Initiation rites. "In secret cults all over the world, the novice is placed in painful and oppressive situations, tormented and ridiculed. He resists; but when he surrenders, his defeat is only apparent, for a resurrection follows."[8] Examples of initiation rites are found among shamans in northern Siberia, among American Indians, and among the islanders of the South Pacific.

6. Solar myths, in which all peoples of the world have shared, from the Aztecs, who offered their prisoners' hearts to the deity, to Emperor Julian, the pagan revivalist in fourth-century Rome. A Persian version was that of the god Mithra, whose worship was especially popular among the Roman legions.

7. The myth of the soul's migration through several incarnations until it is so purified that it may go to the Elysian Fields, nirvana, or union with the deity.

8. The myth of humanization. In the cult of the Cabiri at

---

7. The aquatic element may also be indicated by a serpent. In one Christian variation, St. George slays a dragon.

8. See Carl Kerényi, "The Mysteries of the Kabeiroi," translated by Ralph Manheim, in *The Mysteries*, vol. 2 of *Papers from the Eranos Yearbooks*, edited by Joseph Campbell, Bollingen Series no. 30 (New York: Pantheon, 1955), p. 56.

The Pagan-Christian Conflict

Samothrace, for example, men were represented as grotesque dwarfs who could be brought to a higher realization through feminine influence. According to Carl Kerényi, "Women elevated the warlike, death-dealing men to the function, the dignity, the consciousness of the source of life."[9] Through the Orphic mystery, this idea penetrated not only the pagan world but Christianity as well. A late echo may be found in the medieval Provençal cult of chivalry, and an even later one in Goethe's *Faust*, which credits the "eternally feminine" *(das ewig Weibliche)* with drawing man upward to noble deeds.

9. The myth of dark and light, ecstasy and restraint. A transparent indication of this is the Dionysian mystery cult, which entered from Thrace into Hellas as far as Attica and Delphi, in which Dionysus, profiting from Apollo's absence, takes over the oracle. This myth was later resurrected by Nietzsche in "The Birth of Tragedy," in which he distinguishes between Dionysian passion and Apollonian serenity.

All these myths, translated into, or rather born in and with, their cultic expression, suggest an extremely rich sacral existence in pre-Christian times. Much has been written about the "mythical consciousness," and much effort spent, from Lucien Lévy-Bruhl to René Girard, from Sir James Frazer to Joseph Campbell, to understand the "myth-making" mentality. It may be said that mythic thinking necessitates a concept of time that does not distinguish past and present but rather puts on the same level both what happened then—*in illo tempore*—and what happens now, both filled with an always identical content. As an example, foundation rites, when reenacted in the sacred time of the present—made sacred because the rites re-presented and re-performed the original act of foundation—were events that never completely ceased and were never entirely of the present. They recurred, and this very periodicity—always the same rite, at the same time, in the same place—lifted them onto a plane of reality other than the profane.[10]

---

9. Ibid., pp. 58-59.

10. Compare to this "sacred time" our modern desacralized time, which permits holidays to be held only on Mondays so as to prolong the weekends of a work-weary populace. Recently, American bishops asked their dioceses whether a similar displacement of Catholic holidays would meet the approval of the worshipers. We may thus measure the difference between "sacred

If we study the general significance of these myths from the point of view of the people's understanding of life, we find that they are concerned with everything important in human existence: birth and death, life in community, the process of maturation, the genealogy of the gods, the fertility of nature and human beings, the relation of soul and body, and so on. Since the myth is always accompanied by a corresponding cult or cults which may congregate in mysteries (such as the Eleusian, the Orphic, the Mithraic), those who lived in the belief of those myths necessarily lived under religious systems of an overarching importance. Thus for pre-Christian people, and for those still living under a pre-Christian mode of existence (or at least under a mode of existence that combines some elements of tribal-archaic life-styles with elements of modernity), most aspects of existence were and are permeated by the sacred.

In contrast, when modern people mention religion, they have in mind an increasingly marginalized and isolated segment of life reserved for certain acts, gestures, and convictions. In addition, as if they were embarrassed, they try to give a rational explanation to this domain. Yet it is somewhat superficial to attribute this crucial aspect of pre-Christian existence to a "primitive mentality," as Lévy-Bruhl does,[11] or to a "prerational stage" when man "did not yet feel himself to be the originator of his own decisions," as Walter Wili does.[12]

As the studies of Marcel Detienne and Jean-Paul Vernant, Walter Otto, and E. R. Dodds show, even the highly rational Greeks had an "irrational" side to their worldview, something that seems to be an indispensable ingredient in the exercise of rational judgment.[13] Indeed, as C. G. Jung writes in commenting on a Taoist

---

time," in which paradigmatic events, places, and periods are held and are met with awe, and the utilitarian concept of time, in which the work-and-leisure rhythm of industrial society has the overriding validity.

11. See Lucien Lévy-Bruhl, *Primitive Mentality*, translated by Lillian A. Clare (1923; reprint, New York: AMS Press, 1976).

12. Walter Wili, "The Orphic Mysteries and the Greek Spirit," translated by Ralph Manheim, in *Mysteries*, edited by Joseph Campbell, p. 65.

13. See Marcel Detienne and Jean-Paul Vernant, *Cunning Intelligence in Greek Culture and Society*, translated by Janet Lloyd (Atlantic Highlands, N.J.: Humanities, 1978); Walter Otto, *Dionysus, Myth, and Cult*, translated by

text, in myth we are dealing with a consciousness that, though not Western itself, is just as valid as Western thought forms. Its presence is obvious in Plato's lifework. In the seventh letter, in which he informs his Athenian circle of the shallowness of the progress in learning of his friend, the Syracusan tyrant Dionysius, he states: "One cannot express in words the ultimate vision [gained through philosophy]; after a long elaboration of thought it suddenly comes to light like fire, then it will feed on itself" (341D). In other words, *logos* (the rational discourse) could not be what it is without *mythos*, the extrarational. After Plato, Augustine, in Christian language, formulated this truth best: "credo ut intelligam" (I believe in order that I may understand).

Once we recognize (with Plato, Goethe, Jung, and Eliade) that myth, as understood at the apex of its meaning, is inseparable from rational thought, we may measure the loss that resulted from its suppression and weakening by Christianity. There is no question that the early Christian thinkers, the later missionaries, and even fanatical monks—all of whom at various times engaged in the wholesale destruction of manuscripts, monuments, shrines, and other cultic places and the suppression of non-Christian practices—acted in good faith and in the interest of the new religion. They wanted to save souls—a more important endeavor, obviously, than preserving stones and dead letters. It is also true that in the later imperial period pagan religion hardly defended itself: it seemed to be resigned to its defeat by the younger, more vigorous, rival. Nevertheless, we may say in retrospect, although not without necessary reservations, that the change from the pagan, mythic-cultic worldview to the Christian worldview implied serious losses, and hence involved the risk of unbalancing the psychic and spiritual domain.

First, the reservations. As I said earlier, the "wisdom of history" demands that conquering worldviews—and they conquer because they carry a new and more insistent affirmation of life, of truth, of human organization—sweep away the old realities and creeds that obstruct their progress. A good (and here pertinent) illustration

---

Robert B. Palmer (Bloomington: Indiana University Press, 1965); and E. R. Dodds, *The Greeks and the Irrational*, Sather Classical Lectures no. 25 (Berkeley and Los Angeles: University of California Press, 1951).

may be the controversy in the Roman Senate (A.D. 384) about the statue of Victory. The conservative senators, headed by Symmachus, insisted on reerecting the statue, but the project was strongly opposed by Ambrose, the bishop of Milan. The conflict was finally resolved by the Emperor Theodosius with the curt argument that the money that the restoration would require was needed for the army and the protection of the empire's borders. Thus religious and financial considerations got the better of traditional (pagan) piety.

The student of late pagan Rome sees many proofs of the exhaustion of the old cults and cannot but concede the overall beneficial effect of the Christian transformation. But this should not keep him from measuring the loss involved in that transformation. In spite of the new religion's continuities with the old, it introduced a radically new understanding of the world and had little in common with traditional, local beliefs. The old rites had provided natural (astral, agricultural, animistic) explanations for millennia-old observations and experiences, explanations that served as spiritual protection for largely tribal societies. More important, they mixed the rational with the existential, thus bringing to people the feeling that they participated, for better or worse, in natural events that had a "human" side, a personal involvement, through the influence of gods, spirits, chthonian forces, or heavenly beings.

Two further illustrations may serve to underline the difference between the traditional (tribal, cultic, mythic) view and the Christian view (and, by extension, the rational, individual, and modern view).

Ursula Lamb writes apropos of the Spanish occupation of Mexico that before the conquest, the Aztecs had been accustomed to fear and respect the ruler and the priest, and to spend practically every moment of their lives in dependence on idols and sacred practices. When the Spaniards converted them, however, even though they did not understand the change intellectually, they very rapidly became accustomed to new religious practices, particularly to confession, which brought them back to the habit of always consulting the priests and the statues of the holy ones (here, the saints). Yet at the same time they became more sinful. Asked why, an Indian put it this way: "[In former times] no one did his own free will, but what he was ordered to do, and . . . now

The Pagan-Christian Conflict

our great liberty has done us harm, for we are obliged to fear and respect no one."[14]

The second illustration is from Vanuatu in Oceania,[15] where until recently intertribal wars were conducted with great ferocity but always according to a code that also brought periodic peace and intercommunal celebrations: nocturnal rites, bacchanals, and the immolation of pigs. The *tokar*, as this truce festivity is called, was not quite peace; it was rather a continuation of the war by other means, in which the sacrificed animals were substitutes for the warriors who remained alive. But it was at least a long truce. When the missionaries came and attempted to put an end to the tribal wars and enforce civil peace, the violence continued nonetheless—but without the code of truce to periodically interrupt it and limit its damages. Now it is the missionary-trained Christian militias that hunt down the recalcitrant "men of the dark forests" and inflict severe punishment on them. These are still tribal wars of a sort, since the tribal divisions have often not been blunted by time. But now there is no *tokar* to institute peace.

In both the Aztec and the Vanuatuan view of the universe and humanity, one notes the complete sacralization of existence, the juxtaposition and succession of codes of conduct—codes not only for humans, but also for the gods, whose behavior may be similarly predicted, calculated, influenced, and determined by the correct (codified) application of rites and ceremonies, themselves derived from the myth and at one with it. The myth, then, is the paradigm that orders human existence, and since it orders the life of the universe and of nature too, people know exactly where they stand in regard to the totality of existence. As Yves Vadé writes, one should "imagine between the life of man and that of nature a kind of permanent link, a common substratum and mediating agency."[16] This may be water and its symbol, the serpent, but it may be other substances as well, as early Greek speculation sug-

---

14. Cited in Ursula Lamb, "Religious Conflicts in the Conquest of Mexico," *Journal of the History of Ideas* 17 (October 1956): 538n.33.
15. See J. C. Guillebaud's record of a contemporary study tour to Oceania, *Un voyage en Océanie* (Paris: Éditions du Seuil, 1980).
16. Yves Vadé, "Sur la maternité du chêne et de la pierre," *Revue de l'Histoire des Religions*, 191 (1977): 37.

gests: air, fire, the earth itself, even wood and stone. All these substances refer back to a superior power, the real subject of worship.

The poetic insight of D. H. Lawrence captured very directly the processes of the pagan cult, and he made some useful distinctions between the Greek view of myth and mythic rites (which remained intellectualistic even in their spontaneity) and the view of myths held by Mexican Indians, for example. The Greek gods, Lawrence writes, were the witnesses of and the audience for the ceremonies performed in their honor—and this led to the creation of the theater, the place par excellence of impersonation.[17] It is different with the Indians because they do not regard themselves as created by a god external to themselves. All is divine: the god is part of the world-all as are the trees, the rivers, the sky, the animals, and the Indians themselves. Lawrence describes the corn dance and the bear dance in which the participants do not *represent* gods and natural forces but *are* gods and nature. The Indians are even closer to nature than the pagans of the Mediterranean are, for the Indian rites are not mere performances; rather, their rites create an event, they *are* creation in the making.[18]

It is not far from the truth to say, then, that pagan mythology is generally pantheistic, the religious belief that C. S. Lewis called humanity's natural religion. The earliest manifestations of Greek philosophy show a pantheistic tendency, and Thales spoke of the world in which "all are gods"—an indication that polytheism is a variety of pantheism and that the gods are aspects of the world, which thus becomes easier to deal with. If Dionysus represents a mad world and Apollo an orderly one, we may view their conflict as symbolizing the temptation of excess and its just-as-necesary counterpart sobriety, as the two clash and intermingle.[19] For these

17. The mask worn by the actors was called a *persona*.
18. D. H. Lawrence, *Mornings in Mexico* (London: Secker, 1927), pp. 113-15. In his interpretation, Lawrence may have yielded to his own "nature religion," but the pantheism that he attributes to the Indians of Mexico is a universal phenomenon, regardless of whether in this particular instance he overstresses it or not.
19. See Otto, *Dionysus, Myth, and Cult*, p. 136: "The visage of every true god is the visage of the world. There can be a god who is mad only if there is a mad world which reveals itself through him. Where is this world? Can we still

reasons, some form of polytheism is inseparable from pagan mass cults, which establish through it a true reflection of the human condition and, as we saw before, the protection of self and community.

In their respective ways, Jung, Kerényi, Bronislaw Malinowski, and René Girard all agree that myth provides a prophylaxis: it is a moral agent endowing the community with an identity and a set of positive and negative choices. At issue is the cementing together of the tribe, which, in Girard's description, would fall victim to inner conflict if it did not possess a greater-than-life *story*, vividly showing the price paid for cohesion in the sacred time of the past.[20] Before Girard, Jung noted that not only does myth represent the psychic life of the community, it *is* the psychic life of the community, and the primitive tribe would disintegrate if it lost its mythological heritage. The loss, Jung adds, is a "moral catastrophe."[21]

Girard goes even further when he extends the meaning of the myth to religion itself and argues that "the sole purpose of religion is to prevent the recurrence of reciprocal violence."[22] In this manner, as several authors point out, myth is the entire psychic and spiritual life of the community, and the way it is told—that is, the language of the myth—is the community's self-identification. Malinowski sums it up thus:

These stories live not by idle interest, not as fictitious or even as true narratives; but are to the natives a statement of a primeval, greater, and more relevant reality, by which the present life, fates, and activities of mankind are determined, the knowledge of which supplies man with the motive for ritual and moral actions, as well as with indications as to how to perform them.[23]

---

find it? Can we appreciate its nature? For this no one can help us but the god himself."

20. See René Girard, *Violence and the Sacred*, translated by Patrick Gregory (Baltimore: Johns Hopkins University Press, 1977).
21. C. G. Jung and C. Kerényi, "The Psychology of the Child Archetype," in *Essays on a Science of Mythology*, translated by R. F. C. Hull, Bollingen Series no. 22 (Princeton: Princeton University Press, 1969), p. 73.
22. Girard, *Violence and the Sacred*, p. 55.
23. Bronislaw Malinowski, *Myth in Primitive Psychology* (Westport, Conn: Negro Universities Press, 1971), p. 30.

Myth, then, is the spiritual motivating force of a cosmic vision in which the intramundane gods hold sway. As such it reflects a world in which the nearness of the divine requires of human beings a spontaneous, immediate language—the cultic language. In that case, the dominance of myth over the soul might be interpreted as an early phase of history, and the coming of Christianity might be considered a new phase, the phase of the extracosmic, unique God, no longer a dweller in humanity's world but a distant creator of the universe.

The mythic view is characterized by its stability, even more by its conservatism. The myth is not really supposed to save people, but merely to offer them protection against forces and powers that must endlessly be propitiated but whose nature and influence remain unchanged. True, chaos is sometimes overcome through the efforts of the hero, but it is always there, like the Titans overcome by Zeus who still retain an effective influence on humanity (in the Orphic mystery). The conservatism—some might say pessimism—of the myth accounts for the fact that pagans generally subscribe to the cyclical view of history. Indeed, only a doctrine of Eternal Return is compatible with the mythic view, in which there is no progress of the individual or of the community since every one of the great realities of existence remains fixed in its primordial form, as the mythical themes listed earlier indicate by their unvarying features.

It would be hazardous, however, to state that the mythic-cultic view of reality corresponds only to a certain phase of history, the pre-Christian phase. Even if we put matters that categorically, we must admit that with a weakening of the hold Christianity has had on the Western mind and imagination, and even on the Western concept of myth, the myth might reappear in its earlier or in a modified, modernized form. In fact, that is the thesis of this work: the "pagan temptation" is never very far from a civilization organized around the Christian religion. Why this is so will become clearer, I hope, by the end of this chapter, when the discussion of the Christian answer to the pagan-mythic worldview will articulate the points and the junctures at which Christianity confronts, not always successfully, the ever-present pagan imagination. But before turning to the Christian answer, we must leave the subject of the mass cults of the pagans to focus on their elite culture.

The Pagan Sage

Though we know the elite culture reliably only in the Greco-Roman world, we have an adequate knowledge of mass cults there and also in many other parts of the world. This may help illuminate the place of elite culture in those areas as well. Through the work of archaeologists, ethnographers, mythologists, and other scholars who began to study them about a century and a half ago, popular cults and myths are yielding their secrets. Since that time, and with the help of psychology, philology, and the study of symbols, an enormous amount of material has come to the attention of modern scholarship, material now sufficiently organized to permit us to draw some conclusions. We still lack, however, data about how pagan elites thought—we cannot yet enter the minds of the Aztec or Egyptian priests or the mystagogues of the Hellenic mysteries. When we meet the thought of such men as Pythagoras, who was decisively influenced by the Orphic mystery and possibly by others, we are not dealing with a cultic priest but with a philosopher—a member of the elite culture. But we have no way of measuring the gap between the thought of the priest and that of the philosopher.

Let us focus on the representatives of the Greco-Roman elite culture and on the impact that emerging and expanding Christianity had on their class. At the time of the emergence of Christianity in the first and second centuries, the many speculative systems of Hellas had been well examined, so that only the most brilliant and vigorous survived: the systems of Plato, Aristotle (often mixed with Stoic teachings, since Aristotle, like the Stoics, taught that the cosmos is divine), the Stoics, the Epicureans, the Cynics, and the Skeptics. Each school had its Roman representatives, mostly in the person of such distinguished epigones as Cicero (follower of Plato), Seneca (follower of the Stoics), and Lucretius (follower of the Epicureans). These men, some of them deeply cultured, created no original speculation and cannot really be called philosophers if by the term we understand the Hellenic prototype: thinkers who propose an original ontology, epistemology, ethics, and politics.

The Greek and, even more, the Roman publics were impatient with detailed and well-rounded systems of thought, with elaborate philosophies. They favored either brilliant summaries (such as the *De rerum natura* of Lucretius and the various Platonizing dialogues and treatises of Cicero) or the aphoristic approach (such as that of Seneca or Marcus Aurelius). This latter style, and the mentality that dictated it, was more adequate for a different type of wisdom—for practical wisdom, a mixture of moral precepts, social criticism, and a resigned, pessimistic approach to the human condition—than it was for a complete philosophy.

Plato too had been repelled by the impossibility of reforming the human character, but he distinguished between philosophic minds capable of reaching Socratic insights and the pedestrian mentality of the majority of the populace, which can nonetheless be maintained at a tolerable level of moral health by a skillfully organized system of education and by a political regime combining the features of what we today would distinguish as church and state. In other words, Plato's vision, despite the corruption of politics he had witnessed in the Syracusan tyranny and in the democracy of Athens, was able to embrace universal considerations about humanity, the state, the nature of the gods, and the overarching significance of the Good, beyond sense experience and the interplay of interests.

After Plato, it was impossible to maintain this universal speculative vision, partly because Aristotle seems to have exhausted all available knowledge within the Hellenic framework and partly because the situation and the people's consciousness was drastically modified as the result of vast changes in political and ideological perspective. As a consequence, philosophy directed itself away from grandiose and coherent doctrines toward meditation about the place of the individual. And even then, the concern was no longer the place of individuals in the cosmos but rather their place in the midst of the chaotic conditions of tumultuous centuries and historic upheavals.

The state of affairs then emerging reminds one of the transition from the Catholic Middle Ages to the religiously pluralistic centuries of the Reformation. Philosophically, the first period had seen the great summations—those of Aquinas, Bonaventure, Duns Scotus, and Ockham—while the following period, caught between gigantic forces and thus spiritually confused, produced thinkers whose wisdom consisted of prudent eclecticism and speculative self-protection and whose style was aphoristic, unable to sustain any speculative vigor because of the lack of positive and solid convictions. Montaigne comes to mind along with Erasmus and many other humanists. Science would soon displace their timid efforts at formulating *une morale provisoire* (a provisional morality—Descartes); and the systems produced by rationalism—those of Gassendi, Descartes, and Spinoza—were merely competing auxiliaries of the scientific enterprise and method.[24]

The impoverishment of philosophy in the approximately four centuries around the birth of Christ—from about 200 B.C. to A.D. 180—gave rise to a sort of "pagan wisdom," which was mature by the time Christianity came into existence. Christianity was unable to substantially change the presuppositions of elite culture and this pagan wisdom until the end of pagan times in the fourth century.

The nature of these presuppositions is not easy to reduce to a common denominator since, despite the penchant of the age for syncretism, the origins of this new wisdom were very diverse, including Epicurean materialism and agnosticism, Stoic belief in a world-soul, Cynic contempt for the world and society, Plutarchan Platonism, and the mysticism of Apollonius of Tyana—the whole to be crowned, even if not synthesized, by the moral precepts of Seneca and Marcus Aurelius, the two most characteristic figures. But precisely because the age was so eclectic philosophically, and at the same time so impatient for "how to" solutions, pagan wisdom does present itself to us as a possible unity.

Whether the materialism of Lucretius or the Stoicism of Seneca, pagan speculation tended to lock the individual inside a limited and hostile universe from which there was only one escape route: wisdom, according to the wise man (*sapiens*, sage). It is a fact that no part of the Greek philosophy—or of the Roman that followed it—ever came to terms with the idea of integrating all people into the sapiential commonwealth: Greek philosophy remained forever

---

24. We should note that the Cartesian thesis was a way of helping the changeover from the Aristotelian to the modern (Galilean) worldview. Descartes—but Galileo before him—opted for the geometric descriptiveness of the sublunar world, in contrast to the Aristotelian view that geometry was valid only as a description of celestial, pure forms. Descartes thus contributed to the "homogenization" of space, displacing Aristotle's notion of a qualitative hierarchy. On the entire problem, see Alexandre Koyré, *Etudes d'histoire de la pensée scientifique* (Paris: Gallimard, 1973).

an elitist speculation in which the philosophic soul was regarded as the endowment of only a few exceptional men, and the teaching of wisdom was reserved to exceptional disciples.

From Plato to Plotinus it was held as axiomatic that souls dwell eternally in a kind of divine-royal court. Their descent into and participation in the material and human world was either inexplicable or explained as a punishment—at any rate it was a plunge from the One to the multiple. Thus the best human beings are the contemplatives, fixing their eyes nostalgically on the home their souls had left. As a consequence, Greek systematizers never ceased classifying souls according to the degree of their purity (immateriality), and only the highest category was judged as able and worthy to reach the ultimate vision of the Good.

Plato himself was of the opinion that the Supreme Being was hard to find and impossible to describe to the brutish minds of the masses, who had to be content with the visible gods, the heavenly bodies. Such doctrines were the most potent factors promoting the success of the Eastern cults with their readiness to initiate any and all. They especially lie behind the success of Christianity, which taught that every soul (brilliantly or modestly endowed, belonging to an emperor or to a slave) is created by God and is equally dear to him. Over against pagan elitism the "democracy" of the Eastern cults, including Christianity, was understandably popular.

However, the concept of the sage as distinct from the philosopher was accentuated with growing uncertainty and instability in the world. First, the feelings of stability were shaken in the two centuries preceding the birth of Christ as the Republic's leading figures and triumvirates struggled for the control of the empire. Then followed several monstrous emperors whose horror-filled reigns are recorded in the pages of Juvenal, Tacitus, Suetonius, and even Seneca himself. The elite were able to live through these times—about four centuries—only by taking the path of the sage, that is, either by physically retiring to country estates or by morally withdrawing into themselves and teaching this attitude to others by example.

What was the content of this wisdom? What kind of a man was the *sapiens?* The several centuries during which this wisdom and the concept of the sage were in the process of elaboration brought forth a variety of doctrinal ingredients. First of all, there was a cosmogony stressing the immutability and eternity of the universe, which thereby became a mechanism indifferent to the living as the gods themselves were distant and uncaring. Since time too was eternal, and thus everything that was to happen in the universe had already happened, the endlessly recurring time cycles were merely repeating the same events, the same people, the same arrangements. Nothing was or could be new; the universe was old, although ageless, and all things were worn down.

The clumsy Epicurean-Lucretian attempt to account for variety is philosophically unacceptable. From this school came the theory of the *clinamen*, the idea that atoms continually arrange and rearrange themselves in random patterns and thus form an ever-changing array of new and unexpected objects thanks to their fortuitous agglomeration. But this theory is instantly refuted by the simple observation that animals and human beings, as well as the objects of the inanimate world, present themselves in virtually unchanging shapes throughout the ages—a rock resembles another rock, not a bird; the offspring looks like the parent; and even hybridization has narrow limits.

In this basically unchanging universe and ever-repeated history (which is really not history since nothing new happens and human freedom, insofar as one may speak of it, exhausts itself not in making *history* but in seeking detachment), the highest ideal for humanity is conformity to the universal law of self-withdrawal. Augustine understood this dreadful resignation well when he warned Christians not to fall prey to the cyclical or circular *(circuitus)* view of life taught in his time by the Neoplatonists but to accept the *via recta*, the linear view, which accounts for novelty in the world brought about by God's coauthor, free-willing man. "We do not want to walk in a circle with them," he admonished readers of *The City of God*. True, the pagans also saw the untenable nature of this position. Long before Pythagoras they had been tempted by the Brahmanic theory of metempsychosis, the soul's migration through an infinity of bodies, which provided an answer to the everyday experience of change and renewal. But even so, the migration of souls had no impact on collective history; it only served the infinitely slow purification of the individual soul from earthly temptations and appetites.

The aspiration of the sage, then, was very different, not only from that of the Christian in general and the saint in particular, but even from the ideal of classical Greek philosophy. Socrates never ceased teaching the best way to become good men and showed with his death that there is full compatibility—even more, an obligatory relationship—between being good men and being good citizens. For Aristotle, the contemplatives possess the highest attainable virtue, but they have acquired it through participation in community life. They are political animals because they are beings of reason—which is basically the Socratic message as well. The entire philosophic passion of Plato is marshaled in the story of the cave in the *Republic*. Here the wise man is also the pedagogue, not resting until he tells his foolish fellows that outside the cave, in which they see only the shadows of shadows, there is a world of real objects, and then a world yet higher, the beatific vision.

None of these reflections was seen as viable and valid by the pagan elite of Christian times, although many quoted their philosophic ancestors and paid sincere compliments to the depth of their insights. Naturally there were pagan *sapientes* who were also exemplary, or at least active, leaders in public affairs—Cicero, Pliny, Plutarch, and Marcus Aurelius come readily to mind. We may remember others as well, mostly Stoics, who showed great courage in facing the emperors, courage to the death in defending the interests of a class, of an institution, of the empire itself, and of justice. But theoretically the ideal of the pagan sages was conformity to the divine model of detachment: to become a god even in life, that is, to be unaffected by human passions and vicissitudes.

The speculative foundations of this attitude and ideal are more elaborate and older than they appear at first sight; they are in fact deeply rooted in pre-Christian pagan concepts. I will take the two most directly influential teachings, Epicureanism and Stoicism, as my point of departure, I will then look farther back to yet older doctrines, and finally I will look forward once more, as far as Plotinus. This approach reveals the core of pagan wisdom, and the period under consideration shows itself as typical. Subsequently, it will become easier to measure the novelty of the ideas Christianity introduced and to evidence their break with pagan speculation as far more important than their continuity with it.

In certain respects, Epicurus was a disciple of Plato, insofar as it was the older philosopher who had cleared Olympus, and thus mythology, of its anthropomorphic elements. For a long time, the Greek intellectual elite had found it scandalous that the Homeric stories, from which generations had derived poetic delight as well as their formal education, should be regarded as true. They were about promiscuous, vengeful, and otherwise passion-filled gods and goddesses. It was Plato who first cleansed the heavens of these deities and pointed to the real God beyond sense experience and intellection.

As often happens, a subtle teaching was radically reinterpreted; where Plato suggested that God can be reached by a "kind of spiritual contact which transcends understanding,"[25] Epicurus concluded that the universe contains only matter and void, and that human beings, their intelligence and volition, are an accident of organic life. Although purposive beings, humans are the product of a nonpurposive nature—in other words, of chance. This is the well-known essence of materialist systems, from Epicurus to the present, proceeding through a series of non sequiturs and speculative hiatuses.

In fear of the consequences of teaching atheism in a still-pious society, Epicurus recommended in the *Letter to Menoikeus* that his disciples keep the core of the doctrine secret and that they act according to the prevailing mores: "Let us sacrifice reverently and properly where it is required, and let us do everything properly in accordance with the laws, not distressing ourselves over popular opinions in matters regarded as the highest and the most solemn." In this letter he explicitly enjoins his circle of friends to hold in public that God is a living being, immortal and blissful, for such is the common conception of mankind. But at the same time, behind the public disguise, he encouraged scientific study even more daring and more modern than what Aristotle had authorized in the matter: Epicurus proposed the study of celestial bodies as "agglomerates of fire"—in other words, as neither divine beings nor material bodies moved by divine beings.

The Epicurean sages are, then, withdrawn from the world, not merely because they intend to pursue their studies undisturbed by hostile scrutiny,[26] but also because their own thinking recognizes

---

25. The expression quoted here is from A. J. Festugière, *Epicurus and His Gods*, translated by C. W. Chilton (Oxford: Basil Blackwell, 1955), p. 5.
26. This withdrawal from scrutiny was the personal strategy of many thinkers apprehensive about popular opinion. Descartes's watchword was *"larvatus prodeo,"* which can be translated as "I go about wearing a mask."

no meaning in the universe. Everything is matter and void; the eternal ideas and divine reason are absurdities. Only corporeal reason—that is, human intelligence—is left. Yet not even reason can establish direct contact with reality. Reason is active only because the sensations stimulate it, which leaves the senses as the only criteria for judgment. Action thus precedes thought.

What is of interest here is the physical-ontological justification for the sages' choice, because from it follows their ethical and political attitudes. If the universe is a product of chance and no higher purpose prevails in it than the fortuitous shuffling of atoms in the vacuum, and if even intelligence is a "corporeal reason" exercised in the same way muscles are exercised, then, after the sages have satisfied their intellectual curiosity, the best strategy for them is indeed to cultivate, undisturbed, their gardens and minds. They do not become gods because there are none; but by doing what the universe is doing they are as close to the status of pure inquiring intellect as it is possible to be. And in a godless universe, *this* is the supreme status.

What I have just described is a pattern of thought that will also be found, with variations, in most other pagan speculative systems. One more ingredient will make them complete: the thesis that matter is uncreated and evil, the great obstacle in the way of God (if the system recognizes such a being) and in the path of human intellectual and moral detachment. Matter, then, is regarded as the opposite of God, equal to him or even greater in power, and thus absolutely evil. All the great philosophers of Greece believed this—Plato included—with the exception of Aristotle (and the materialists, of course).[27]

This belief is the great flaw in Greek thought, and we must realize how deeply embedded it was if we are to understand the revolutionary impact of the Christian teaching about the Incarnation. For pagan thinkers the Incarnation was nothing less than a scandal. The closest they came to such a concept, but with a purely negative connotation, is the teaching of Pythagoras and Empedocles that souls fallen from the divine estate are subse-

---

27. "The vision of the one eternal, passionless Spirit, far removed from the world of chance and change and earthly soilure, was the conquest of Greek philosophy, travailing for 800 years." See Samuel Dill, *Roman Society from Nero to Marcus Aurelius* (London and New York: Macmillan, 1925), p. 419.

quently incarnated in animal forms as a punishment. But it was inconceivable that God, the spiritual being par excellence, should assume materiality[28]—a thought as distasteful to their contemporaries as the idea of creation ex nihilo, which meant that matter too was God's creation and did not preexist creation as a separate and evil principle.

As our image of the pagan sage slowly takes form, we begin to see that their wisdom involved mainly insistence on exclusive intellectuality and rejection of appetites, passions, and ordinary worldly interests. The Epicurean view was that the sage's intelligence was supposed to be impassionately directed at purely intellectual comprehension, just as much as is needed for self-protection against involvement in mundane matters.

At first sight, the Stoic sages were more human than the Epicurean, since they possessed a more rounded physics and cosmology and therefore a wider moral view. The Stoic sages do speak of God, not in order to hide their real opinions, but because they find him everywhere—though more like an all-permeating gas than an all-sustaining personal providence. The existence of this God, however, is ascertained in human beings only by a feeling of reassurance, not by any positive injunctions emanating from a personal and conscious agent. In short, God is universal reason, or, as the Stoics put it, universal fire, part of which is everyone's share, as it is the share of everything else as well. This explains the Stoic belief that all things are in communication with and will ultimately rejoin the universal spirit-reason-fire, which may be called God or Zeus. This teaching of the way to wisdom is essential to paganism, and it has antecedents long before Greek philosophy.

One of the intriguing tasks of scholarship in this area is to examine the exact nature of the relationship and influence between the

---

28. There are typical reactions to the idea of the Incarnation in such pagan intellectuals as Porphyry, disciple and biographer of Plotinus, and Arnobius. "How can one admit," asks Porphyry in *Against the Christians* (frag. 77), "that the divine should become an embryo, that after his birth he is put in swaddling clothes, that he is soiled with blood and bile, and worse things yet?" And Arnobius writes in *Adversus nationes* (2.37): "If souls were of the Lord's race, they would permanently dwell in the king's court, without ever leaving that place of beatitude. . . . They would never come to these terrestrial places where they inhabit opaque bodies and are mixed with humors and blood, in receptacles of excrement, in vases of urine."

Hindu-Brahmanic Eastern doctrines and Greek philosophy—and, even more, that between the Eastern doctrines and Hellenistic, that is, post-Alexandrian, philosophy. We have abundant material, researched and published by Henri-Charles Puech, about spiritual developments in the last centuries of the empire—about Indian, Persian, Egyptian, Syrian, and other influences on Gnosticism and Manichaeism. For the earlier Eastern influence on Pythagoras and Plato, however, we have only conjectures. At any rate, the Greek world had no reliable knowledge about the East until Alexander's conquest of vast territories stretching to the Indian subcontinent. Yet the great teachings must have penetrated somehow, unless we assume that there was already a kind of harmony, a common religious ideology, between Upanishadic and Greek wisdom.

As can be expected, there is a considerable difference of degree between the two. The Brahmanic sage, because he has overcome the individuating principle, is more thoroughly immersed in the world-all than his rationalist Greek counterpart. But the similarity between the two doctrines of wisdom is obvious. The Upanishads teach that the fall of the souls, particles of a totality, into bodies is a cosmic rupture and a state of misery for the separated souls, because in the body they become limited and divided into individuals, fragments of the whole. Individuals say: "I am such and such, this thing is mine." They distinguish themselves and become part of a network of separate existences.

The aspiration of these unfortunate souls[29] is to be reabsorbed in the world-all in order to surmount the evil of personal existence. In the Brahmanic and Buddhist Orient, this reabsorption is achieved through initiation into the secret doctrine, reserved for the elite, and through the ascetic method of purification: detachment from the senses, from worldly involvement, and even from intellectual stimulation. The sages looks inside themselves in order to become one with the Absolute, but in the process they give up the notions of elementary morality, since they are no longer interested in other people and the world around them. They are indeed

---

29. This may be the origin of the Hegelian concept of the "misery of consciousness" and of the Marxist concept of "alienation." The soul was born elsewhere (*allogenes*, in Greek Gnostic literature) and is now in exile from its real home.

"beyond good and evil"; absorption in the Absolute cancels and replaces all human preoccupations.

Claude Tresmontant compares with a luminous clarity the teachings of the Upanishads and of Christianity. He writes that the Christian tradition establishes a personal and moral relation between the transcendent Absolute and the human being, whereas the Upanishads prompt the sage to overcome the illusion of personal existence as well as the ethical demands that follow from it.[30] This is, of course, the extreme form of the sage's withdrawal, but it shows that the attitude of the sage (and we can extend the analysis to the Greek sage as well, although mitigated by an altogether different cultural milieu) is ultimately motivated by a counterontology, a denial of the real world. The world is an illusion, and the illusion itself is the result of a fall from the Absolute (absolute nothingness, for the Oriental sage; the One, for Plotinus and other Greeks) into a veiled existence. It is understandably urgent that this existence be terminated and that, in the meantime, its demands be reduced to a minimum.

With only few exceptions, found among the Greek philosophers of the classical age, pagan wisdom emphasized these features: namely, that individuation is a source of suffering because it is the consequence of a fall of the soul into a material body, really a tomb.[31] The soul itself is not a unique thing, let alone God-created. It is rather a mere particle of the Absolute, detached and drifting for reasons hard to clarify but variously ascribed to "desire," "temptation," or a vague "discontent." The aspiration of the sage to return has nothing to do with the Christian soul's desire for salvation. In Christian teaching the individual soul will rise to a state of contemplation, the beatific vision. The pagan sages in contrast expect to be liberated from the burden of individuality; their spirit *(pneuma)* will be reintegrated with the Absolute.

For the pagans, the burden of personhood is difficult to carry since in the entire universe only the sage is endowed with thinking, and thinking too is a symptom of the fallen, individuated state. In the Hebrew and Christian religions God is the most active thinker;

---

30. Claude Tresmontant, *La Métaphysique du Christianisme et la naissance de la philosophie chrétienne: Problèmes de la création et de l'anthropologie des origines à saint Augustin* (Paris: Éditions du Seuil, 1961), p. 265.

31. "Body" in Greek is *soma;* "tomb" is *sema.*

he conceives and plans creation, witnesses and admonishes, judges and pardons. But in the pagan systems the "spirit" is not personal; it is not an anthropomorphic god. Its characteristic qualification, from the Brahmans to Plotinus, is that it is One. Thus the spirit does not think; it merely is. Thought, reflection, and discursive reason entered the world through humanity and are marked with the seal of sin, evil, and the Fall. The products of thought are mere illusion, and they encumber the universe, which aspires to calm. The ideal of the sage in this evil world is contemplation, which is not active reflection or reasoned thought but a state of tranquility in which humans let themselves be suffused by the vanity of things and of being—and in the last stages, by nothingness.[32]

Whether the Greeks learned their formulas of wisdom from the East cannot be reliably established. But their ideal was often similar to that of the East. Pythagoras, who was closest to the Oriental doctrine, taught that the human soul is a daemonic, immortal being, cast down from divine heights and confined for its punishment within, yet with no real relationship with, the body. Similarly, Plato writes in the *Phaedrus* that the soul, tempted by the appetitive impulse, falls from its home and loses its cognitive faculty. It is Plato's genius that he did not stop at this desolate conclusion but elaborated (in the *Meno*, among other dialogues) the theory of anamnesis—even in the body, the soul can be reawakened; it is able to relearn what it knew in its blessed state. How else could a slave boy follow the Socratic demonstration? Anamnesis opens the door of reason and serves as a bridge, which other pagan sages dared not cross, from the soul's alienation in this world of the senses to its capacity to assume the body and plunge into the surrounding world.

But Plato was the great exception. His philosopher is still very much the sage who thinks only of the soul's salvation and has only contempt for passions, interests, "ships and harbors, city walls and taxes," and for practical affairs in general, including the affairs of the state, which is "corrupt and founded on deception." At the same time, Plato reflected at great length on how the philosophers

---

32. One might say that this state is the opposite of Christian mysticism because the latter stimulates positive actions and charity. See the example of the great mystics, Paul, John of the Cross, Francis, Teresa of Avila, and others.

could still share the preoccupations of their fellow citizens—not as experts in this or that, but as members of society concerned with the supreme well-being of the community as a whole, that is, with justice. As he states in the *Republic*, when it comes to dealing with practical, earthly matters, those who possess the highest virtue, philosophy, will have all the others added to it.

This was, however, a unique and ingenious compromise, an exception, not the rule among the wise men. The increasingly evil political conditions during those four centuries around the birth of Christ, especially the decay that thickened from about 100 B.C. to A.D. 100, provided further motives for withdrawal and a search for personal tranquility. The protection and cure of the soul became the first consideration, and the weakening speculative power sought no metaphysical justification. Even in Seneca, who stands out in an age of approaching mediocrity, eclecticism prevailed. In various writings of Seneca we find different views of God: as the creator of the universe, but also as incorporeal reason, an all-permeating divine breath, or an immutable chain of interlinked causation. The central concern for Seneca and for his contemporaries and successors is the moral life—not of the ordinary citizen, however, but of the one who aspires to the supreme wisdom.

As a consequence, the irresistible tendency of pagan speculation to depreciate the world and to exalt the self-seeking spirit was, if anything, strengthened during the last centuries of struggling and already agonizing paganism. If one may speak of a new element in this time, it was a cheapening of the solution for which the sage had been looking. The question was how to establish a link between the distant divine and those who suffer here in the world in the prison of the flesh. It was not an altogether new question, but it was now put more urgently than before since earlier Greek thought was now nearly submerged in the flood of Eastern sects and systems, which brought with them their crude recipes for salvation. Not even the severest decrees of the emperors were able to drive out the astrologers, necromancers, diviners, and various one-man oracles. The population thus had its imported cults, but the more demanding elite clamored for a religion that would be neither the system of Mithra or Serapis nor one presenting an impossibly radical break with Greek philosophy.

What they found was yet another new version of the old, not satisfactory to increasingly tortured minds. On the one hand, there came about a religious revival of sorts, the chief elements of which were the ideas of Pythagoras and Plato, but now less in a philosophic than in a religious garb. On the other hand, there was a proliferation of magic and occult systems, based mostly on daemonology—the belief in the daemons, supernatural beings intermediate between the gods and humans. The two combined in what Samuel Dill calls a "pagan theology," through the elaboration of "a celestial hierarchy in which the Deity, removed to an infinite distance, was remotely linked to humanity by a graduated scale of inferior spiritual beings, daemons, and heroes."[33] Later, these daemons were turned by the church into the "bad daemons" opposed to Christ and his angels. For the still-pagan world, the good and evil spirits at least filled the gap between the aloof deity and suffering humanity, the beginning of a religion in the new, Christian, sense.

Although one cannot say that this situation prepared the way for a monotheistic approach to religion, and even less for the victory of Christianity, it is a historic fact that the process of dissolution had begun for the hard core of paganism. The process hardly affected philosophy, the tenets of which were vigorously affirmed by epigones from Celsus to Julian, and, in a much more nuanced fashion, by the last great pagan sage, Plotinus.

Celsus belongs to another part of this chapter, since his reputation rests on the fact that it was he, of all late Romans, who for the first time and most systematically opposed the Christian religion whose literature he knew quite well. It is thus even more significant that the basic features of pagan wisdom are also present in his anti-Christian tract, in which he pursues altogether different objectives. Celsus speaks of evil and sin as inherent in matter, of man as incidental to the universe, of God as "never irritated by men as he is never irritated by monkeys or flies," and of the fate of each being as absolutely determined. His is Lucretian determinism, the foundation stone of Roman elite culture, which we thus find still asserted at the end of the second century, although by this time it is most often mixed with Pythagorean Eastern speculative elements.

This mixture shows the tremendous effort of thinkers in the late imperial period to come to terms with a new religious worldview

---

33. Dill, *Roman Society from Nero to Marcus Aurelius*, p. 459.

by transforming the philosophical enterprise into an auxiliary of religious speculation rather than allowing it to remain a hindrance. Seneca, Marcus Aurelius, and Epictetus, as well as such secondary thinkers as Plutarch, Maximus of Tyre, and Apollonius of Tyana, all show a speculative and quasi-religious effort to break through pagan presuppositions. In the absence of a philosophical genius (until Plotinus), the moral intelligence shows prodigious advances in breaking the intellectualist seal with which pagan thought is generally, and at times monotonously, stamped. However, to expect a breakthrough is less than fair when we consider Plotinus's teaching. As is the case with all geniuses, not only did he come close to effecting the expected radical change, but even his failure to do so is instructive—as if he passed by the last opportunity to say the decisive word.

Plotinus had advantages that others lacked. By the time he left the school of Ammonius Saccas in Alexandria and formed his own in Rome, the great battle had been joined between an increasingly self-assertive Christianity and the Gnostic movements that radicalized both Christian doctrines (in the direction of heresies) and the doctrines of Greek wisdom. And there were other paradoxes as well. Christians were still jailed when found out and were sometimes rounded up to be fed to the beasts in the circus. But at the same time, they were welcomed in many households, their writings scrutinized with an intrigued curiosity, and their thinkers (among them the Church Fathers) accepted as worthy discussion partners. In the early years of the third century, the emperor Alexander Severus had in his private chapel an image of Christ, next to those of Abraham, Orpheus, and Mithra, as a great and respected religious teacher.

Plotinus knew of the Christian teaching and had studied it, and he was well-acquainted with the Gnostic theses, upheld around him everywhere from the marketplace to the schools. Irenaeus tells us that places where discussions were held were teeming with Gnostic disputants, one more vehement than the other, and that each sect leader tried not only to outduel the others every morning with a new and startling theory, but also to take recruits away from competitors.

Plotinus did battle against the Gnostics, whom he reproached for their belief that one can leave the human condition at will and join God "on the wings of dreams." And indeed the Gnostics were radical Greek sages, more directly influenced by the Eastern systems than other sages were. They believed that the world is the creation of the devil, who holds the good God in bondage, and that the Gnostics or Pneumatics *(pneumatikoi)* possess the secret of escaping this evil world so as to be reunited with the divine substance. The average Gnostic teacher, as one would expect, was thus mostly concerned with the description of the "escape route," the avoidance of the *archontes* (guardians) and the *aiōnes* (powerful forces), who secure the rule of the evil prince, the dēmiourgos, and prevent the rise of the soul.

The leaders of the Gnostic movement—Valentinus, Basilides, Arnobius, and others—propounded a more grandiose design, the essence of which was the old scheme: the sage (here called the *pneumatikos*, the depository of the spiritual or divine particle) despises the world (a material entity, the devil's work), withdraws even from procreation since it only produces more of earthly life, and focuses on efforts to end his exile and liberate his part of the spirit through death, and before that through self-torture and asceticism.[34]

This is a caricature of the sage, but it is significant that even in such a degraded version the concept and the ideal remained unchanged. Plotinus is not comparable to his Gnostic adversaries; his teaching is the crowning speculative glory of a no-longer speculative age. Yet it culminates in just another expression of traditional wisdom. In truth, we may speak of a regression if we compare Plotinus with his deeply admired master, Plato. Plato was on the verge of recognizing a personal God, but Plotinus was unable to conceive of anything other than the impersonal, abstract One, above intellect and the Good, locked up inside nonqualification.

Plotinus must have been aware, surrounded as he was by salvation systems genuine and cheap, that it is not impossible for the human mind to postulate a being not only immortal, but also alive, personal, and creative. Nonetheless, the Greek in him could not find the link between the One and the Nous (the divine reason or intelligence) to which creation, or, rather, emanation, is entrusted. Emanation may be described as a forced and ultimately unex-

---

34. Through a logical inversion of the motive of asceticism, many Gnostics abandoned themselves to obscene sexual gratification, arguing that since the spirit is safe in its purity, the body, contemptible as it is, cannot affect it.

plained productivity, without love, the result of which is a series of distillations—humanity ends up somewhere on the descending ladder, and the material world on the lowest rung.

Perhaps because Plotinus's style is so soft and high-flying—no longer the vigorous style of the Greek classics—we are able to discern more clearly the central flaw of Greek thought. The first cause, the *archē*, must as the One be so far removed and confined that it is impossible for it to be the source of the many. Furthermore, the One must also be beyond thinking; otherwise it would contain multiple forms. Thus, as in all philosophers in the Platonic tradition, there are in Plotinus two breaks in the system: between the One and the Nous,[35] and between the Nous and the chain of being.

But we may also speak of a third break, by which Plotinus looked to Hinduism, with which his thought had natural affinities and which had influenced him directly (he had enrolled in the army of Emperor Gordian, doing battle in Parthia, in order to encounter Persian and Indian wisdom). For in the end, according to Plotinus, the chain of being—which is borrowed, not generously given by a personal God—is reabsorbed into the One. The cosmic drama is over; the ladder is pulled up. All that happens below is without meaning because the individual self is not really expanded while separated from the One. Joseph Katz calls Plotinus, perhaps too severely, "a Gnostic *manqué*" since it is the divine spark, a Gnostic notion, that enables the self to be reunited with the One. But the supreme part of the psyche had never even left it.[36]

There are noble and beautiful texts in the writings of Plotinus that reveal him not only as a sage but also as a mystic aspiring to be united with God. Yet the meticulous critique of Marcel de Corte detected the flaw. The Plotinian sage is so thirsty for union with the Totality that he purges himself of body, of morality, of all the "accretions" to his pure self, thus preparing for the encounter with the supremely pure One. The faults he committed were not his.

---

35. The One engenders the *Nous* by "turning to face and contemplate itself."
36. Joseph Katz, "Plotinus and the Gnostics," *Journal of the History of Ideas* 15 (April 1954): 289.

They had no real being but were only matter of a sort that stuck to the pure self.[37]

In other words, the Plotinian sages, like the others of the pagan world, detach themselves from the world in their rush toward reabsorption; they do not recognize the imperfections of the human state. For them, "salvation is not to be achieved. It is achieved. For its realization it is enough that the individual should become conscious of what he is already in his inmost nature, where Intellect which is beyond the virtues identifies itself with true being and with the idea which one forms of the self, of the world, and of God."[38] There is no becoming, no history. De Corte summed it up thus: For Plotinus

the real man is not the flesh-and-blood creature, or the reasoning man who seizes things from the outside only. The real man is intelligible man whose steely eyes review, without damage, the infinity of his own being since "infinity is to be found in intelligence," since "to possess oneself is to possess all things. . . ." Intelligible man is the universal man; anything that particularizes him into this or that man is a mere addition of non-being.[39]

Admittedly, such a status is not very different from the divine, and Plotinus did indeed express this ambiguity when he wrote that "to be attached to the One is to be God."[40] Book One of the *Enneads* is liberally studded with passages in which the distinction between the sage and the divine is blurred: The sage lives at the highest peak of himself, lending to the inferior levels only the scantiest attention, just enough to preserve life. The moral effort is no longer a struggle, it is rather a victorious flight. The sage does not live the human life, even if he possesses some social virtues; in truth, he has left this life, having chosen the divine life. The true man is pure of all that touches upon animality; he possesses the contemplative

37. See Marcel de Corte, *Aristote et Plotin* (Paris: Desclée de Brouwer, 1935), p. 222.
38. See Paul Henry, *Plotinus: The Enneads*, translated by Stephen MacKenna, 4th ed., revised by B. S. Page (New York: Pantheon, 1969), p. xxxix.
39. De Corte, "Tonalité du mysticisme de Plotin," *Hermes*, no. 2 (December 1933): 5.
40. Quoted in Maurice de Gandillac, *La Sagesse de Plotin*, 2d ed. (Paris: Vrin, 1966), p. 252 n. 49.

virtues, those which reside in the soul, and the soul itself secedes from the body.[41]

This attitude of self-divinization prevailed until the end of pagan times: The sage was bodily in the world, but his spirit had fused with the ineffable One. It is not a religious feeling but rather a speculation about the divine. For comparison, here are two brief lines from an early Christian hymn expressing the spirit of the new religion as it defies the postulates of the old: "The Invisible One is seen, and is not ashamed; / The Incomprehensible is laid hold upon, and is not indignant."[42]

Yet pagan speculation, reinforced by Plotinus, did not surrender. Neoplatonism, in its last great effort, oriented it toward a form of henotheism, the adoration of the One, usually the sun. We may thus speak, as Hugo Rahner notes, of "a solar pantheism, centering round the ascent of the salvation-hungry soul by lunar ways to a blissful hereafter, which is no longer conceived as a subterranean Hades but as an astral-celestial heaven."[43] By the fourth century paganism had developed a moral sphere of its own, but this was clearly an imitation of the Christian religion, a last attempt to compete with it. And under Augustine's intellectual hammer blows, paganism finally collapsed.

THE SAGE AND THE SAINT

Instead of giving an overview of pagan philosophy, I have preferred to focus on the figure of the sage, to use the ideal type to give a general impression of the pagan speculative enterprise. The sage expresses the highest aspirations of pagan philosophy and elite culture, just as the myth and the myth-interpreting cult translate the inner world of the pagan mass cult. Confronting elite culture and the mass cult, Christianity did not and could not behave like other schools or sects. It did not become their rival, proposing yet another method of withdrawal from the world or yet another mys-

---

41. Plotinus, *Enneads*, 1.2.7.
42. Quoted from Hugo Rahner, "The Christian Mystery and the Pagan Mysteries," translated by Ralph Manheim, in *Mysteries*, edited by Joseph Campbell, p. 372.
43. Ibid., p. 348.

tery of purification. Instead, it was obliged by its worldview to challenge the culture and the cult on all essential points, and either to renew the bases of philosophical speculation and humanity's approach to God or to disappear without a trace.

Although I have mentioned in passing the conflict between paganism and Christianity, I have not analyzed it systematically. The remainder of this chapter, then, seeks to explain the inevitability of the conflict and to suggest that by winning it Christianity not only devastated the pagan mode of thinking but attacked certain deeply rooted forms of imagination and aspiration that, though externally suppressed, survived in the soul. Not only have they survived but, embedded in the recesses of Christianized consciousness, they have continued to put pressure on the Christian worldview and Christian speculation. If these weaken and fail to perform adequately the function of permeating the soul and mind, paganism reappears as if its dwelling place were just below consciousness and as if it were the natural alternative to Christianity.

C. G. Jung diagnosed the case, writing that during the centuries of its assured triumph a self-satisfied Christianity failed to elaborate its own myth and refused to lend an ear to those who brought forth and expressed the obscure notions of mythical representation. According to Jung, the subconscious is teeming with popular images that were forced into hiding, so to speak, by various modes of thinking and feeling that had evolved in past civilizations. Likewise, the Christian system has imprinted itself on our psychic and irrational personality, displacing the images that had accumulated in pre-Christian times and have remained undissolved ever since.

It seemed to Jung that the pre-Christian, ancestral images ought to have been integrated by Christianity into the Westerner's irrational household, so as to ensure a richer, more balanced psychic life. Jung, unlike Freud, did not deny the prophylactic effect religion had on his patients. He suggested, however, that the religious sphere should not be an exclusively Christian reserve but should be open to all nonrational influences.[44] Indirectly address-

---

44. In his autobiography, Jung tells of a semiconscious self-interrogation: In what myth does modern man live? One may say in the Christian myth. Do you personally live in that myth? Honestly, no. Then, we no longer have a myth. What is your own myth?— At this point, the inner dialogue broke off. *Ma Vie* (Paris: Gallimard, 1966), p. 199.

ing the issue we are discussing, Jung argued that modern people need to open the floodgates through which pagan sensitivity and the pagan mythical imagination may enter from the collective subconscious.

Two responses to Jung's views are pertinent at this point. One was a direct answer to the psychologist, the other carried his suggestion further and made it more specific. Martin Buber, opposing Jung from the point of view of a person of faith in the monotheistic tradition, argued that the question is not about the therapy of patients who may need this or that cure, but about the verity of the object of faith, the one God. The various archetypal images and their usefulness for the health of the human psyche is one thing; the truth of religion and God's revelation is another. The psychologist should strive to cure the sick but should not meddle in the higher issue of God's truth.[45]

The second view has as one of its chief modern spokesmen Ernesto Buonaiuti, who gives a sympathetic hearing—as Jung recommended that Christians should—to the heresies of the first centuries, to those of Marcion and the Gnostics, for example. Buonaiuti believes that these heresies expressed Christ's true teaching, which was later distorted by the church. He suggests that the "highest prophetic wisdom" demanded of the first Christians a life according to the unwritten laws of revelation, not an obedience to outward laws. "The idea," he writes, "that a long interval must precede the coming of the kingdom, and that this interval requires the foundation of a visible, hierarchically ordered Church, is utterly alien to Christ's central thought."[46] Buonaiuti sees the *ecclesia spiritualis* as having sprung up spontaneously around the figure and teaching of Christ over against the institutional church, which was the work of doctors, scholars, hierarchs, and bureaucrats.

Whatever we may think of Buonaiuti's thesis, it is a fact that the heresies that the church has anathematized (expressly or implicitly), from the earliest days until the present, carried with them

45. Martin Buber, "Reply to C. G. Jung," a supplement to his *Eclipse of God* (New York: Harper, 1952), pp. 131ff.
46. Ernesto Buonaiuti, "Ecclesia Spiritualis," translated by Ralph Manheim, in *Spirit and Nature*, vol. 1 of Papers from the Eranos Yearbooks, edited by Joseph Campbell, Bollingen Series no. 30 (New York: Pantheon, 1954), p. 227.

much material that derived from pagan myths and pagan culture. We will mention just a few, with the proviso that we recognize that these are shorthand terms for vastly complex products of popular imagination and elite theorizing: belief in astral dependence; hermetic-magical manipulation of heaven; the alchemical reproduction of the world drama in which opposites are reconciled; and symbols like the serpent, signifying the universe without beginning or end. Were we to follow Jung's direction of thinking, we would hold that all these images, beliefs, techniques, and practices express the permanent psychic realities, motives, and needs of humanity, and that their suppression results only in their being stored in an increasingly crowded depot from which they seek liberation.

Taking the above examples as typical of suppressed material, we may put ourselves in the place of pagan cultists and state that the first, the belief in the stars' influence on our destiny, expresses an indestructible sense of human dependence on unfathomable forces; that the second represents an effort to manipulate the stars from here below; that the third intends to help us overcome the rupture in the human condition by bringing together in the alchemist's furnace the opposite elements, sulphur and mercury, whose fusion, it was believed, accelerates the reconciliation of opposites on a cosmic scale.[47]

The road from chaos to cosmos, the integration of the individual into the community, the initiation of youth, the submission to higher forces, the magical manipulation of the same forces—all these profound needs of the human inner economy were given symbolic and cultic expression in the pagan myths. The question is whether Christianity, in suppressing them, was capable of replacing them with other myths or another equivalent. Buber's argument indicates that this could not be the case because monotheistic religion deals not with myths but with truth. Yet biblical

---

47. Eliade writes in *The Forge and the Crucible* (New York: Harper, 1971) that ancient and even medieval people accorded the miner a semisacred status because, by extracting metals, he was supposed to speed up the turning of all metals into their highest form, gold. Natural forces in the depth of mountains do this work at their own rhythm, but the miner does nature's work faster. The alchemist is semisacred for a similar reason: he accelerates the fusion of opposites so that universal harmony might reign. The Christian alchemist saw it as his objective to bring about the reign of Christ.

scholarship has insisted for centuries—in fact, since Philo Judaeus—that many of the Old and New Testament stories are allegorical and that they translate immemorially ancient pagan mythical themes into biblical language. Modern exegesis, too, claims to detect, behind the Gospel episodes, mythical elements derived from pagan mysteries: Christ as the new expression of the solar myth; his temptation by Satan as a parallel of the earlier myth of the hero passing through the underground; the virginity of Mary as a common element according to which the religious hero is born from a virgin mother; and so on.[48]

This is a labyrinthine debate that should not absorb our attention. All things considered, the great difference between pagan myths and the Gospels is that most of the latter's stories are historically factual,[49] and mythical elements touch only the inessentials. The question remains, however: Does Christianity fill the imagination of the masses of people the way pagan myths once did?

Every doctrine, worldview, speculative system, or religion possesses an inner consistency that cannot be violated without the system's falling apart. The kind of syncretistic soul that Jung envisions as an ideal would be partly Christian but would carry within itself many alien and incompatible elements as well. The formula *lex orandi, lex credendi* (loosely, one believes the way one prays) suggests that a religion prescribes its content and its form to the practice of liturgy and prayer. We are thus led to the conclusion that it was consistent with Christianity to eliminate and abolish cults that depended on such beliefs as that nature is animated; that matter is evil; that the supreme human aspiration in this world is gradual spiritualization; that history runs in cycles and lacks meaning; that the spirit, as a divine substance, is superior to the soul; that God (or the gods) is indifferent to humanity and history; and that God is coeval with his opposite principle, evil. When the

---

48. Note, for example, the story of Romulus, the founder of Rome, who was born of Rhea Sylvia, a vestal virgin whom the god Mars had visited in prison, and the story of Buddha, who did not know his father.

49. In his book *Redating the New Testament* (Philadelphia: Westminster, 1976), J. A. T. Robinson, retired Anglican bishop of Woolwich, argues that the texts of the New Testament were written between the years 47 and 70, not 50 and 100 as the most commonly held thesis stated. If his hypothesis is correct, the authors of the New Testament were witnesses of what they describe or could at least have interviewed the actual witnesses.

Hebrew prophets suppressed the cult of Baal and when the Spaniards destroyed the Aztec gods, there was behind these acts a doctrinal understanding that idolatrous practice prominently includes the devil as a force equal to God and demanding worship. Idolatry indicates the duality of God: one good, one evil.

Nevertheless, the answer to the earlier question, whether Christianity was able to fill the place of the abolished pagan myths and cults, must be at least partly negative. We saw the presence of nature, real and imaginary, in these myths. It would be easy to argue with the early Christians that myths were inspired by the devil, or to argue with the thinkers of the Enlightenment that mythical thinking was the science of the day. The truth seems to lie elsewhere, and this is also the argument of the most recent scholarship: that mythical imagination is a unique way of thinking and is a natural human expression.

Some call this way of thinking mythopoesis; others, Henri Bergson, for example, *fonction fabulatrice* (the impulse to fictionalize or turn into a story). Jung and his school describe it in great detail. One is dealing here with a conception of nature that Christianity could not tolerate, for reasons given above. The fertility cult, the influence of chthonian spirits, and the cycle of rebirth have a specific value for the imagination that Christianity can only partially replace, or against which it can only juxtapose its own rituals and images.[50] The point that Jungians and many others make is that even though the old myths and cults were abolished in the public sphere, their suppression was not quite successful in individual souls, where they continue to struggle with Christian images.

One aim of psychological analysis (*not* psychoanalysis) is to bring forth and make manifest the ancestral shapes and impulses that the patient spontaneously draws on paper or carries out in acts. Such drawings and acts reach back, far behind Christian imagery and symbols, to the domain of the quasi inexpressible, to

50. This was brought vividly to my attention at a Sunday Mass held in the high plateau of Guatemala. While the (white) priest officiated at the altar, the Indians were engaged in quite different activities—addressing and lifting candles for ancestors and talking to the statues of saints in the manner in which one might address idols. One can have similar experiences in southern Italy. Eliade argues that the belief of the "Danubian peasant" has preserved a great deal of pre-Christian cults.

humankind's "primordial estate."[51] In contrast, the Gospel stories and the lives of saints are, as we said, predominantly historical and rational, and they call very sparingly upon the miraculous, and hardly ever on the primordial myth, the occult forces, the earth spirits, or the natural powers. When one compares the story of Jesus from Incarnation to Resurrection with the Gnostic myths or with the luxuriant Hindu or Mesopotamian lives of religious heroes, one finds that the miraculous element is by no means the point of the story, and that there is no place for animism, spirits, and other deities, or for the personified natural forces that abound in the others.[52]

The risk involved in the suppression of myth should now be obvious. Pagan myth seems to withstand the erosion of time better than the Christian religion, for all its truth. Nature, with its inexhaustible mysteries, is always present in myth. It interprets the primary human experiences and it influences human souls without intermediaries. The myth thus does not wither easily; it has great resources, and it is able to assume new shapes. There are even modern myths operating in industrial societies that, though differing from traditional myths in content, reveal the same need for nonrational explanations and solutions.

In contrast, the Christian religion, so delicately positioned on the collaborating edge between faith and reason, demands human cooperation in both areas. There is no supportive nature on which people can rely for understanding; Christianity expects everyone to make the effort to comprehend their own existence in the light of reason and faith. Hence the indispensable support of the church, its traditions, sacraments, saints, and teaching. Thus instead of

51. The expression is René Guénon's from "Oriental Metaphysics" (n.p., n.d.), in which he argues that the West, and Western Christianity, has abandoned the road of wisdom, still preserved in the Oriental systems. For more on this, see Chapter 5 below.

52. Yet one cannot underestimate the myth element in Christianity, despite Christian insistence that the Incarnation, Resurrection, and Ascension are historical events. Many people believe that the latest discoveries about the Shroud of Turin, for example, bring more factual data and thus further confirmation to this historicity. Yet the myth remains, and through such elements as the liturgy, the imitation of Christ as a model, and the eternal renewal of past events in the sacraments of the Catholic Mass, Christianity is integrated with mystical thought.

nature, an institution; instead of the permanence of the first, the social fragility of the second.

But an institution, or an institutionalized collectivity, risks becoming overly rationalistic; or, what is practically the same thing, the collectivity may become unfaithful to the sacred framework of its existence, allowing it to be desacralized. There then ensues a collapse, what Titus Burckhardt calls "a mummification of the symbols" that the collectivity had assumed at the beginning.[53] This process is not merely a phenomenon of the community—it is also reflected in the individual psychic life of every member. As we shall see further on, Christianity is subject to such an erosion in two exposed areas, reason and faith. Having sponsored rational thinking about the universe and nature, a Christian civilization may turn excessively rationalistic and lose its sacral character. The suppressed need for myth may then reappear in order to prevent desiccation. But these suppressed myths would then encourage the development of a different civilization, a different belief system, perhaps even a new religion.

If we now examine some of the speculative positions elaborated by Hellenistic-Roman elites and compare them with the Christian position on these issues, we will notice a thorough incompatibility and the need for one of the rivals to yield. For pagan thinkers from Aristotle to Plotinus, the heavens were immutable and the planets were moved by divine forces, themselves eternally the same and filling the universe with their conscious presence and will. According to Pierre Duhem, the failure of Greek science (to continue on a path to modernity) was due to the influence of this kind of theological postulate. Christianity made possible the progress to modernism, not because it was scientific, but because it denied the divinity of the universe, thus laying it open to rational research. True, the enterprise of Epicurus was similar, and Anaxagoras suggested in the time of Pericles that the sun was a fiery body the size of the Peloponnesus (a statement for which he was forced to flee Athens); but to the Epicurean theory of all-is-matter, Christian thinkers

---

53. See Titus Burckhardt, "Cosmology and Modern Science," in *The Sword of Gnosis: Metaphysics, Cosmology, Tradition, Symbolism*, edited by Jacob Needleman (Baltimore: Penguin, 1974), p. 173.

opposed an extra-cosmic God, creator of a soul, who did not permeate the universe. Thus God left the heavens open to scientific investigation.[54]

Celsus himself, the first systematic opponent of Christianity, attacked the Christian view on another point. A God who descended in person from heaven and assumed a human body would upset the orderliness of the universe and cause catastrophe. He also argued against the Incarnation on the grounds that it was self-contradictory: it would involve a diminution, hence a change; but gods, like nature, are unchangeable.

There was the same incompatibility on the concept of matter. The thrust of the pagan sages, from the Hindus to the Neoplatonists—that is, for thousands of years—was to rid themselves of the impurities of matter and to turn increasingly to the spirit. The sages indeed defined themselves as quasi-pure spirits who develop techniques of controlling the body and thus avoiding bodily and mental suffering. Nascent Christianity then came and exalted the spirit that was made flesh in an act of special divine grace for the sake of mankind (just the opposite of what was desired by the pagans!). Moreover, this spirit made flesh was the central object of worship as a God-man who suffered torments in his flesh, shed tears, felt betrayed, and predicted with an infinite sorrow the destiny of his religion's holy city. In the eyes of pagan philosophers, the true sage is above such preoccupations. For the Gnostics in particular, even the soul was a mere appetitive, and thus impure, entity, certainly not worthy of divine solicitude. The *psychoi*, those whose highest faculty was the soul, were regarded as too deeply integrated with life's impurities and as inferior to the *pneumatikoi*, possessors of the spiritual particles, a divine guarantee of future reabsorption into God ("salvation").

The pagan thinker regarded the soul as subtly material: the Stoic sage considered it part of the fiery world-soul, and the Epi-

---

54. In fact, the issue was not so easily settled. Most Christian thinkers agreed with their pagan contemporaries that the heavenly bodies were alive and intelligent. As late as the thirteenth century, Bishop Tempier of Paris saw the need to condemn the rather widely held position that celestial bodies have a soul. See Richard C. Dales, "The De-Animation of the Heavens in the Middle Ages," *Journal of the History of Ideas* 41 (October-December 1980): 546.

curean postulated no soul at all but only material particles—cohesive heaps of them, as Lucretius suggested. The pagans were never very sure of the origin and destination of the soul, although the question of its cure eventually became virtually the focus of their speculative effort. The most they were able to conceive was the soul as a part of the divine spirit, tending to return from the material world to its place of origin, not by any (moral) merit but through successive purifications in the course of its migrations. The merits, as said, were not good deeds but degrees of dematerialization, of distancing from mundane concerns. For the Gnostics, who were the last and most radical of the pagan sages, dematerialization was not a mere noninvolvement with gross appetites and a life spent in sensual gratification; it was aloofness from family and civic life as well. In the best cases this led to asceticism; in others, to an obscene indulgence of the senses as too lowly for the pure spiritual person to worry about.

On this point, too, Christianity advocated the opposite. Christians believe that the soul's origin is in the creative act of God, and that every soul is endowed with the knowledge of what God means by good and evil, with an inclination to follow the good yet with a free will to do either good or evil. There can be no metempsychosis: the soul is neither independent of the body nor imprisoned in it, desirous of escaping. Instead, the body and soul together form an indissoluble psychosomatic unity, a person who is morally responsible as long as life lasts.

This view of the person leads the Christian saints, in contrast to the pagan sages, to make use of their powers and of the grace they have received to promote the spiritual and material well-being of the community of Christians—in truth, of the whole of humankind. Where the sages withdraw from the concerns of the world, the saints show their charity in words, acts, and prayer. Indeed, one of the saints' responsibilities was to oppose the pagan sages' excessive affirmation of the self, as Augustine did with these words: "An assertion of selfhood involves the danger of fatal misapprehension. The presumption of man may, indeed, lead him to suppose that, in his consciousness of existence and of activity, there is evidence that he embodies a scintilla of the divine essence, the mere possession of which constitutes a prima-facie claim to divinity, lifting him above the natural order of which he forms a part."⁵⁵ That is, human folly may suggest that human limitations are external and not inherent.

The core of the educated pagan worldview was that the world contains more evil than good and that the balance inexorably tips toward evil, the dominant element, because the universe is eternal. Since it is impossible for the human mind to deal intelligibly with eternity, pagan speculation divided it into cycles or Great Years. Yet in order to avoid inconsistency, the pagans also postulated the repetition of these cycles, so that in each, eternally, the same things recur. As Augustine viewed it, this is to assume that through countless ages, again and again, Plato sits in the Academy of Athens, teaching the same pupils in the same school, and all of this is destined to be repeated through countless ages of the future. He adds: "God forbid that we should swallow such nonsense. Christ died, once and for all, for our sins."⁵⁶

Augustine's exclamation brings out the inability of Christianity to adopt the theory of Eternal Return, as it was similarly unable to adopt the doctrine of migrating souls, evil matter, and other basic pagan presuppositions. The Christian position ultimately depends on seeing God as the all-powerful creator (not a mere shaper) whose love of being (as opposed to nonbeing or nothingness) brought forth the universe. The pagan on the other hand saw the gods as enormously powerful natural forces, limited only by the similarly powerful forces of other gods. Even in the most refined version of paganism, in Plato and Plotinus, God is consubstantial with souls and did not create matter, which was made by another, essentially hostile, power. In the view of the more radical pagans, the Brahman and the Gnostic, being itself is evil, and its emergence is a flaw in the universal nothingness. While God and his human cocreators maintain the universe in existence, expending prodigious efforts to make it better and to embellish it, it is incumbent on the (radical) pagan sages to cause the annihilation of the universe, first of all by causing it to weaken in themselves.

There is no doubt that, at its best and most noble, pagan phi-

---

55. Augustine, quoted in Charles Norris Cochrane, *Christianity and Classical Culture: A Study of Thought and Action from Augustus to Augustine* (Oxford: Clarendon, 1940), p. 406.
56. Augustine, *The City of God*, 12.14.

losophy composed beautiful and moving texts honoring God—note the mystical raptures of Plotinus or the hymn in which the Stoic Cleanthes addresses himself to father Zeus, master of nature, governor of the universe, provider of all things. But Zeus is a supreme organizer, not, finally, a creator. Plotinus, in turn, celebrates the incomparable beauty his soul contemplates as it escapes from the body in moments of self-awakening. Yet in such passages he also speaks of his soul's great vocation of "settling in the divinity, above the other intelligible beings" (*Enneads*, 4.8.1).

Compare these summits of pagan theology with Augustine's statement as he speaks of nature, which, even in its fallen state, remains so beautiful and good that had it been created by God after the Fall, it would still be proof of its author's infinite wisdom. Let us keep in mind that for Augustine the Fall is the fall of humanity, and it is the fault of humanity. But for the pagan sage, the Fall is the fall of the world, simply because it came into existence; ultimately, it is God's failure.

It is understandable, then, that pagan speculation was plagued by the central difficulty of establishing the nature of the relationship between God and the universe. In one description God was compelled from outside to bring forth the universe; in another, the One engendered the Intellect by "turning to face itself"; in yet another, the origin of the universe is simply chance, a given agglomeration of atoms working themselves out, taking a certain shape in the eternal flow of time. It is this indefinable and uncertain cosmological relationship that accounts for the hesitation of the sages and for their final withdrawal from a world that does not make sense. Even at their most consistent, the hypotheses setting forth the nature of this relationship remained within the confines of astrology.

Since the God of the pagans remained a fundamentally aloof figure—he did not appear interested in humanity once he had set the laws of the universe in motion—he could not be regarded as the fountainhead of and a participant in history. History was either inconsequential mythology or the tale of the foundation and major events of cities and states. Thus Arnaldo Momigliano's point is well taken when he writes that Christian chronographers, explaining to pagan converts the antiquity of Christ's teaching (in order to compete with pagan antiquity), were obliged to present a philosophy of history, a "model of providential history." "The convert . . . was compelled to enlarge his historical horizon: he was likely to think for the first time in terms of universal history."[57]

In contrast, Jesus was a historical figure, and Paul said that the quality of history changed for Christians by God's saving act. The linear, not cyclical, concept of historical time made sense for the first time of the novelty of things in everyday experience, for which no philosophical explanation could be given by pagan wisdom. With novelty intelligible, other notions now entered the new conceptual world: progress, regression, decadence, and, primarily, the uniqueness of individual historical acts.

This all pointed to the contingency of events, not only of human action, but also of the universe. While paganism advocated determinism and necessity, compatible with the aloofness of the gods, Christianity and Christian philosophy stressed two crucial novelties: first, the idea that the universe is *contingent*, which means that it was not created under some compulsion endured by God; and second, the idea that God, once he created the universe, remained *consistent* in endowing it with unchanging laws and sustaining it with his providence.

The first of these tenets indicated that God is outside his creation and that no part of the universe, humans included, can claim to possess "divine parts," not even the psyche or the *pneuma*. It also emphasized the dependence of the universe on God; and since this God is good, there is no reason for sages to train themselves in the techniques of detachment.[58] Finally, the contingent character of the universe made way for the scientific investigation of nature and for participation in history, since the contingency of creation gave a new importance to the human endeavor.

The second tenet confirmed the first. Contingency does not mean that the universe and nature are capriciously organized and that the laws of nature and the nature of humanity vary unpredictably. Miracles are extremely rare. Jesus himself was reluctant to perform any, and believers today must investigate the reports of

57. Arnaldo Momigliano, "Pagan and Christian Historiography in the Fourth Century A.D.," in *The Conflict Between Paganism and Christianity in the Fourth Century*, edited by Arnaldo Momigliano (Oxford: Clarendon, 1963), p. 83.

58. It is rarely noted that the Oriental, the shamanic, and other techniques of detachment are predicated on the assumption of an evil God wanting to harm humans.

miracles at length before accepting them as genuine. It is significant that the question of God's inconsistency arose again with the emergence of neopaganism at the end of the Middle Ages. (Ockham and the late Scholastics called this inconsistency *potentia absoluta*, an ambiguous term; the opposite is *potentia ordinata*, that is, once God created he remained within the limits of creation.) Questions about God's purposive intelligence and nature's susceptibility to scientific investigation surfaced, among other thinkers, with Descartes, who took special pains to deny that God may be so evil as to play games with the trusting human mind.

In practice, the Greeks acknowledged consistency in nature. After all, they formulated many scientific laws. Yet the reason their science did not advance beyond the beginning of profound and brilliant insights may be that this acknowledgment was not elevated to the status of centrality in their worldview—in other words, they did not combine consistency in the universe with the contingency of a created universe. As Stanley Jaki writes: "The Greeks were profoundly aware of the rationality of nature and of the measure in which consistency gives rationality to reasoning. They were the first to construct formal ways to the ultimate in being, and Aristotle even perceived something of that aspect of the contingency of things which was implied in the fact that not all that was possible did in fact exist."[59]

Jaki's remark concerns science, whereas I have tried to describe an entire worldview; there the Greeks were more deficient. In the course of the description we reviewed and compared the pagan and Christian conceptions of the heavens, matter, the soul, history, creation, and God. These are indeed the salient elements of a philosophy: cosmology, physics, psychology and ethics, history, the problems of origin and finality, and theology. The pagan worldview, particularly in its Greek version, is a coherent whole that had to put up a struggle on all fronts against the Christian worldview, likewise coherent. We have become aware of the weaknesses of the former, but we must also examine the weaknesses of the latter. These weaknesses make it susceptible to break-ins and influence by the pagan worldview, which has remained the standard recourse of minds dissatisfed with Christian religion and civilization.

59. Stanley Jaki, *The Road to Science and the Ways of God* (Chicago: University of Chicago Press, 1978), p. 320.

CHAPTER 2

The Pagan Revival

People use the expression "the Dark Ages" to refer to a thousand-year period of embarrassing near-vacuum, during which nothing outstanding happened except in a negative sense: the misguided Crusades, the Inquisition, invasions, and myriad acts of social injustice within the framework of a rigidly fixed feudal structure. This stereotypical view of the period has been dispelled through the efforts of specialists who have pointed to two phenomena: first, the continuity, and even development, of the period from antiquity to the Renaissance in political theory, philosophy, and science; and second, its outstanding original achievements in literature (note Dante's *Divine Comedy*, the troubadour's art, and the literary rendering of Celtic, Viking, and other legends), in architecture (the cathedrals), in philosophy (the works from Boethius and Alcuin to the great summas), and in science (note the theorists Jean Buridan, Nicole d'Oresme, Albert of Saxony, and Nicholas of Cusa, precursors of Kepler and Galileo, and also the more immediately practical inventions of the harness and navigational instruments, and the explorations in geometry).

Scholars have paid much less attention to the revival, in the last centuries of the Middle Ages, of the opposition between the supposedly extinct pagan worldview and the Christian worldview under the weary but generally tolerant eyes of the church. One might surmise that this aspect of late medieval times receives less attention than expected because the Middle Ages are still regarded as a more or less blank spot between two luminous periods, pagan antiquity and the Renaissance revival of paganism. Insofar as it is believed that the medieval church simply would not have tolerated pagan thought, the revival of the pagan-Christian conflict is ascribed wholly to the Renaissance, with the consequence that people overlook the pagan speculation that had continued throughout the medieval period and that had in fact been incorporated into Christian thought.[1]

The overlapping, in numerous instances, of Christian and pagan thought does not mean that the Middle Ages were not Christian. In the Roman world, paganism was officially suppressed in the period between the Roman emperor Constantine and the Byzantine emperor Justinian (from the fourth to the sixth century).[2] Farther to the north and east, it was suppressed even longer, as the territories between the Franks and the Slavs, roughly between Aachen and Kiev, became Christianized. In these politically amorphous territories—from Charlemagne's empire to the principalities of Kiev and Novgorod—the pagan cults were exterminated, so that very little survived except what was preserved in sagas, art objects, grave sites, and other minor remnants. Thus repaganization could not make much progress, except in areas previously dominated by Greco-Roman civilization, in the south and west of Europe.

It is impossible to speak of a suspension of cross-influences here, much less of a civilizational rupture. In philosophy, Neoplatonism continued to influence not only the mystics, who felt its impact in the works of Pseudo-Dionysius the Areopagite, but also the philosophers, who were exposed to it in Arab and Hebrew commentaries on ancient texts. In science, the two worldviews, the Christian and the ancient pagan, could hardly be separated, since Aristotle's view of the heavens and the sublunar world prevailed throughout the entire period, and far into the seventeenth century.

---

1. Some of the authors who in recent times have studied the continuity from ancient times through the Middle Ages to the modern age are Raymond Klibansky (Platonic philosophy), Herbert Butterfield (science), Joseph Strayer (politics and the state), Walter Ullmann (papal and secular political structures), and Erwin Panofsky (art and architecture).

2. The latter name and date are legitimately chosen. In 529 Justinian closed Plato's Academy in Athens. (Some of the resident scholars found refuge in the Persian court.) The same date is connected with the founding of Benedict of Nursia's first monastery in the Western style (at Monte Cassino) and his authorship of the Benedictine Rule. A new kind of educational institution—the monastery as opposed to the academy—had begun.

The Pagan Revival

Long before this, toward the end of antiquity, Emperor Julian and his entourage of pagan sages and mystics, Neoplatonic philosophers, and other public figures attempted a pagan revival, Julian himself going so far as to reconstruct the temple, an enterprise abandoned when he died after a very short reign. It is difficult to tell whether these somewhat pathetic figures were truly committed to a revival of philosophical speculation and pagan sects—the cult of Serapis, of Mithra, of Magna Mater—or whether they were simply grasping at the waning traces of Roman grandeur. The fact is, Julian's rekindled paganism, sun worship and all, proved too cerebral for a populace that was no longer racially Roman (Italo-Latin),[3] and he was unable to sway the people so recently impressed by a victorious Christianity.

If this was the case when paganism still had some political and philosophical force behind it, paganism in the later medieval centuries could only be an adjunct of Christianity, in the sense that it affected the elite culture alone. Let us repeat this all-important fact: the medieval worldview was Christian, even to the point of Christianizing the pagan position. Thus, although Augustine was certainly a Platonist and others, in large numbers, were Neoplatonists or Aristotelians, it is important to understand that these were still essentially Christian thinkers, mystics, and savants who carefully selected what they took from their pagan predecessors, adopting only what was compatible with Christian doctrine and the Christian worldview.

We have already indicated that up to the Renaissance and beyond—in fact, until the eighteenth-century research into and revival of folklore beginning with the German Johann Gottfried von Herder—very little was known about the pre-Christian mass cults of Europe. When we speak of a pre-Renaissance and Renaissance "pagan revival," we are in fact focusing on the reemergence of the Mediterranean myths, particularly in the forms in which they found expression among the intellectual elite of the period. This elite attempted a fusion of late pagan mythic speculation and late pagan philosophical syncretism. They attempted at the same time, however, to synthesize this with Christianity, jettisoning the

---

3. Funeral inscriptions testify that throughout the last centuries of the empire few Latins inhabited the towns and the countryside of Italy.

Christian element and allowing the pagan element to dominate when such a synthesis proved impossible or undesirable.

The success of this repaganization is in large part due to a weakening of the Christian faith and symbology, which was later emphasized by the split in the body of Christendom. The pagan tradition and speculative view in contrast appeared to be of a piece. Over against the dissension among various Scholastic systems,[4] pagan philosophy could present itself as a unity; it was a unity often based on a mistaken interpretation, but this was not recognized at the time. For example, through errors by Arab commentators, Aristotle was credited with the authorship of important Neoplatonic texts, and thus the two greatest speculative figures of antiquity were erroneously reconciled.

Neoplatonism incorporated certain ancient esoteric doctrines, not only in the Christian world, but also in the wider Mediterranean sphere, which included Arabs, Hebrews, and Persians, who lived in an intellectual dialogue with Christians. Myron Gilmore mentions, for example, that Neoplatonic elements entered the Zohar (Jewish cabala) with their "theory of emanations, by which was explained the relationship of a transcendent god to the world," a thesis as much in dissonance with Hebrew as with Christian theology.[5]

On the level of symbolic representation, paganism, through Neoplatonic postulates, began to gain ground. In rebuilding the abbey church at Saint-Denis in the twelfth century, the French churchman and statesman Suger had introduced the quintessentially Christian Gothic architecture to Western Europe. By the fifteenth century, ecclesiastical architecture began to translate into physical form the new syncretism of ideas sponsored by Neoplatonism. The Italian Leon Battista Alberti experimented with symmetrical circular churches, paying tribute to the current interest in the perfection of the circle (a Platonic heritage), which represents

---

4. Already in Dante's *Paradise* (1315-1321), we find reconciled the great Christian systematizers Thomas and Bonaventure, but also the great dissenters Joachim of Fiore and Siger of Brabant. That Dante regarded such an imaginary reconciliation as necessary—in the same way that the reconciliation of the "two swords," church and empire, was necessary—suggests the depth of the rift at several crucial points in the *Respublica Christiana*.

5. Myron Gilmore, *The World of Humanism, 1453–1517* (1952; reprint, New York: Harper and Row, 1962), p. 195.

The Pagan Revival

through a microcosmic reference the harmony of the macrocosm. God was viewed, not as a creator wholly external to creation (a point insisted upon by Aquinas), but as an all-permeating, possibly mathematical, harmony, better evidenced in a circular construction. Again in Gilmore's words:

> In a circular church the altar was at the center, equidistant from all parts of the circumference, corresponding to the position of an almost pantheistic God in a symmetrical and mathematically ordered universe. . . . A theocentric interest had been substituted for a Christocentric one; God the Father, the Pantocrator, had replaced the Man of Sorrows as the religious center of the Renaissance.[6]

If we consider that the basilica church of St. Peter, at least before the Reformation the fulcrum of the Christian world, was built on the circular model, we see the extent of neopagan penetration. It can be remarked that this model underemphasized the concept of mediation so central to the Christian religion and substituted for it a quasi-pantheistic concept in which everything participates in the divine.

This penetration testifies to the strength that Neoplatonism had gathered in spite of the decadent aspect it was already displaying by the end of the pagan period. I have already mentioned the resistance of the pagan thinkers to the inroads of Christianity from the second century onward, and in Chapter 1 I gave glimpses of their varied and brilliant efforts to elaborate suitable responses to the Christian challenge—to such an extent that by the third century a considerable transformation had taken place in the area of pagan speculation. There developed a pagan spirituality and mysticism, even a quasi monotheism.[7] But at the same time the speculative foundation did not change, could not change: even after the establishment of the medieval Christian commonwealth, it remained the richly supplied storehouse of anti-Christian argu-

---

6. Ibid., p. 240.

7. It was not quite monotheism, for monotheism denotes belief in only one personal God, *creator omnium*. The pagans did not, even in exceptional cases, go beyond henotheism, the worship of one power without denying the existence of others. But what the pagans believed in was an impersonal power, unable to create unless compelled by an extraneous agent.

ments, usable by Christian thinkers to influence doctrine and philosophy in the directions they desired.

Thus one may speak of an undercurrent of pagan thought among ecclesiastics and teachers, at times sporadically represented, at other times swelling in prominence and persuasive power. Pagan thought, though easily detected, remained elusive and difficult to grasp. Only as heresy could it be identified and opposed because the heretics, radical in attitudes and impatient in their enthusiasm for instant salvation, usually gave themselves away. But pagan thought could not so easily be identified when it appeared woven into the fabric of an otherwise orthodox speculation, treatise, disputation, or university course. Erwin Panofsky characterizes the situation well, although he is speaking of times closer to the Renaissance proper, when he contrasts the medieval and the Neoplatonic. The first "endeavored to *incorporate* whatever seemed admissible of classical ideas and yet to draw as sharp a line as possible between faith and reason"; the second "attempted to *fuse* two cultural worlds clearly recognized as distinct from each other."[8]

The consequence was the fusion of philosophies, religions, and magic, whatever their content and style: Hermetism, Orphism, Pythagoreanism, cabala, and the endless and amorphous mysteries of Egypt and India. The combination was clearly a throwback to a thousand years before, to the syncretism of the late pagan period. It is significant that one of the chief works of this fusion bears the title *Theologia Platonica* and was written at the Medici court, by Marsilio Ficino. This was the same man who undertook the translation of Plato's dialogues and was then commanded by his employer, Cosimo, to turn his attention to the freshly arrived *Corpus Hermeticum*. This example provides a brief glimpse into the play of influences.

It is not surprising that in such an atmosphere the tone of Christian writers became muted. Although openly anti-Christian literature was still a few generations away (the above episode of Ficino dates from the 1460s), there was a growing tendency toward a new syncretism, a "universal religion." Ficino himself was

---

8. Erwin Panofsky, "Artist, Scientist, Genius: Notes on 'Renaissance-Dämmerung,'" in *The Renaissance: Six Essays*, edited by Wallace K. Ferguson (New York and Evanston: Harper & Row, 1962), p. 129.

The Pagan Revival

fascinated with the great hidden—prerevelation—interpreters of the divine, putting on the same level Plato, Zoroaster, Pythagoras, and Hermes Trismegistus. Giovanni Pico della Mirandola, a disciple of Ficino, also subscribed to this *pia filosophia* (philosophy of religiousness, or sacred philosophy), writing that "all the Greeks among whom is found something of the divine, such as Pythagoras, Plato, Empedocles, and Democritus [the materialist forebear of Epicurus], had the Egyptians for masters. The philosopher Numenius says that Plato is none other than an Athenian Moses."[9] One cannot help comparing this demarche by Ficino, Pico, and many of their humanist contemporaries with that of the Roman emperor Alexander Severus, who around A.D. 235 placed the images of Moses, Jesus, Zoroaster, and other great religious personages in his private chapel. The emperor was prudent enough to distinguish his private beliefs from official worship, as were Ficino and the prince of Mirandola.

At first, in the early part of the fourteenth century, what came to be called "universal religion" had as its objective furthering the truth and glory of Christianity. The thesis was that all religions of the earth contained parts of the divine revelation, but in an incomplete, often crude, form. Christianity, however, was set apart at the top of the hierarchy of religions, and one studied the others precisely in order to discern the incomparable purity of the Christian religion, which the truth value of the others merely confirmed.

With Pico at the end of the fifteenth century, and with Jean Bodin (see below) a hundred years later, the emphasis was to change. Thinkers began to view all religions as of equal value (they are all errors agreeable to God, wrote Bodin); they saw all as different aspects of the one "natural religion," shared by humanity through time and place.[10] Ficino, Pico, Johannes Reuchlin, and others were convinced of the unity of all religions. Christianity, they thought, stood out among them, but it did not teach an essentially different truth. Even Erasmus, though he was Luther's

---

9. Pico della Mirandola, quoted in Frances A. Yates, *The French Academies of the Sixteenth Century* (London: The Warburg Institute, 1947), p. 3.

10. Jean Bodin, *Colloquium of the Seven about Secrets of the Sublime (Colloquium heptaplomeres de rerum sublimium arcanis abditis)*, translated and edited by Marion Leathers Daniels Kuntz (Princeton: Princeton University Press, 1975), p. 251.

most prestigious Catholic adversary, believed that, apart from the faith in Christ that gets one to paradise, the distinctive elements of the Christian faith were not essential. Christianity was thus reduced to a system in which the ethical commands were admirable and useful, but in which both the doctrinal and the historical elements were for all practical purposes expendable.

I discussed in Chapter 1 the divergence between Christians and pagans in their interpretation of the nature of the heavens, creation, time, history, God, the soul, matter, and so on. The single pagan thesis that underlies all the rest is that at the hierarchical top of the universe there is an abstract entity—variously called the Infinite Spirit, the First Principle, the Original Mover, or simply the One—in whose spiritual substance all other spirits participate, including the human soul. Pagans for the most part consider human life to be a temporary interlude (in which the individual spiritual particle separates from the Infinite Spirit, though the *why* of the separation is never satisfactorily explained) between original union with the Infinite Spirit and its eventual reabsorption into it.

Implicit in this conception is the admission that neither the Infinite Spirit nor the individual soul possesses a clear status. The former is never entire since souls keep deserting its substance, and the latter has merely a borrowed, nostalgic existence. One may detect behind this vagueness the pervasive influence of Hindu speculation (which I will discuss in Chapter 5). The optimum state of the world, in this interpretation, would be nonbeing. If nevertheless the world is, it is the consequence of a fall, the fall into being. Hence the Infinite Spirit points to something else, outside itself, which compels it to originate the world. To use Scholastic language, the Infinite Spirit does not exist *a se*, of itself; it exists under a compulsion, which reveals that it is a negative thing, a wretched condition. Likewise, the soul. It has detached itself from the Infinite Spirit, either by curiosity or punishment, and it is now imprisoned in a material body. Thus its existence is also the result of a fall—hence its misery.

Why is this deeply pessimistic world picture, included in pagan speculation from the Hindus to the Neoplatonists, attractive to Christian thinkers when their religion presents an altogether different, positive, and life-affirming worldview on these essential issues? We noted that the pagan philosophical elite from the time

The Pagan Revival

of Celsus reacted against Christian teaching and rejected the idea of a personal God. They rejected the God who was made man, who is the good creator in whom believers are to put their faith, who created not only the heavens and the earth but also time, matter, and the soul, who is not subject to an evil counterforce, and who commands humans to do good.

Now the worldview of many thinkers in the Christian centuries did not differ essentially from the pagan worldview. Christians too were embarrassed by the idea of an incarnate God as contrary to the laws of nature; by the doctrine of creation instead of the belief in a universe brought into existence by chance;[11] by the anthropomorphic features attributed to God;[12] by time as a divine creation instead of being inert and eternal; by the immortality of the soul instead of its disintegration at death into component atoms. Consequently, a number of Christian philosophers, motivated by a combination of veneration for the great thinkers of Greece and philosophical conviction, kept the tenets of pagan speculation alive. This veneration did not have to be camouflaged except when its objects were such notorious materialists as Epicurus and Lucretius or such skeptics as Pyrrho.

One may legitimately speak of a "pagan temptation" as one surveys certain intellectual movements as chief illustrations of pagan thought. I shall discuss three such movements, in just enough detail to show both that there was a continuous pagan influence which, with time, grew increasingly coherent, self-assertive, and organized, at least from the fourteenth century on;

11. Thomas Aquinas, perhaps more than other thinkers in the church, insisted on creation ex nihilo as God's act, impossible for humanity. A few of his predecessors were similarly categorical, using for human work such expressions as "imitation" (of God's work), "elaboration," and "production."

12. Plato and his contemporaries, Sophists and philosophers, were similarly embarrassed by the crude mythology as shaped by Homer and Hesiod. The anthropomorphic conception of the gods was a scandal in thinking circles. The issue became much deeper with the Christian religion where God, by definition, is "anthropomorph," having spent years among human beings who saw and touched him. The deanthropomorphization of Christ is thus not a difficult but an impossible enterprise, which increases many times the Christian thinker's embarrassment—if he is embarrassed by the assertion of God's nearness to human beings. For a discussion, see my book *God and the Knowledge of Reality* (New York: Basic Books, 1973), Part I.

and also that this pagan influence, which amounted to a revival, prefigures a similar occurrence in our own century. This is, after all, the thesis of this book: that the pagan worldview persists behind the Christian worldview and that favorable circumstances, among which the most important is the fading of Christian truth as symbolized myth (see Chapter 3), allow it to manifest itself with a renewed vigor.

Given its psychology, paganism always distinguished between the elite mind and the vulgar mind, the first penetrable by the light of knowledge, the second never reaching the threshold of wisdom. This view was classically expressed by Plato in his threefold division of the Republic's citizens. There is also a radical version in Gnosticism, which divides humanity into three categories according to the possession of spirit *(pneuma)*, soul *(psychē)*, or matter *(hylē)*. In contrast, Christianity teaches the equal worth of every soul, the soul's reciprocal relationship with the body, and the capacity of all humans to understand and follow God's precepts. In Christianity there is no distinction between a "secret doctrine" or *gnosis* reserved to the initiated and another, popularized part available to the unreflective and the profane.

The separation of faith and reason began plaguing Christian speculation, however, when large doses of Greek philosophy came to the attention of medieval Christian thinkers through the Arab-Syrian rediscovery of hitherto unknown texts. The problem had been there all along, since the dimension of faith seems to be in contradiction to the dimension of reason. Such extreme statements as *credo quia absurdum* (I believe because it is unreasonable), though they may be reactions to extreme rationalist pagan critiques, highlight and discredit the relationship between faith and reason. The deeper and truer statement *credo ut intelligam* (I believe in order that I may understand) also needs considerable explanation for its application in both sacred and profane knowledge.

Moreover, the problem of faith was one of the few issues for which pagan speculation offered no precedent since, although the Greeks examined the phenomenon of knowledge from every angle, they never faced the companion phenomenon, faith. This is understandable, for faith can arise only where there is a personal God, good and generous, who creates the world and humanity with a view to establishing with both a relationship based on his

The Pagan Revival

own transcendence and personalness. Faith is elicited by the transcendent God, who demands that his people accept his promises grounded in rationally unprovable truths and commit their lives thereto. Faith is intensified by the personal God, who grounds human faith in him existentially by giving a vital demonstration of his own commitment to his people and the world.

The Greeks recognized no such God and could not envisage a history in which God manifested himself from his transcendence, helping humans to overcome the temptation of evil and the temptation of unbelief. <u>Yet only such a God can call forth faith—that is, an exacting yet trustful personal relationship based on both mastery and charity. Not even at its most subtle and probing was paganism able to produce this kind of relationship</u>. "The older Stoicism," writes Samuel Dill, "provided no object of worship. For worship cannot be paid to an impersonal law without moral attributes. . . . The sage may for a moment have a superhuman triumph, in his defiance of the temptations or calamities with which Nature has surrounded him, but it is a lonely triumph of inhuman pride."[13]

The inability to reconcile faith and reason was pivotal, then, in the challenge that pagan philosophy leveled against the Christian worldview. Ingenious solutions and reconciliations were opposed to the prevailing orthodoxy, but none were satisfying. It was finally the Arab world that produced an answer known as the doctrine of the "two verities," usually attributed to Averroës.[14] In the Arab philosopher's own words: "Of the things which are too hard for ordinary believers to grasp, God gave them signs and symbols. . . . Thus divine things are divided into the exoteric ones [accessible to the masses] and esoteric ones reserved for the philosophers."[15]

Though the doctrine of the two verities was unacceptable to the

13. Samuel Dill, *Roman Society from Nero to Marcus Aurelius* (London and New York: Macmillan, 1925), p. 512.

14. Averroës wanted not so much to heal the conflict between faith and reason—for which he blamed the Islamic theologians and their endless disputes—as to pacify the vulgar crowd by offering them a literal reading of the Koran and reserving esoteric teaching for the thinkers.

15. Averroës, *Traité décisif sur l'accord de la religion et de la philosophie* [Decisive Treatise on the Agreement of Religion and Philosophy] (Algiers: Carbonel, 1942), p. 18.

church, it was eagerly seized upon by the philosophers at the University of Padua, which subsequently became known for this option while continuing, nonetheless, as a center of Aristotelian studies. From Padua, Averroism spread to many places in Europe, particularly by the end of the fifteenth and during the sixteenth centuries when Italy was opened to the outside world through the wars on its soil by Spaniards, Germans, and the French. Partisans of the Averroist doctrine, leaning on the authority of Aristotle, who, so the saying went, "could not err," possessed a great advantage from the point of view of the "paganizers": they could pacify church authorities with assurances of orthodox faith, yet free themselves for the elaboration of a materialist system.

Several motives may be distinguished in the Paduan teaching. Officially, the Paduans discovered two parallel ways of interpreting religion. But in fact, there was not much question of parallel ways since the faith dimension was abandoned to the nonthinking orthodox and to the untutored masses. The philosophers held as valid for themselves only that area on which reason could operate unobstructed. This led, in time, to two divergent courses. One was fideism, in which faith renounced the claim to understanding and was therefore encouraged by the Paduan philosophers as a safe blind alley for the religious-minded; the other was rationalism, which, if well directed, could lead to science. The scientific enterprise was thus freed in advance from religious interference. Instead of reconciling reason and faith as advertised, or at least recognizing the validity of their respective paths, the Paduan teaching effectively drove a wedge between the two, depreciated the value of faith, and thereby broke the medieval harmony between theology and philosophy.

The Paduan theses read like a pagan catechism. In the first half of the sixteenth century, when the university was at the height of its reputation, the groundwork was laid with attacks on Christian ethics, on the concept of creation, and on God's providence. In the second half of the century, the Paduan philosophers chose their targets more daringly: immortality, miracles, and eventually even the fundamental dogmas, the Incarnation and divinity of Christ.

A few illustrations may be in order here. Bonaventure Des Périers, a French disciple of Padua, asserted that God created the world from all eternity, because to think otherwise would mean a God with unrealized potentialities. The Italian mathemati-

The Pagan Revival

cian Girolamo Cardano taught that the heavenly motions prove the perfection of the world whose God is at rest. The so-called spiritual libertines believed that Christians well-advanced in their faith become absorbed by God and are deified; they are separated from their fellow Christians by being saved already in this life and by being thus incapable of sin. Pietro Pomponazzi, the main Paduan figure around the turn of the sixteenth century, elaborated a humanistic ethic on the basis of the soul's mortality because, he argued, a person liberated from preoccupation with an immortal soul is more likely to adopt a way of life in conformity with the values held dear by the humanists.[16] Such arguments did not prevent Pomponazzi, a follower of the two verities hypothesis, from believing, as a Christian, in the soul's immortality.

These were Paduan statements, and Padua put its stamp on the greater part of Renaissance rationalism. We see clearly the traces of the Paduan spirit in the successive positions occupied by Montaigne in the second half of the sixteenth century: Epicureanism, Stocism, and Pyrrhonism, among which it was difficult for him to choose because of their very similar legacy. Giordano Bruno, Montaigne's contemporary, was an exemplary neopagan who taught a cosmology in harmony with the main thrust of pagan speculation. We find in his works *(The Ash Wednesday Supper* and *De la causa, principio et uno)* a crude pantheism and the mechanical model of Epicureanism, a mixture that would astonish readers if they did not know that in the Renaissance the magic-hermetic element often fused with mechanistic theories, both having originated in the mental laboratories of paganism.

Bruno discusses the idea of an infinite number of worlds and an infinite number of beings in them and proposes as his main thesis that all, worlds and beings, are parts of the divine substance called the One. In this he followed Averroist-Paduan speculation, one

---

16. There were more startling suggestions as well. Etienne Dolet, an alumnus of Padua, proposed several changes in the terminology of the religion—instead of the "church," one should speak of the "republic"; instead of the "pope," one should speak of "Jupiter's *flamen*"; the cardinals should be renamed *"patres conscripti"*; and the devil should henceforth be known as a "sycophant." This is grotesque, but it points to the weight of fashion, no less heavy today than yesterday. For an overview of Paduan influence, see Henri Busson, *Le Rationalisme dans la littérature française de la Renaissance (1533–1601)* (Paris: Vrin, 1957).

important tenet of which was that the act of thought consisted in overcoming the individual self's isolation so as to allow its fusion with the one Absolute Intellect. Only this fusion can explain the process of thought and establish its validity. The true thinking subject is not the self; it is the nonpersonal being common to all thinking beings.[17]

This position, vigorously asserted by Bruno, explains why Frances A. Yates calls him a magician.[18] The Averroist position conforms to the Hermetic teaching that the world-all is so criss-crossed with occult forces that the macrocosm (the universe) and the microcosm (the human being) are able to influence one another. Many of Bruno's statements suggest not only that he believed in this cosmic unity and these reciprocal influences—*Natura est Deus in rebus* (Nature is God within objects)—but also that he expected to use these magic forces to reach eminence in this world.

He did not seek a mere speculative eminence, for his ambition went far beyond that. His project, "heroic" as he imagined it in *Eroici furori* (Heroic Frenzies), was to restore the "great original religion," identified as that of Moses and Pythagoras, truer and more venerable than Christianity. As he wrote in the *Spaccio della bestia trionfante* (The Expulsion of the Triumphant Beast), the Copernican sun will dispel the darkness and help humanity enter into a great living universe with magical forces vibrating through it. Bruno's wandering through Europe and his visits to universities suggest his intention, for the places he visited were the focal points of anti-Catholicism (London, Geneva, and Wittenberg) and of heretical teaching (Toulouse and Padua). He expected to become the chief organizer of a new dispensation, under the sign of the *pantheos*, a deity identified with the infinite universe, a pulsating, self-renewing animal rather than an orderly cosmos.

---

17. This was one of the crucial theses of Averroism and was based on a confusion between Aristotle and Stoicism. Thomas Aquinas, in confronting this position, sought to refute it by pointing out that the intellect is not outside us but is rather a power of the soul. Were this not the case, the will, too, would be outside human beings, and the principles of morality would thus be invalidated. See Thomas Aquinas, *De unitate intellectus contra Averroistas*.

18. Frances A. Yates, *Giordano Bruno and the Hermetic Tradition* (London: Routledge and Kegan Paul, 1964), p. 202.

The Pagan Revival

To what magical forces are we referring apropos of Giordano Bruno and his age? The pagan influence that penetrated the thought of Christian philosophers under the tag of Averroism manifested itself at about the same time as certain Hermetic teachings became available as a corpus (the *Corpus Hermeticum*) to Western speculation and research. I have discussed elsewhere the impact that this vast collection of documents (brought to Italy from Constantinople after its fall to the Turks in 1453) had on philosophy in Europe.[19] Its immediate impact on the Medici court was such that Prince Cosimo, as previously mentioned, instructed his philosophical adviser, Marsilio Ficino, to abandon his work on the translation of Plato and to devote himself to unraveling the Hermetic writings (this was about 1460–63).

These writings were supposedly the work of the mythical Hermes Trismegistus (Hermes thrice greatest), an Egyptian sage, and contained his conversations with his son Thoth. The names are significant. Hermes, the Greek messenger god, was an intriguing figure, a curious explorer and investigator; Thoth was an Egyptian deity—in fact, the Egyptian Hermes. Bringing the two figures together shows a late pagan redaction, typical of the Mediterranean area. This was an attempt to acquire credibility through the attribution of the documents to the Egyptian Hermes Trismegistus, since Egypt was regarded as the fountainhead of very ancient, pre-Mosaic wisdom. The presence of Thoth lends the work its local color, and the content of the instruction and conversation culminates in recipes for the magical manipulation of cosmic forces.

The *Corpus Hermeticum* did not appear alone. During the same period, prompted to some extent by historical events—the fall of Constantinople, the arrival of Spanish Jews in various parts of the Continent, and the Reformation, which encouraged the surfacing of sects and esoteric teachings—other occult writings and practices flooded Europe, opening up new fields for scholarly study as well as opportunities for exploitation and abuse by charlatans. Alchemy, apparently as old as the mining profession from which it took its origin, suddenly became an object of inquiry, partly for the gold it promised, but also, in the eyes of the more serious, for

---

19. See Part II of my book *God and the Knowledge of Reality*.

its unlimited possibilities for bringing about the fusion of opposites, not only in metals, but in all things.

The coming "Christian state," a kind of earthly kingdom, for example, was regarded by some as a product of alchemical operations. Another indication of the climate of the times was the interest in the hermaphrodite as the fusion of male and female. One may readily see how these ideas excited the imagination of the semi-educated, and of the educated as well, and how the link was established among the Hermetic recipes of astral manipulation, the alchemical fusion of opposites that yielded the enigma of the universe, the secret cosmic influences discovered through astrological signs and numbers, and the cabalistic formulas by which the most ancient wisdom could be explored.

Ideas such as these were among the important preoccupations of the elite.[20] I have already mentioned Cosimo de' Medici's command to Marsilio Ficino. Kepler for his part dealt so seriously with alchemy that Emperor Rudolf engaged him more for the promise of gold than for astronomical investigations. And Spinoza described a visit to an alchemist's laboratory in one of his letters, in sufficient detail to demonstrate his interest. Astrology was the rage of Renaissance society, probably because of the controversy between the Aristotelian view of the heavens and the emerging mechanistic theories. Hermetism was counted as a science, and Pico della Mirandola regarded it as a gift of antiquity similar in value to the Bible and Greek philosophy. Jean Bodin, the learned judge and legal authority and the first great formulator of the theory of royal sovereignty, wrote a long and abstruse account of a fictional symposium on the topic, "the secrets of the sublime." In this volume, one of the participants declares, with an obvious reference to Hermetic secrets, that "the oldest leaders and parents

20. Mircea Eliade remarks in his diary that the vogue of Hermetism among Renaissance humanists shows their impatience with and reaction against the Aristotelian rational system, which imprisoned Catholic thought in a "ghetto." Through studies of magic and the occult, they aspired to transcend Christianity in the direction of a primordial and universal doctrine. Eliade explains the Renaissance popularity of the cabala in a similar fashion: the cabalists reacted to the centuries-old formal religiosity (of the Talmud, etc.) by working out a "cosmic religiosity" with ancient symbols, feminine elements in the divinity, and such dramatic episodes as the exile of God. See Eliade, *Fragments d'un journal* (Paris: Gallimard, 1973), pp. 407-8, 504-5.

of the human race had no other religion" than nature, and that "they left the memory of a Golden Age."[21]

Bodin's is a curious book: an encyclopedia of all knowledge, a tract on religious tolerance, a pamphlet expressing Renaissance ideology—all of it studded with intimations of a secret doctrine. In religious matters Bodin recommends ecumenism. One of the participants in the symposium, the author's obvious mouthpiece, relates that he has visited all the shrines at which people worship the Deity and found that all religions—the natural (scientific) one, the Greek, the Indian, the Tartar, the Moslem, the Hebrew, and the Christian—"are not unpleasing to eternal God and are excused as just errors."[22] Another participant, who also enjoys the author's favors, declares that it is ridiculous for a God to remain incorporeal for infinite times, then suddenly to place himself in a woman's womb, suffer punishment, be buried, and then take "to heaven a bodily mass which was unknown there before."[23] Celsus could not have been more grossly sarcastic.

It is certain that Bodin, like Pico and Bruno, was an avid reader of the Hermetic corpus. He credits the great heroes, "Pythagoras, Hermes, Plato, Zoroaster," with the possession of a secret knowledge, a wisdom transcending the all-too-profane religion of Christianity and common to only a chosen few. It is not surprising that, from the vantage point of this secret knowledge (*gnosis*), Bodin, again like Pico and Bruno, comes out in favor of tolerance among the derivative religions, Judaism, Christianity, and Islam. His own preference, however, seems to be for Judaism as the oldest, and therefore the closest to the "most ancient wisdom," humankind's true original religion, about which Hermes Trismegistus reported such striking things. Yet in Bodin's handling, tolerance quickly turns into indifference: "If true religion is contained in the pure worship of eternal God, I believe the law of nature is sufficient for man's salvation."[24] Indifference, in turn, becomes disguised as generosity; it encourages fideism, as the Paduan conception and even the personal faith of Erasmus indicate.

The main intention, here as elsewhere, is to substitute pagan

21. Bodin, *Colloquium of the Seven about Secrets of the Sublime*, p. 225.
22. Ibid., p. 251.
23. Ibid., p. 327.
24. Ibid., p. 225.

wisdom for the Christian religion, which would be a gain for the political commonwealth. Senamus, one of the participants in Bodin's fictional symposium asserts that when the Christian religion began, the sacred rites of the gods had been put aside, and the states and republics of the world began to struggle with violent upheavals. This was the reason why Greeks and Latins offered serious objections to the Christian deity.[25] This was also Machiavelli's central argument: namely, that the Christian religion and an efficiently ruled state are incompatible.

If Bodin himself was not completely engrossed in popularizing the Hermetic corpus, the elite for several generations made occult literature their religion. The main tenets of this cult (in which the influence of Pythagoras and Plato's *Timaeus* was dominant) asserted that the universe and humanity, the macro- and the microcosm, are constructed in the same harmonic proportions, so that the reciprocal influence was a potential to be exploited by the magician.

This potential had been put to use by some precursors of Renaissance magic, among them Roger Bacon in the thirteenth century, who claimed to direct operations compelling angels and the spirits of planets to do extraordinary things. Almost four centuries later, Tommaso Campanella constructed a model of the heavens in a previously fumigated, sealed room, with white cloth spread out and seven candles lit (for the seven known planets), and proceeded with a religious ceremony directing the angels, especially the sun angels. This, the seventeenth century, was also the century of Galileo, whose work finally overcame the Aristotelian worldview in the universities and laboratories. Yet Campanella's example shows that even Galileo's contemporaries—unorthodox from the church's point of view (Campanella was a long-imprisoned heretic)—followed Aristotle's theory that the celestial bodies were, if not alive, at least moved by living agents.

Aristotle, Plato, Pythagoras, and then the mythical and Oriental sages Hermes and Zoroaster, were recruited by some in the Renaissance to validate a religion counter to Christianity. These men were supposed to have been the beneficiaries of a wisdom more ancient than that of Christianity—and thus of a truer wisdom, since in the Renaissance antiquity was the equivalent of

25. Ibid., p. 160.

truth. Though what was put in the mouth of the Hermetic and other prophets was not necessarily what they had actually said, the wisdom of pagan antiquity was nonetheless enhanced by the *Corpus Hermeticum* and other writings.

The magicians of the Renaissance had two objectives: to secure human power over nature and thereby to remove God as a provident, efficacious being. The magic view is based on the supposition that the universe is an agglomerate, not only of the mental and material, but also of the spirits and spiritual substances—in sum, that there is an *anima mundi*. The universe is thus one substance (this is monism), self-sustaining, self-sufficient; indeed, as Bruno suggested, it is a big vibrant animal, full of life forces and with every part interconnected. Sages (or magicians) are in possession of certain words, formulas, talismans, and techniques by which they are able to call forth the corresponding and appropriate spirits.

Two illustrations of this Renaissance magic point of view may help make the point clear. The Venetian Francesco Giorgi described in 1525 the magical use of the sun to distribute "celestial life": "This celestial life is distributed by the sun 'through a certain vital spirit, by which . . . the whole world lives, continually drawing it in, together with the spirit and power of the other stars. Man, especially, does this through his own spirit, which is by its nature similar to them, and can be made more akin to them by art and foresight, by many rules and aids, of which true sages treat rather by word of mouth than in writing.'"[26]

Somewhat later, in 1586, the Venetian Fabio Paolini wrote in his *Hebdomades* of the magic effects of Orpheus's music on humans and animals—but also on stones and trees. He "believed that, just as a proper mixture of tones could give music a planetary power, so a proper mixture of 'forms' could produce 'celestial power' in an oration." In one of his lectures, Paolini "described how this celestial power was obtained in oratory by attracting the *anima mundi*." The latter contains, Paolini wrote, "seminal reasons, corresponding to the Ideas in the Divine Mind." "By collecting together a suitable set of things one can attract into them the corresponding

---

26. Francesco Giorgi, quoted in D. P. Walker, *Spiritual and Demonic Magic from Ficino to Campanella* (Notre Dame, Ind.: University of Notre Dame Press, 1969), pp. 113.

seminal reasons . . . by which they were originally shaped." By means of this magic, magicians can give a planetary character to a thought or mental image which would then obey them.[27]

After the high tension in Catholic thought in the period between the twelfth and fourteenth centuries—the age of Scholastic summas, cathedrals, doctrinal clarifications, political formulations, and literature—the fifteenth century was a time of malaise, doubt, and reformulation before the advent of medieval decadence and Renaissance reformation. The pagan revival, channeled by the Padua school and by occult literature, was not alone in signaling the change. Another symptom was the *theologia negativa*, which also reached back to a pagan Neoplatonism. But this Neoplatonism was "Christianized"—first by the works of Pseudo-Dionysius the Areopagite and John Scotus Eriugena, then, after a long period of quasi silence, by the sermons and essays of the Rhineland mystics, foremost among them Meister Eckhart. Still later, Thomas à Kempis was an influential representative of an offshoot of the negative theology, the *devotio moderna*, as was Jean Gerson, the rector of the University of Paris.

I will mention only two impulses behind negative theology, both of which suggest the coming dissolution of belief in God into a *visio intellectualis*, best represented by Nicholas of Cusa, who lived in the first half of the fifteenth century. The first impulse or source is the thesis proposed by Pseudo-Dionysius in the fifth or sixth century that we should not strive to apprehend God concep-

27. Fabio Paolini, quoted in Walker, *Spiritual and Demonic Magic*, p. 139. All these speculations, of unquestioned pagan inspiration, were variations on a theme to which great as well as less important philosophers of antiquity had subscribed. The theme was the *living universe*—one big yet limited cosmos, stratified into qualitatively different spheres, permeated with spirits and forces, ordered as an organism. This was Aristotle's worldview, and it was accepted not only by ancient scholars but by many medieval scholars as well. It penetrated all endeavors, from art and science to politics. Only through a combination of the slowly changing speculation of powerfully inspired minds and of the undeniable data of observation did this general view of the universe change. See Jean Seznec, *The Survival of the Pagan Gods: The Mythological Tradition and Its Place in Renaissance Humanism and Art*, translated by Barbara F. Sessions, Bollingen Series no. 38 (Princeton: Princeton University Press, 1953).

tually, by ascribing attributes to him that are but exalted versions of human attributes: goodness, wisdom, intelligence, providence, and so on. We ought, rather, to deny these concepts and epithets and refrain from applying them to God because they humanize him. It is best to speak of God negatively, until the anthropomorphic character disappears and only the ineffable God remains, stripped of the habitual words of praise and adoration, and thereby magnified.

Negative theology then received another impulse after the passing of the age of High Scholasticism, which had seen the triumph of Aristotelian philosophy—the categories, the metaphysics, the logic—which rendered speculation about God too rationalistic, logical, and dry. Reacting against the discussion of God as a mere object of science (as was the case with degenerative forms of Scholasticism), Gerson, Nicole d'Oresme, Thomas à Kempis, and others insisted on more piety, immersion in prayer, and a deeper adoration of the mystery.

Nicholas of Cusa (Cusanus) appeared at this juncture. The German philosopher and mathematician, who received a cardinalate for his ecumenical efforts with the Eastern Church, was one of the most complex thinkers of his time. In fact, the full impact of his thought reaches us only today. The core of his speculation may be called a dialectics of the finite and the infinite for which he gave mathematical and geometrical formulations, applying the formulas to theology as well. For Cusanus the infinite God is so far above our speculative powers—in fact, so far above the world of reality—that we should conceive of him only as we do of mathematical abstractions: God is the unattainable limit toward which all finite things tend, just as certain geometric sequences tend toward a limit, and certain curves approach an asymptote.

We come nearer to God, Cusanus writes in *Of Learned Ignorance* (1.26 and elsewhere), by the process of elimination and by the use of negative propositions. He is infinite, that is, *not* limited, *not* finite. Thus God is neither truth, intellect, and light nor Father, Son, and Holy Spirit. In his *Vision of God* (chapter 13) we find a prayer of such an intellectualist tone that it could have been taken from the *Meditations* of Marcus Aurelius:

He that approaches you must ascend above every limit and finite thing. But how shall we attain unto you? Does he not enter, by ascending over the limit, into the undefined and confused, and thus, in regard to the intellect, into ignorance and obscurity? So that the intellect ought to become ignorant and abide in darkness if it wants to see you. But what, oh my God, is this intellectual ignorance? Is it not a wise, a knowing, ignorance? You, God, who are infinity, can only be approached by him whose intellect is in ignorance, to wit, by him who knows himself to be ignorant of you.

With this reduction of God to a speculative abstraction—indirectly following Pseudo-Dionysius, to whom he recognized his great debt, but depersonalizing Pseudo-Dionysius's God much more radically—Cusanus left the study of divine things to concentrate on the conditioned world of finite objects. While the domain of absolute truth is ruled out as inaccessible, and thus left to faith (fideism), reason which cannot reach the essence of things can nevertheless organize and systematize them. It is endowed with the power to establish science, although in this endeavor it receives the help of metaphysical speculation about God as limit.

The truly original element in Cusanus's thought is the proposition that the infinite is enclosed in the finite. All things, without any mediating agency, depend directly on the Absolute Being, but this Absolute Being has only one mode of manifesting itself: through finite things. Such a quasi-Plotinian conception situates Cusanus among the early precursors of Kant and of modern phenomenology. God exists, Cusanus claims, but his only mode of expression is through humans and objects: all participate in the totality which is in them. God is the limit of speculation, he is unity and perfection, but he is only passively present in the things of the world, which are limited and multiple.

We recognize the essential pagan modus operandi: relegate God to a phantom existence—or with Cusanus turn him into an abstract postulate, a requirement of the scientific mind—without positive and existential ties with the world and humanity. This is justified by the need to remove all trace of anthropomorphism, which is a pollution of the divine figure with mundane frailties. The God that results is the pure and abstract God of Plotinus and of the entire Greco-Roman pagan world, not the towering and thundering God of the Old Testament or the loving God of the Gospels. It would indeed take an act of faith, then, to hold that Cusanus's God is the world's creator, if for no other reason than that the act of creation would be a limitation (creating this world rather than another) imposed on the unlimited and infinite. More probably, Cusanus would say that creation was a lapse of the infinite into the finite, another Neoplatonic position.

The point in this discussion is not whether Cardinal Nicholas of Cusa was or was not a man of faith. The point is rather that it was almost natural for excellent minds to fall back upon pagan premises, since they were repelled by certain tenets of the Christianity they otherwise professed. We saw that one of these tenets was the immortality of the soul, which Pomponazzi denied philosophically but still professed as a Christian. The doctrine of the Incarnation was another hard-to-swallow tenet, as it necessitated a certain degree of anthropomorphization of God, which would limit him and deny his infinity. The importance of faith as the cornerstone of religion was also distasteful because it blocked the free movement of reason, and of science in particular.

What we have called the pagan thrust is the ambition of many thinkers, past and present, to remove these obstructions and to formulate a natural religion, as it came to be called. And where is this natural religion to be found ready-made if not in pagan antiquity, where the sages had repudiated the Homeric pantheon, relegated the gods to a position of inaction and indifference, and endowed the natural forces with philosophical tags so that there could be no question of faith in an impersonal cosmos?

The success of the pagan revival was stupendous, whether in the studies of the occult or of wisdom. We must look for the root of this success in the relentless efforts of so many thinkers not only to unearth ancient writings but also to formulate arguments against the Christian religion. Pagan speculation itself was supported by prestigious doctrines of the Orient, which display a spectacular and attractive variety of arguments grounded in pantheism, Gnosticism, and atomism. These Eastern doctrines are not just philosophies; they are worldviews, speculative but also lived visions—religion, ethics, and epistemology in one. This makes them full-fledged rivals of Christianity.

Yet facing them, Christianity seems to be like an arrow, boldly penetrating into a hostile mass. It may be overcome, or it may be victorious, but it is never won over to the cause of other side. It always remains isolated, in contradiction to all others. The explanation that Christianity brought to the permanent questions about God, creation, soul, and matter, the rational realities behind the cosmological tales, stunned all other civilizations and decisively shaped that of the West. Yet those things that are characteristic of Christianity—the personhood of God, his becoming a man and returning to heaven, the independence and freedom of the soul even in its creaturely status, a faith that does not contradict but promotes the inquiries of reason—all this can be grasped by thinking people, but it can also be rejected as too demanding and too disruptive of our reflective capacity.

Thus Nicholas of Cusa, standing at the intersection of modern influences in his century—*theologia negativa*, Occamism, mysticism of the Rhineland, Averroism in its Paduan version, the "secret knowledge" of the occult—provides an excellent illustration for the impact of pagan thought on the Christian religion and civilization. Maurice de Gandillac writes that a long apophatic tradition[28] had preceded Nicholas—Plotinus, Pseudo-Dionysius, Meister Eckhart, and his disciple Johannes Tauler—which accounts for the ideas of divine infinity, of knowledge through "unknowing of God's immanence in finite things, of the mystic's renunciation of discursive intelligence."[29] In this manner a noetic vacuum was created around God—again, in harmony with pagan thought—and filled in such a way that the universe appeared as the work of the human mind, a progressive accomplishment that imitates the gradualness of divine creation. Cusanus's *visio intellectualis* "presupposes self-movement of the mind as well as original force in the mind itself that unfolds in a continuous process of thought."[30]

28. Apophasis is the teaching of the Eastern Church about the impossibility of approaching God with words, names, and other means of discursive knowledge. Let us note here that Nicholas of Cusa strongly influenced Pico and, in particular, the generation after him, including Giordano Bruno, who quoted him at length. Pico himself elaborated his own conclusions from negative theology but remained in remarkable concordance with the ideas of Cusanus. Yet Pico had a Paduan training and Paduan sympathies. For the interrelatedness of these late medieval thinkers and their common link to the tradition of Neoplatonism see Edgar Wind, *Pagan Mysteries in the Renaissance* (New Haven: Yale University Press, 1958).

29. Maurice de Gandillac, *La Philosophie de Nicolas de Cues* (Paris: Aubier, 1941), p. 109.

30. Ernst Cassirer, *The Individual and the Cosmos in Renaissance Philosophy*,

De Gandillac does not hesitate to label the human mind in Cusanus's conception a "second God" because it does not work on a previously given model but, through a permanent subjective effort, "adopts the inner formative forces to the indeterminacy of pure experience."[31] In other words, in the course of intellectual discovery increasingly capable mental tools are applied to the just-grasped world of experience. In the "absence" of God, humans create their own world and thus come to know it intimately.[32] More than that, although humans are but finite points, as are the objects of their knowledge, the infinite God's immanence in the world of the finite guarantees the progression of this knowledge, not from one truth to another, but through never-ending approximations.

One consequence of negative theology was that God, stripped of names and attributes and of an external, objective existence, could be discovered only in the human soul. This old thesis was powerfully renewed by the striking poetic images of the sermons and treatises of Meister Eckhart, who had gone so far as to declare that God would not *be* without man. Cusanus supplemented this point with his theory of the immanence of God in all things, including the privileged place of the soul, the "childbed" of divinity as he called it, in which incarnation occurs and keeps recurring. In the same way that human beings generate in themselves the knowledge of the world, shaping it with their conceptual instruments and without a preexisting model, divinity generates itself in the soul without a preexisting model. Just as knowledge of the external world grows (science), so does God. He *becomes* rather than *is*. Grace, said Tauler (in the fourteenth century), is not a gift; it is the discovery of the Ineffable, slumbering in the "mysterious ark" (the soul).

The Gnostics were similarly convinced that God, hidden and imprisoned by the evil creator of this world, remains active in the

---

translated by Mario Domandi (Philadelphia: University of Pennsylvania Press, 1972), p. 14.

31. De Gandillac, *La Philosophie de Nicolas de Cues*, p. 153.

32. One is reminded here of Giambattista Vico's epistemology three centuries later. According to Vico, human beings know only what they make with their own (mental or physical) instruments. Thus, although in a sense they remain ignorant of nature, they know history because they shape it.

spirit or *pneuma* of the elect, which is indeed a divine particle. It was the task of the Gnostics—their religious commandment, if the term is apt—to let this inner God grow; that is, it was the task of the elect to become ever more spiritual. For the Gnostics, there was a final objective—the restitution of their part of God, the divine scintilla, to the now-captive and diminished God. We do not know exactly what Cusanus meant by God. From his theoretical writings we obtain nothing more than striking and intriguing labels satisfying the savant: God is the immanent Infinity, the object of learned ignorance, the One above all contradictions, as the infinite circle is above the curve and the straight line. And the word for Christ is the "maximum-man."[33]

To conclude this discussion of the pagan worldview—its elaboration in ancient times and its revival in the late Middle Ages—it is necessary to take stock of certain of its features in order to put into perspective the rise of the pagan temptation in the contemporary world, the topic of the next three chapters. I will note here three features. First, the pagan worldview was a continual, if not constant, element of Christian civilization through and after the Middle Ages; second, the acceptance by Christian thinkers of the two verities drew from and encouraged the revival of the pagan worldview; and third, the decline of belief in the immanent presence of the supernatural, whenever it occurred, merely strengthened the pagan temptation.

I discussed in this chapter the continual presence and periodic revival of pagan speculation up to the fifteenth and sixteenth centuries. Needless to say, the story does not end there. Continuity past that point was assured by a long line of Paduan rationalists; by their intellectual descendants, the libertines, in the seventeenth century; and, in that same century, by the continued progress and popularity of the Hermetic doctrine, which issued in Rosicrucianism, Freemasonry, and varieties of alchemical and astrological arts. Lucretius, who was rediscovered and grew in prestige at the beginning of the fifteenth century, exerted an influence on Hobbes, Gassendi, La Mettrie, and Voltaire much later. The popularity of the occult too lasted long beyond the chronological

---

33. In some of his intellectual procedures and terminology, Cusanus often reminds us of Teilhard de Chardin.

The Pagan Revival

limit of this chapter, as many scholarly works indicate. Yet we have good reasons not to argue that pagan speculation has been equally and uniformly intensive and influential from the fourteenth century to the present. Rather, it appears that there have been periods of latency and revival.

We must ask why the pagan perspective continued to be strong for so long and why it periodically exerted an increased influence on Christian civilization. That the Paduan school eagerly seized upon the Averroist thesis of the two verities suggests that many people then, and many others since then, have found the Christian tension of faith and reason unbearable. The Western tradition inherited from the Greeks a strong penchant for science; and, as we saw in Chapter 1, this inclination was decisively strengthened by Christianity, which made strenuous efforts to clear the way still clogged by the Greek view of things above and below the heavens. It was assumed that if science was to progress, faith had to make concessions, and eventually yield. Whether this view was correct or not, it is how many in the late Middle Ages saw it, and it may explain the popularity among many scholars—and less educated people—of the Paduan theories.

Now it is interesting, though not surprising, that Greek speculation never developed a doctrine of the two verities. There are several reasons for this. One is that the Greeks were already divided between what I have called the mass cult and elite culture, so that there was no need for the elite to elaborate a diluted version of their doctrine for the masses (recall the belittling statement of Averroës above), while keeping the difficult, secret part intact for themselves. The only Greek thinkers among whom we observe a doctrine along the lines of the two verities or the division of one belief into two divergent doctrines are the Gnostics. But for them Greek speculation actually took second place behind Oriental influences. They believed that the *pneumatikoi* (the Pneumatics, who could supposedly escape the world of matter) were superior and that the *hyloi* (those made of matter, bound in the world of matter) were inferior, with the two groups eventually separating into two different and divergent sets of belief, much as the castes are separated in India.

The Christian religion by contrast was the same for all believers; thus it is understandable that the impatient ones felt the need to pacify the masses—as well as, at the other end, the official guardians of orthodoxy, whom they also regarded as intellectually dull—by allocating faith to them and reserving reason for themselves. Christianity never divided into two separate religions—mass cult and elite culture—but it did divide into two aspects of the same religion—two truths. The tragedy is, of course, that the Christian thinkers who fostered this development attempted to separate two aspects that at heart are inseparable. Indeed, their artificial separation leads each time to two unorthodox positions: some version of fideism on the one hand and some version of rationalism on the other.

Another explanation for why Greek speculation (except for Gnostic thinking) had no need for two verities and why Christian thinking did is that the Greek, even at its most intellectual, was supported by myth, or at least by material which could be mythicized. The pagans' mythopoeic readiness was greater than that of the Christians, who, as was pointed out earlier, needed no myth since they possessed history and supernatural truth. The strongly bound unity and organic wholeness of the Christian religion, from which the speculative theses, demonstrations, and conclusions logically followed, rendered the elaboration of special myths superfluous—even more, forbidden. Paganism was on the popular level an indefinitely stylized interpretation of nature and on the educated level a protection against nature's "calamities and temptations." The pagan could afford to live in two worlds, the mythical and the speculative. The Christian could not, however, because Christian faith was articulated not only by a well-rounded philosophy but also by an elaborate theology. This, perhaps more than any other factor, explains the tension in the area we are discussing.

This leads to one last feature of the revival of the pagan worldview, which I will introduce with a question: What is the general condition that would foster a pagan revival in a Christian civilization? To answer that the necessary condition is the weakening of the Christian myth is somewhat ambiguous, because in Christianity the place of the pagan myth is taken by the supernatural. If Christ did not rise from the dead, said Paul, Christians are but poor fools. Thus the condition for a pagan revival in a Christian civilization is the weakening of the belief in the supernatural and of the mythopoeic elements that translate the supernatural, even in Christianity, into sacred symbols and myths. Like the pagan myth and its cultural expressions, the Christian belief in the supernatural needs the strong, visible presence of the cult and cultic symbols: prayer, ritual, a sense of the sacred community, sincere piety, the élan of the clergy, and the unquestioning confidence that earthly authority is in touch with God through words and deeds.

The belief in the presence of the supernatural—always a mediated, veiled presence—does not weaken without reawakening the latent temptation of paganism. The pagan myth—the occult, the magical, the idolatrous love of nature, immanentist philosophies—begins to awaken among the masses by exerting an imperceivable influence on the unconscious; only then does it make its appearance in consciousness and in rationalistic systems. The pagan mythos begins to replace the Christian mythos.

Among the elite, the situation is even more confused. The elite had already, for the most part, discarded the mythicization of religion in favor of a more rationalistic system. But even so, in a Christian culture, the elite too benefit from a vigorously asserted supernatural. They too need channels through which higher truths are communicated to the values of culture, scholarship, or aesthetic admiration. In Christianity it is belief in the supernatural that keeps the element of the sacred alive and publicly active.[34] Its fatigue, its listlessness or indifference, opens the way for a revival of the pagan alternative.

---

34. In a religious culture, the sacred place is the public place. In modern secular society, religion has fallen into the private domain, which is now the last refuge of the sacred. However, it may be a contradiction in terms to speak of a "private sacred."

CHAPTER 3

The Christian Desacralization

In his book *The Crisis of the Modern World* (1946), René Guénon writes that the true Middle Ages, by which he understands a civilization loyal to the Christian tradition, began with Charlemagne's rule and lasted until the beginning of the fourteenth century—some 500 years in all. I have expressed the view in this book that the earliest publicly noticeable stirrings of the pagan revival began with Paduan Averroism in the early fourteenth century after the culmination of the Scholastic period, the era of vast summas and great debates. One might say that Christianity began to retreat after that time, shaken by certain decisive events in that century: the schism in the Catholic Church and the Avignon papacy, the conflict between popes and the radicals among the Franciscans, the rapid rise of Ockhamism in philosophy, and the ever-increasing efforts at secularization led by Marsilio of Padua.

Other movements followed: the subtle systematization of negative theology by Nicholas of Cusa and the vogue of occult doctrines, partly in combination with Neoplatonism. The general weakening of the church over some 150 years facilitated the popularization of these trends in which the fundamentals of pagan revival—the early traces of Neoplatonism, pantheism, and Epicurean materialism—are recognizable. It is indeed difficult to fault Guénon's diagnosis that beginning with the fourteenth century the decadence of Christianity became unmistakably obvious.

My thesis has been that a similar phenomenon is taking place in our own time and that the immediate and remote causes of today's

The Christian Desacralization

conflict between Christianity and paganism can be identified as surely as those responsible for events six, or even nineteen, centuries ago. The conflict assumes almost identical forms in different eras: it is again possible to distinguish an elite culture and mass cults, both existing at the expense of Christianity and deeply affecting Christian civilization. In the next two chapters I shall examine both as I discuss neopaganism and the new occult. But before that, I will examine the retreat of Christianity itself, and the consequent repaganization of Western culture.

I argued in Chapter 2 that the church was never able, or perhaps was never willing, to eliminate manifestations of paganism. It was always the church's unofficial but steadily held position that one may learn even from hostile doctrines and that the development of a living body of traditions depends on intellectual contact with opponents. It is also useful for those in possession of truth to test that truth in the fire of controversy. This attitude is expressed in the formula *haereses oportet esse:* it is necessary that there be heresies. There is no danger in such a position, but the condition for sustaining it is that the church remain unquestionably loyal not only to dogma, doctrine, and magisterium—the intellectual component, so to speak—but also to the element of myth in the church's life that manifests itself through cultic and symbolic forms—the sacred component.

Unlike pagan religion in which the philosophical and theological element is not joined to the cultic core but is freely floating or nonexistent, the Christian religion incorporates the seeds of a civilization that, when mature, turns against its religious framework. The seeds are the combined tendency to rationalize (to reduce to the rational) and to desacralize.

I suggested at the end of Chapter 2 that paganism is, in the final analysis, a form of nature worship. As is evident from the following examples from ancient writings, human beings adored the forces manifest in nature and allowed their imaginations to be impressed by its myriad varieties. "From Ymir's flesh the earth was made, from his sweat the seas, the mountains from his bones, the trees out of his hair, and his cranium formed the vault of heaven" (from the *Edda*, a Scandinavian saga). "The moon was born from the consciousness of Purusha, his stare created the sun, from his mouth Indra and Agni [fire] were born, and from his breath the wind. Air issued from his nombril, the sun came out of his head, and the earth from his feet. . . . This is how the world was arranged. Purusha is the father of all."¹

Note that the pagan creation story is in a sense much more concrete or physical than the creation accounts of the Hebrew and Christian religions. In the latter God's Word (the Logos) creates as if by remote control while in the former the universe is made out of the god's body. Consequently the pagan worshiper adored nature directly, and in it the god. But the main spiritual preoccupation of the pagan elite eventually became to protect itself against the inexorability of nature. The members of the elite seemed to believe that it is best to come to terms with nature through a withdrawal into a small personal area in which one may remain unaffected. This is the ultimate message of the pagan systems of wisdom, whether Hindu, Stoic, Skeptic, Epicurean, or late imperial syncretistic.

This is very different from the intent and content of Christian philosophical-religious discourse, and hence Christian civilization as well differs from the pagan. The pagan (nature) myth always remains stable: it does not change, does not evolve. When reforms are attempted—such as Siddhartha Gautama's reform of Hinduism half a millennium before the birth of Christ that resulted in the formation of Buddhism—they generally fail. Buddhism itself was gradually reabsorbed into ancient Hindu forms, and Gautama (Buddha) himself came to be adored like other gods. Hindu reformism had to wait until the nineteenth century when the Hindu elite—primarily the Brahmanic leading caste—came into contact with Western religion and values and became captivated with the British style of life and political institutions. True, only the surface of Indian society was affected; religious and ethical conservatism has survived to this day and shows no sign of change except in those few sects which have adopted a kind of ambiguous monotheism (for example, worshipers of Brahmo adapt, under nineteenth-century Western Christian influence Brahmanism to monotheism).

What makes pagan religions permanent and unchanging? A careful answer points, I think, to their worship of nature, itself unchanging despite its seasonal and other rhythms, thus integrat-

---

1. From the Sanskrit treatise, *Rig-Veda*, quoted by G. Locchi in *Le mythe cosmogonique indo-européen* (n.p., n.d.).

ing movement with an overall permanence. Under the impact of an apparently static nature, even Aristotle's sophisticated cosmology insisted on the immobility of celestial bodies. But since mobility could not be denied in the face of observation, Aristotle assumed—on the basis of a supposed ideality—that the celestial bodies moved in the most regular motion, the circular, the motion that eventually will bring everything around to its original position. The same is true of the Hindu Great Year and Eternal Return: by such conceptions the Hindus reduce change to a minimum and postulate it only at such intervals that it is beyond human imagination and conception. Strictly speaking, then, there is no change or novelty, merely the recurrence of the same events.

In this cosmic, spatial, and temporal permanence, myth thrives because it too remains changeless in its description and narration. These descriptions and narrations share in *sacredness*, the condition of eternal sameness infinitely transcending the transitoriness of individual human experience. In fact, human experience becomes meaningful only when compared to permanence—cosmogonic, cosmological, ontological—which is ultimately personalized in the divine. Standing underneath the great drama of the birth of the gods and the world-all (cosmogony) and facing the constant sameness of the starry sky above (cosmology), human beings came to the conclusion that there is a certain structure of being (ontology), which is "isness" itself, guaranteed by God or by the gods.

Paganism thus sacralizes the world, and if we study Greek speculative thought, we discover that philosophy from Thales to Plotinus (eight centuries) consisted of a succession of systems in which the universe (nature) was described in different ways but always as divine. As such, with a few exceptions, nature or the cosmos was considered the ultimate reality, and thus always sacred. It is understandable that the human response to nature expressed itself in unchanging cults and symbols since the mythical-natural substratum itself was held to be permanent. Furthermore, it is no surprise then that neopagans, upon facing the desacralization of nature inherent in Christian thought and civilization, connected the cause of the sacred with the rehabilitation of paganism. Misusing the term, perhaps deliberately, they spoke of a restored "transcendence" that only a return to paganism would be able to effect. They believed that a vigorous, self-asserting civilization needs the sacred and that only a pagan turn to nature and to myth may posit it again, over against a Christianity whose sacred sources have become exhausted.

What about Christianity and the sacred? We have seen that the pagan myth was not concocted from mere superstition and that there are common themes in pagan myths all over the world. As several disciplines inform us, the myth is so great a mental-spiritual requirement of the human being that when it is erased from the public consciousness and driven from the public place—that is when the public place (religion) is no longer seen as in contact with the sacred—it seeks refuge in the individual's unconscious and expresses itself through personal myths, symbols, dreams, tales, and acts. To quote C. G. Jung: "All ages before us have believed in gods in some form or other. Only an unparalleled impoverishment of symbolism could enable us to rediscover the gods as psychic factors, that is, as archetypes of the unconscious. . . . Heaven has become for us the cosmic space of the physicists, and the divine empyrean a fair memory of things that once were. But 'the heart glows,' and a secret unrest gnaws at the roots of our being."[2]

Do Jung's words point to a flaw in the Christianizing of our civilization or to a failure of Christianity to cover the expanse of the mythical imagination? I think that the latter answer is more accurate. It makes little sense to say that Christianity has failed in forming civilization when in fact it is the primary force behind the present shape of Western culture. For centuries, it has supplied poets, artists, painters, architects, composers, playwrights, and scientists with an inexhaustible reservoir of inspiration, hypotheses, themes, forms, and styles. Museums, churches, public buildings, the theater, literary genres, and much more display works of Christian inspiration and accomplishment as powerful as anything that the pantheons of the Greeks, Egyptians, Chaldeans, or Hindus ever produced. Though styles of art and architecture changed—Roman, gothic, baroque, romantic—throughout the Christian era the contents have focused on Christian topics and values. In 1802, Chateaubriand devoted a memorable book, *Le Génie du Christianisme*, to the analysis of how Christianity remolded Western aesthetic sensibilities and filled the Western imagination

---

2. C. G. Jung, "Archetypes of the Collective Unconscious," as quoted in Joseph Campbell, *The Hero with a Thousand Faces*, Bollingen Series no. 17, 2d ed. (Princeton: Princeton University Press, 1968), pp. 104-5n.24.

with sacred history from the Bible, from the lives of saints, and from stories in permanent vogue among the cultured and the uncultured populace. In the face of so much evidence, obviously impossible but also unnecessary to marshal here, it is a challenging enterprise to find the opening through which the pagan imagination was able to penetrate.

Two such openings may suggest themselves. The first stems from the inseparable attachment of the myth to the ever-recurring variations and rhythms of nature, as we saw above. Thus myth was a repeatable story, as permanent as nature itself—and as unfathomable, too, always presenting itself in forms as tangible as nature yet as mysterious as the powers behind it. Thus without denying the mysteries in nature, the myth and the cult allowed their followers to deal on a direct, comprehensible level with nature and everyday experience.

To be sure, the great pagan mysteries and cults had their dogmatic side and their strict cultic observances; yet the cult—for example, the Eleusian mysteries—was linked to one particular place and routine, and it did not possess the power of enforcing dogmas and practices, the core of which was the initiation ceremony, enjoining the initiated to guard the secret of what they had heard. In a way the secret was not a precise content but rather the fact of bringing the worshipers together. The pagan imagination was able to remain strong and to penetrate the Christian imagination because it had no dogmatic edifice, no organization, especially no speculative effort, and no anguish about the intellectual task of reconciling reason and faith at every step. The Christian imagination, on the other hand, had to deal with theological subtleties—those of the Nicene Creed, for example—and had to reconcile them with the observations of nature.

The pagan myth according to which a king becomes a sacrificial victim destined to die, either by his own or by another's hand, substantiates my point here. In such myths the king had to die for various reasons. To restore fruitfulness to the land or to expiate the sins of the community are just two. In both cases, the worshipers in the cult could come to terms with the mystery through their own instincts and knowledge of nature, a kind of direct vision (though later researchers, who deal with the "cooled-off" event, may try to offer other explanations). Now compare this myth with the story of Christ dying on the cross. What was natural in the pagan myth, or at least accessible to natural observation and imagination, is here replaced with the supernatural (the prior incarnation of divinity, his earthly existence, and his subsequent resurrection), which necessitates infinite reflection, careful handling of symbols, and their separation from the historical event.

Pagan beliefs about growth and development, to cite another example, also combine concrete observations of nature with a belief in the mysterious forces behind those natural events. The passage of the seed through the subsoil and its bursting into bread-giving wheat give rise to a myth that is intertwined with the observed operations of agriculture. The Christian sacred story, on the other hand, does not allow such a combination. Historical reality demands of the worshipers that they deal with natural events, but also that they deal with the theological subtleties expressed therein as reality and not as myth. History and factual material are ready to be dealt with by science, first of all by the science of theology.

Compare Christ with the heroes of paganism—Gilgamesh, Odysseus, Hermes, Hercules, Jason, Theseus, Buddha, Faust. One could attribute numerous further traits, adventures, and imaginative elements to the pagan heroes without really altering their stories; but nothing further can be attributed to the hero of Christianity. Christ's story cannot be changed after the fact because in distinction to those of the pagan heroes his acts are historically ascertained: his story is true.

The apocryphal "lives of Christ" were carefully excised by the church from the official story at a time when "lives" abounded in literature and when various sects presented their own versions of the career of the central character. Many, in their interpretation of the life of Christ, not only embroidered on the canvas of the gospel story; they also transformed the figure of Christ, making of him a phantom (the Gnostics, who rejected the Incarnation), an amiable young poet (the rationalists, including Ernest Renan), or today a revolutionary (Christian Marxists). Popular imagination has, of course, gotten hold of the Christ figure throughout the centuries and in every area into which his religion has penetrated. This imagination has further shaped and elaborated the image of Christ; yet this elaboration has been tolerated in the belief that there was hardly any danger that history—the supreme guarantee—would be modified in the process.

The Christian Desacralization

The question is whether the sacred can be sustained in a Christian civilization exposed to all sorts of stresses, philosophical controversies, and rationalistic critiques.[3] Christianity draws part of its strength from its close connection with human mythical archetypes, even though it also relies essentially on historical documentation. The virgin birth, for example, is so universal that the early Christian missionaries were forced to think that the devil himself had preceded them to mock their efforts. Universal too are the quest for the father, the ordeal, the atonement, the heavenly triumph of the true son, and other elements essential to Christianity.[4] While such elements cannot be uprooted from the sacred tradition of humanity, new variations on the fundamental themes can be accepted without undue difficulty. Thus in most instances Christianity was able to overcome paganism by successfully superimposing its own story on the existing tribal, animistic, and collective myth.

Yet—and this is the second opening that paganism found in Christianity—the Christian religion challenges its own myth and the entire edifice of its sacred, cultic, and symbolic affirmation when it counterposes its mythic and its rational components. As we saw, nature cannot very well be denied; it can only be embellished or degraded through the work of imagination. This is difficult with the supernatural because neither reason nor the senses readily admit it. Reason remains forever recalcitrant; and the senses, though they may be amenable to grasping the supernatural and may even show an eagerness to bathe in its glow, will accept it only if it is mediated by symbols, themselves embedded in cultic life and a mythic infrastructure. Thus, more than pagan religion, which at all times draws sustenance directly from nature, the Christian religion requires the mediating presence of symbols,

---

3. The extreme form of rationalistic critique that opposes Christianity is the denial that Jesus existed at all. Rationalism, unable to deal with things outside its narrow scope, prefers to deny an *idée claire et distincte* (a clear and distinct idea), the Cartesian litmus test, rather than probe beyond the boundaries of the immediate data. Although rationalists may agree that witnesses to any event may describe it in various, even contradictory ways, they see the differences in the Synoptic accounts of the life of Christ—and the divergence between the Synoptic Gospels and the Gospel of John—as proof that the Gospel authors were not witnesses of any significant event.

4. See Campbell, *Hero with a Thousand Faces*, p. 312.

which transmit the unseen and untouched reality of the supernatural.

There is a point beyond which the sacred does not operate—namely, when faith in the supernatural weakens or reaches the vanishing point. Christian civilization constantly produces such occasions of desacralization because its rational component by itself does not know the limits beyond which it turns into a desiccating rationalism and begins to contest the other components: faith, the reality of the supernatural that justifies faith, the domain of mythopoeia and symbol, and in the end the historicity of the gospel itself. In "normal" circumstances, the church guards itself against attempts at demythologization and desacralization, just as it guards itself against the opposite attempts, the overemphasis on faith at the expense of reason. But there are periods when the holders of the magisterium themselves become hesitant, probably even doubtful, and allow the equilibrium to be broken in the face of an overwhelming and sustained skepticism.

We find a good illustration of the process of desacralization in a dialogue between Karl Jaspers and Rudolf Bultmann.[5] The subtitle of the volume in which the dialogue was printed—"An Inquiry into the Possibility of Religion without Myth"—indicates the intent of desacralization as the modern world undertakes it: it is a search for a religion that is a wholly private affair, no longer embarrassing in a rationalistic and scientific environment.

Jaspers, the existentialist thinker, and Bultmann, celebrated for his demythologizing of Christianity, do not appear very friendly in this exchange of views. Then suddenly it dawns on Bultmann that they have been in total agreement all along—which indeed had been obvious to the objective reader. Bultmann writes:

[Jaspers] says that the belief that "God manifests himself at a given place and time, that he has revealed himself at one place and time and only there and then, makes God appear as a fixed thing, an object in the world." Very true! It is also true that the Christian churches often interpreted and still interpret the revealed faith in that way. But does not Jaspers see that such a conception of the revealed faith has been fought against repeatedly? Does he not know that what I am fighting against is just this fixation

---

5. The dialogue is found in Karl Jaspers and Rudolf Bultmann, *Myth and Christianity: An Inquiry into the Possibility of Religion without Myth* (New York: Noonday, 1958), pp. 67, 70.

of God as an objective entity, against misconceiving the revelation as an act accomplished once and for all? Does he not grasp that the purpose of my demythologization is to interpret the mythological eschatology of the New Testament in such a way that the process of revelation is given its genuine meaning of an "eschatological" process? . . .

The "demythologized" sense of the Christian doctrine of incarnation, of the word that "was made flesh," is precisely this, that God manifests himself not merely as the idea of God . . . but as "my" God who speaks to me here and now. . . . Christ is not merely a past phenomenon, but the ever-present word of God.

These are crucial passages because they show that when myth is liquidated, religion, deprived of the sense of the sacred, becomes a private and uncommunicable affair—it ceases to function as a religion. I am not arguing here for a strict rational control of the content of faith over against the existentialism of Bultmann and Jaspers. As I said earlier, excessive rationalism applied to the gospel story and to doctrine risks obscuring the mythopoeic component with which religious truth must be suffused if it is not to degenerate into a mere philosophical, psychological, or sociological system. The speculative character of the Christian religion, when placed in different historical contexts, can lead at times either to a rationalist devastation or to a retreat into a personal myth. In either case there is a loss of the material that supplies the imagination with symbols and myths.

Until our century the danger of this loss was present much more in Protestantism than in Catholicism. As Jung states, Protestantism did away with dogma, liturgy, ritual, and the sacrificial importance of the priesthood, thus opening the way for the strictly rational, the utilitarian, the streamlined. It pulled down many a wall that had been carefully erected by the church and thus immediately began to experience the disintegrating and schismatic effect of individual revelation. As soon as the dogmatic fence was broken down and ritual lost its authority, humanity was confronted with an inner experience without the protection and guidance of dogma and ritual, which are the unparalleled quintessence of Christianity as well as of pagan religious experience.

The Christian religion is exposed to the temptation of an excessive rationalism because of its well-defined doctrine and documented historicity. By eliminating the pagan myth and replacing it with a story with truth content, Christianity compelled the mythopoeic impulse either to leave the domain of public imagination or to curb itself within certain limits. Jung himself insists in all his works that by removing the collective archetypes the rationalist worldview has forced modern people to retreat into a world of personal archetypes and myths. The pathology of the situation becomes manifest in that these archetypes are not the fundamental experiences of humankind, limited in number yet basic for the constitution of the psyche, but personal fantasies, magnified and manipulated by the individual who cannot participate in a reassuring common experience and its symbolization.

Symbols, writes Eliade, "converge towards a common aim: to abolish the limits of the 'fragment' man is within society and the cosmos, and, by means of making clear his deepest identity and his social status, and making him one with the rhythms of nature[, to] integrat[e] him into a large unity: society, the universe."[6] The point is that not being able to draw from the common fund, human beings retreat into a world of personal obsessions, without contact with the world of other people. It is obvious that in all civilizations such contact on the interhuman level is normally supplied by religion, which remains linked with an infinitely rich store of symbols and images. If religion cuts its ties with symbols and images, it no longer fulfills one of its essential functions: the rooting of human beings in the mysterious being of the universe and through it in God—or, as Jung puts it in obviously non-Christian language, in the oneness of the cosmos.

The Christian flaw, as I call it, consists in bypassing the universe of nature in the direct linkage of human beings in a relationship with God. The flaw of Greek paganism in contrast, as also of the Hindu, was that though the linkage to the natural universe, the cosmos, was abundantly elaborated and asserted, it was not extended to establish contact with the transcendent. Not recognizing an extra-universal, personal, creator God, Greek speculation led, in a sense, nowhere: its gods either were indifferent or were mere abstract entities like the One of the Plotinian conception. But while it is existentially possible for human beings to have only vague ideas about God's identity, since God is surrounded by mystery and awe, it is hard for them to renounce their ties with

---

6. Mircea Eliade, *Patterns in Comparative Religion*, translated by Rosemary Sheed (New York: Sheed and Ward, 1958), p. 451.

nature. Christianity did not pay sufficient attention to this need for the nourishment that nature provides to the soul, and it consequently yielded such preoccupations to rationalists and scientists, who took from nature its mysteries.

Scholars are agreed that the break between the Christian and the modern worldview occurred at the time of, perhaps with, Galileo. The Christian worldview was still Aristotelian, which means that Christians, along with Aristotle, held that celestial bodies were moved by living spirits or gods and that the supralunar sphere contained no matter—and was hence incorruptible and unchangeable. Galileo, in contrast, and Kepler before him, saw the celestial motions in terms of mechanics and discovered laws that owed nothing to divine consciousness and will. From that moment on, science and the rational spirit that sponsored it and underwrote its methods and conclusions conquered nature and neutralized it. Nature could no longer serve the human imagination on its way to God.[7]

The desacralization of nature by Christianity necessarily led to a similar desacralization, or "disciplining," of the imagination, something that the Christian religion could ill afford since nature, in the form of myth and symbol, was needed as a mediation toward the supernatural. Yet this desacralization was hardly avoidable because, as noted in Chapter 1, a well-defined doctrine must organize those external manifestations of inner life that involve the imagination, from problems of morality to architecture and music. In this respect the church maintained a generous and resourceful policy. Under the church's patronage, imagination found myriad artistic outlets that remained uncurbed, even when they clashed with the Christian spirit, or were encouraged, when they did not clash. This "half-disciplined" imagination resulted in the great literature and art of the Christian centuries, from the revolutionary architecture of Suger of Saint-Denis to Dante's *Divine Comedy*.

Yet the Church rejected the limitless freedom of the imagination because it may produce images and symbols that conflict with those that Christian teaching can approve. Gilbert Durand, who is critical of this curbing of imagination, observes that the church

---

7. At the time of the first landing on the moon in 1969, journalists asked an old Zulu in South Africa what he thought of it. He told them sadly: "Men have pierced one eye of God; he will soon be blind."

was similarly vigilant, even suspicious, with regard to the mystics' claims of visions of God,[8] and we have already noted Ernesto Buonaiuti's complaint that the early church excluded the representatives of the *ecclesia spiritualis* for calling into question the rational rendering of prophetism. Agreeing with the Jungian perspective, Durand sees in the rationalization of the Christian message and the destruction of the communal mythopoeia the main cause of the ossification of symbols in our time, and therefore the main cause of the success of various psychological therapies that try to reintegrate the individual's symbolic imagination with the great collective archetypes.[9]

The problem of desacralization is hardly solvable, and it may never be adequately analyzed or formulated. Criticism of "ossified" symbols generally arises when a new system emerges that either gives existing symbols a new interpretation or finds altogether new symbols. Christian symbols remained operative for many centuries and were able to renew themselves many times and were even able to assimilate alien sets of symbols. We cannot now judge whether, as Buonaiuti implies, second- and third-century heretics (whom he includes under the tag *ecclesia spiritualis* but who manifestly taught things contrary to the church's magisterium) would have developed symbols harmonious with Christ's teaching. It is very unlikely.[10] For the rest, Christian symbols have stood the test of time, and it is perhaps too early to tell whether they are now changing—that is, adapting themselves temporarily to new realities—or are actually fading.

8. Gilbert Durand, *L'Imagination symbolique*, 2d ed. (Paris: Presses Universitaires de France, 1968), p. 38.

9. Durand observes, however, that Freud's system is too intellectualistic to achieve for his patients a salutary contact with the collective symbol. See ibid., pp. 42-43.

10. In a heretical symbology that began with Christian symbols there would probably soon be a degradation into a wholly pagan system. For example, in the early centuries after Christ there developed a desire to "soften" the remote figure of Christ through an emphasis on Mary's role not only as the mother of God but also as herself an effective intercessor for sinners. Though Christ's historical and redemptive qualities were firmly fixed in dogma and doctrine, the relatively blurred figure of Mary could have been manipulated by heretics had the church not been vigilant. In fact, in the fourth century, there were cases of inadequately instructed converts worshiping Mary as a goddess alongside Christ.

What we see is that new church architecture, art, and music are making concessions to the spirit of an industrialized civilization and thus to a style stamped more by the utilitarian engineer than by the inspired artist. This may explain why large numbers of believers turn away from an overly rationalized, prosaic, and symbolless liturgy, from music that does not elevate them, and from architecture the like of which they find every day of the week in their office buildings, factories, and functional schools. It may also explain the popularity of the charismatic movements. As one observer has pertinently remarked, the movement comes from the too-long frustrated desires for the supernatural.[11]

Is there an explanation? The church, and the Christian religion in general, may have exhausted the spiritual energy that great world movements, institutions, or empires seem to possess, then exhaust. This would be an explanation in the tradition of Giambattista Vico, Oswald Spengler, and Arnold Toynbee. There is another explanation as well: that is, that the rational ingredient that is part of the substance of Christianity produces a civilization in which rationalism may reach such excessive proportions that it

---

Furthermore, imaginative attempts were made in the depth of the popular psyche to combine Mary with the female deities of other cults, such as the Egyptian Isis, the Magna Mater of northwestern Syria, and the Palestinian Ashtarte among others. According to students of myth, the chief female deities represent the lunar element of the cosmos and thus are rivals of the chief male deities, who represent the solar element. The desire, pagan in inspiration, to establish an equality between Christ and Mary would, if successful, have brought back into play the age-old mythical struggle in which the solar god defeats the lunar goddess, compelling her to accept an inferior but always potentially rebellious position.

The church resisted this, perhaps natural, surge of the feminine myth that supported Mary's ascent to equality with her son. The "solution" gradually imposed itself, and we see it represented in certain Sienese paintings: The dead Mary, surrounded by the apostles, is taken up—in a diminutive form to indicate that it is her soul that is being represented—to Christ, who descends from heaven to receive her. As H. Zimmer points out, there can be no mistake: the divine son carries Mary with him as the *mater purissima*, the most pure mother, not a goddess. See Zimmer's article "The Indian World Mother," *Eranos*, 1938, pp. 70-102, esp. 82 and 83.

11. See W. A. Marra, "A Cautious Look at the Charismatic Movement," *Christian Order*, May 1980.

devours the symbolic meaning (which we have also called mythopoeic or simply mythical). It is not without justification that Alain de Benoist, the leading thinker of neopagan speculation, writes: "Judaeo-Christian monotheism appears as a religion without myths, deprived of the element which has characterized all religions. . . . According to the Bible, the world must be desacralized, nature is no longer animated, the gods no longer inhabit. The opposite of monotheism is the religiously permeated cosmos."[12]

The two explanations offered here are not in contradiction to each other. They both point to the phenomenon discussed in this chapter: the opening of the gates in a Christian civilization to pagan sensibility and the pagan mode of thought.

The thesis that the increasingly unstable equilibrium between Christianity and paganism broke down decisively during the Enlightenment is certainly plausible. Up to that time church and state, even civil society, clearly recognized the portents of the breakdown, whether philosophical, scientific, or political, whether embedded in heresies or utopias. They were also vigorous enough to undertake countermeasures such as public refutations and excommunications or the formation of counterorganizations: religious orders, new art forms, the Council of Trent itself. But in the eighteenth century things began to change with a notable suddenness. One important sign of the degree of the change in society was the increasing number of intellectuals who turned from the church and Christianity. By intellectuals I mean not only the outstanding ones in the growing anti-Christian battle—Pierre Bayle, Lessing, Voltaire—but also members of the clergy who openly or in private detached themselves from the doctrinal and moral presuppositions of the Christian religion and the church.

This is an important and intriguing turning point, the first large-scale desertion of Christianity by its clerical personnel.[13] In an age

12. Alain de Benoist, *Comment peut-on être païen?* (Paris: Albin Michel, 1981), p. 147.
13. This turning point has been investigated in numerous works, including Peter Gay, *The Enlightenment: An Interpretation*, 2 vols. (New York: Knopf, 1966, 1969); Paul Hazard, *The European Mind: The Critical Years, 1680–1715* (New Haven: Yale University Press, 1953); Cyril B. O'Keefe, *Contemporary*

The Christian Desacralization

of rationalism they are the first ones tempted by the need to put forward speculative arguments as part of apologetics, to explore their religion's historical background in the light of the latest research data, and to study (I am now speaking of the present) psychoanalysis, Marxist social analysis, or the structure of myth. In this respect, too, the Christian clergy is in an altogether different position from its pagan counterpart. We cannot imagine a Brahman priest, or a Greek or Roman servant of the nation's altar, engaging in learned theological disputations with the help of findings brought in from various up-to-date sciences.

Theology, if we may use the term in a discussion of pre-Christian and nonmonotheistic areas and times, was the field of abstruse reflection for philosophers, poets, and dramatists. The fathers of Greek theology are the poets Hesiod and Homer; others who engaged later in such speculations were already philosophers. The Christian priest, on the other hand, is expected to be doctrinally and theologically well versed, as is the Christian thinker. Their temptation, in discussion with critics, is to proceed along the line of pure reasoning since their opponents accept no arguments based on faith, and probably not many based on history. In an age when new ideologies are constructed around myths and their psychological or sociological reverberations, reference to faith and history may often be counted as a drawback. From one step to another, impatient debaters or apologists concede the battleground and argue on the critic's terms; they slip into an excessive rationalism, and ultimately into their opponent's own position, fired by the illusion that their thesis is now irrefutable. Alas, their thesis may also no longer be Christian.

This is what happens on the level of discourse and argument. It is more difficult to follow the traces of desacralization on other levels. Why, at a certain time, is the sacred no longer believed? Once the myth is removed from under it, does the cult become a listless routine, and are symbols then perceived as representing nothing? I suggested before that the Christian sacred must be

---

Reactions to the Enlightenment (1728–1762): A Study of Three Critical Journals, the Jesuit Journal de Trévoux, the Jansenist Nouvelles ecclésiastiques, and the Secular Journal des savants (Geneva: Slatkine, 1974); and Ira O. Wade, *The Intellectual Origins of the French Enlightenment* (Princeton: Princeton University Press, 1971).

firmly rooted in the supernatural; it is imperiled when the supernatural is reinterpreted as natural, when explanations are found for the former in the latter. These explanations are inevitably couched in the prevailing favorite terminology, which today is mostly scientific and sociopolitical. At that stage the necessary distance between the supernatural and nature, the sacred and the profane, the reverential and the coarse, disappears. As the sacred descends from its accustomed height, which was supposed to be permanent, to the pedestrian, it becomes the object of a mock deference and subject to human manipulation.

Examples of the abolition of this distance abound. Latin as a sacred language is eliminated from liturgy; the consecrated host no longer changes substance, only significance, a diluted version of sacredness; the clergy no longer wear the distinguishing cassock, and the sign of difference and of distance is restricted to a hardly perceptible minimum; the distinction between priest and layman becomes blurred, until the two become interchangeable; sermons rarely focus on the salvation of the soul, more often on psychological and ideological issues. The justifications for the changes often lie in ideology, sociology, science, and other nonreligious grounds—which only means that the devalued sacred takes second, third, or tenth place behind the day's fashionable theories. One is tempted to say that a new sacred had been found, overshadowing the Christian sacred.

The character and modus operandi of the contemporary transformation of the sacred may be instructively studied in the recent works of Hans Küng. The case is instructive because it shows the rationalistic turn a Christian scholar may take in attempting, not merely to update or modernize the religion and the church to which he belongs, but also to establish, once and for all, for past and present, a satisfactory harmony between that religion and the alleged requirements of the modern mind and scholarship. Let us keep in mind that Christianity in its doctrinal universe and apologetic method actually demands the use of reason in its service. Christianity differs from other religions in its self-confident reliance on faith, reason, and history together; it never renounces any of them.

Küng asks in several works how one can and should be a Christian in today's world.[14] In his lengthy answer he insists on the

14. See especially Küng's major work, *On Being a Christian*, translated by Edward Quinn (Garden City, N.Y.: Doubleday, 1976).

The Christian Desacralization

following points. The acceptance of Jesus as a norm[15] must be an absolutely personal decision (this excludes, for one thing, infant baptism). Human action, though centered in the law of God, follows not from immutable human nature but from experimentations with projects that seem humanly good. Mary's virginity is not to be taken in a physical sense but as symbolic of a new age. The Christian message cannot meaningfully contradict the philosophical and scientific achievements of the Enlightenment. One should refuse to believe in supernatural interventions, which are contrary to the laws of physics; and one should thus adopt a unitary conception of God and the world. The Holy Spirit is essentially the spirit of freedom. The church is the community of those engaged in witnessing for Christ and for the hope of humanity, according to the ideals of liberty, equality, and fraternity.

All of these statements may be summarized in the following paraphrase, a kind of Küngian profession of faith: The struggle for God must be regarded today differently from the way it was regarded by Christ's contemporaries. The scientific explanation of the universe, the new concept of authority, the critique of ideologies, humanity's awareness turned to this world rather than the next, humanity's polarization of the future—all these factors have strongly influenced our conception of God.[16]

Two things are remarkable here: first, Küng's effort to give a rationalistic interpretation of Christianity and second, the striking parallel with Pico della Mirandola's efforts at a Hermetic-occult interpretation. The clerical critic five centuries before Küng believed that in order to harmonize Christianity with "the spirit of the times," one must achieve a synthesis with the popular data that had become available. The clerical critic today is of the opinion that such a harmony with the world at the end of the twentieth century can be achieved through a synthesis with the latest available data. In both instances the contemporary new data—the occult for Pico and the scientific and sociological for Küng—are regarded as valid enough to prompt the adjustment of religion, doctrine, and faith to fit with them.

Let us not debate the wisdom of seeking a synthesis between Christianity and the century (or generation) in which the critic

---

15. Nowhere does Küng call Christ "God." His references are to Christ as God's "legitimate mandatory," "personal messenger," "trustee," and "friend."
16. Küng discusses this at greater length in *On Being a Christian*, pp. 81ff.

happens to live; let us rather read the above passages as illustrations of the inroads of rationalism into Christian thinking insofar as Küng's position is not at all an uncommon one in contemporary Christianity. Let us also read these passages with the awareness that religion is not a mere rational system, a speculative philosophy obliged to justify all its statements and practices before a tribunal of reason. Religion is primarily a link with the sacred, and besides reason it appeals to a wide gamut of emotions: awe, the quest for mystery, and the surrender to the cultic performance. We must not ignore all of this in the name of a Cartesian set of "clear and distinct ideas."

The origin and development of every religion give rise to dogma, liturgy, and ceremony, to a certain aesthetic orientation and expression, to sets of symbols, and to the acceptance of a tradition. There are innumerable signs of deep religious roots in the human soul through which the sense of the sacred prepares it for the presence of the deity, for the ability to listen to God's footsteps in history and nature. How can one—to return our attention to Küng's rationalistic passages—decide then, by reason alone, that children should not be accepted in the ecclesial community before becoming "self-committing persons"? How can one decide alone, without guidance, what is good? Is it possible, is it "reasonable," to read Mary's virginity as the "sign of a new age"?[17] Should the Christian message accept as criteria the scientific and political theories—themselves periodically at odds, rephrased, replaced—of the Enlightenment? Does the quest for freedom really exhaust the mystery of the Holy Spirit?

The point of my argument is not to single out one theologian's theses only to suggest that through them the mystery and the sacred character of Christianity are squeezed into the mold of rationalism, an operation that impoverishes not only Christianity

---

17. The universal acceptance of certain basic themes—miraculous birth, exposure of the newborn, unknown identity throughout youth, recognition, glory—ought to make the demythologizers prudent. There is more to the matter than their rationalism can grasp. Furthermore, it is arrogant to claim that Christianity is in all aspects above the level of myth; it seems, on the contrary, that Christianity shares with other religions the inexhaustible gift of impressing itself not only on reason (see Chapter 1), but also on the imagination, which, even if it does not justify faith, feeds and sustains it.

but also the essence and constitutive elements of religion as such. Religion has been exposed to rationalism and the reasoning mind all throughout history, and throughout history it has responded, for its own good or ill, to the rationalist challenge. Joseph Campbell has very aptly enumerated the phases that Christianity underwent in its response to the pressure of rationalism. The "development" of the religion has ranged from primitive Christianity in which the Master was literally followed to the latest phase of liberal Christianity with its "attempt to interpret Jesus as a model human being, but without accepting his ascetic path."[18]

Küng's case is exemplary in that he is obviously embarrassed by the inherent and necessary connection of Christianity to a spiritual substratum that not only is not exclusively rational but is often mythical, prophetic, and supernatural. We fault him not for inventing the rationalist attack but rather merely for having carried to excess some of the features of Christianity that lend themselves to such an operation. His task would not be so easy were he a pagan, because in the pagan cult the domain of the sacred cannot be circumscribed with any precision. When the universe is the only overarching existent, with no God outside it creating and sustaining it, then everything is sacred, as in some varieties of Hinduism, in the Hermetic doctrine, and in Bruno's pantheism.[19] It is then hard to say where the sacred terminates.

The tremendous achievement of Christianity, but one that also involved great risks, was the revolutionary proposition of desacralizing the universe and the corresponding concentration of all that is sacred in God. The Christian worldview thus splits reality in half: a sacred God and a wholly profane universe; a necessary God and a contingent universe. This is a universe in which things happen in certain ways according to divine providence but could also, under the same divine providence, happen otherwise, in a completely different way. The Christian's intellectual temptation is to deny to some extent the contingency of the universe and to understand it as necessary and determined. Reason insists on ex-

---

18. Campbell, *Hero with a Thousand Faces*, p. 320n.4.
19. The pagan concept as an alternative to Christianity is summed up well by Alain de Benoist: "Either God is one and distinct from the world, or the world is one and contains the gods as well as men." *Comment peut-on être païen?* p. 158.

plaining and grasping all, and in the process it disregards both what cannot be explained and what can be explained by means other than reason.[20]

Catholic philosophy throughout history has always recognized this division between an emphasis on reason and an emphasis on faith; moreover, it has always been exposed to the temptation of trying to harmonize dogma, doctrine, and practice with the current state of science and society. Hans Küng is just one theologian who has faced the temptation, but there have been many others in the past. Indeed, since late medieval times, the rationalist streak has often been prominent in theology (usually with the companion phenomenon of fideism) with the result that the elements of mystery and the sacred have been gradually devalued.

In the view of many contemporary students of religion this is among the greatest tragedies of the modern world. "Up until the Renaissance," writes Eliade, "man felt integrated with the cosmos that he accepted and expressed in macro-anthropic images. . . . For modern man, such experiences seem 'alienating' and 'objectifying.' But for men of traditional societies there used to be a porousness among all the cosmic levels." Yet, Eliade continues, the experience of the sacred is indissolubly linked to the human effort to construct a meaningful world.[21] Such a world still exists in relatively untouched societies and, at the other end, in modern, nonfigurative art where attempts are made, perhaps unconsciously, to bring to representational life such primordial images as the *axis mundi*, the egg (the universe closed upon itself), the willed chaos leading to order, and so on. These figures, shapes, and quasi objects live on in our imagination or in our subconscious as the closest things to the sacred cultic objects of old whose value was not in their worth or beauty, but in their participation in suprarational reality. Among countless stones, writes Eliade, one becomes saturated with being. "The object appears as the receptacle

20. De Benoist's critique of the Hebrew and Christian worldviews moves on just this plane. For him, the superiority of the pagan view lies in the fact that there is no opposition between two worlds, one created, the other the creator, but there is instead "unceasing consubstantiality, the convertibility of gods and men." Ibid., p. 89.
21. Eliade, *Fragments d'un journal* (Paris: Gallimard, 1973), pp. 32, 555.

The Christian Desacralization

of an exterior force. . . . It resists time; its reality is coupled with perenniality."[22]

René Guénon, who, as we have seen, also dates the vanishing of the cosmic feeling to the end of the Middle Ages, concludes that degeneracy set in as Western civilization lost its sense of the sacred. The triumph of rationalism, according to him, was not progress but a fall from the height of the spiritual principle. He writes, for example, that it is false to state that astrology "evolved" into astronomy, and alchemy into chemistry, since the latter are impoverished, utilitarian perspectives. It is more correct to say that these and other modern sciences are "degenerate" versions of the former, which used to provide explanations satisfying the deepest quest of humanity.[23] Guénon thus agrees with Eliade that for modern people the cosmos has become "opaque, inert, mute," that it can "transmit no message, . . . hold no cipher,"[24] and that consequently "the mind is no longer capable of perceiving the metaphysical significance of a symbol."[25]

This is all the more catastrophic since symbols signify not temporary but timeless truth and meaning. It seems that many symbols are not the invention of any particular epoch or community but have remained identical since the beginning of human history. Studies have unearthed, in archaeological research as well as in the depths of the psyche, ever-recurring representations of primordial realities that are part of the structure of being that humans have recognized throughout history and to which they remain attached. But if modern people no longer consciously recognize them and are prevented and distracted from manifesting their loyalty to them, a break occurs and they become alienated from their reassuring, even though to some extent controlling, guideposts.[26]

---

22. Eliade, *The Myth of the Eternal Return*, translated by Willard R. Trask, Bollingen Series no. 46 (New York: Pantheon, 1943), p. 4.
23. René Guénon, *The Crisis of the Modern World*, translated by Marco Pallis and Richard Nicholson (London: Luzac, 1962), pp. 36-47.
24. Eliade, *The Sacred and the Profane: The Nature of Religion*, translated by Willard R. Trask (New York: Harcourt, Brace, 1959), p. 178.
25. Eliade, *The Two and the One*, translated by J. M. Cohen (London: Harvill; New York: Harper and Row, 1965), p. 100.
26. We face such jolts of desacralization and alienation in everyday life—for example, when school life is separated from prayer, the singing of carols,

They will, however, not become freer than people of the past since other mechanisms of control assume the task of limiting their actions, thought, and imagination, their "coarse" symbols and myths, and their ideologies, slogans, and insignia.

The same thing is true of myths, as Paul Ricoeur points out. He calls myth an "antidote to distress" that serves in "guarding the finite contours of the signs which, in their turn, refer to the plenitude that man aims at." Thus he offers essentially the same diagnosis that Eliade, Guénon, and Jung do.[27]

An examination of the state of Christianity today reveals a dangerous weakening of many of the elements that keep the religious commitment alive. For centuries rationalism has been penetrating religion to its core, devastating the mythic, the symbolic, and the liturgical and removing the mystery either by ignoring it as superstition unfit for an age of science or by explaining it as reducible to natural causes. This tendency, far from establishing the rule of reason, has turned reason itself into a narrow perspective on the world—with the consequence that our modern sense of reality has become impaired. Reality for people today often means even less than the "tangible"; it often consists of little more than well-advertised propositions or statistical data.

Even Christians are ready to doubt or dismiss the great truths their religion teaches. Some question the historicity of Jesus with one of two arguments: using scriptural exegesis they question many events of Jesus' life by pointing out inconsistencies and suggesting later additions and interpolations; and using the study of myth they establish similarities between the person of Christ and other mythical heroes (see above). The reality of Jesus disappears in a cloud of unknowability—somewhat as Siddhartha Gautama's historicity disappeared behind the figure of Buddha. Catholic believers are further persuaded that the central event of

---

religious imagery, and so on, on the grounds that such things are unconstitutional. The secular concept of the state certainly becomes purer and more precise; yet the entire civilization, whose constitutive parts are fed by many sources, collapses, as it were, from the elimination of the sacred from the public domain and its consequent relegation to the private sphere.

27. Paul Ricoeur, *The Symbolism of Evil*, translated by Emerson Buchanan (New York: Harper and Row, 1967), p. 169.

the Mass, the transsubstantiation of the host into the flesh of Christ, is a scientifically untenable, preposterous assertion. To show that their information is up to date, they accept the thesis of "transsignification" proposed by Edward Schillebeeckx,[28] following the rationalist affirmation that reality, if it exists at all, cannot be known and that only human statements about it make sense. The Mass itself thus turns into a "commemorative event." The entire trend of modernizing the Christian religion by transforming it into a naturally explained rational system points to the decline of a civilization, to what the philosopher C. E. M. Joad, connecting it with the notion of decadence, calls "the loss of object,"[29] and to what Eliade terms "the absence of the sacred objects."[30]

We must, of course, attach some value to historical discoveries, to individualism, to science, to the quest for moral independence from collective passions and judgments. Yet we must also realize that these areas can never form the basis for a true judgment of religion, for religion thrives on other realities, in an area where the divine touches upon the human and penetrates it, seeking a response. If our true being (at least the true being of some) were made up of a spiritual essence as Gnosticism insisted, we might not need the many mediating zones through which religious people reach for the transcendent. But since we are a unity of spirit and flesh, and are, above all, their interaction, we must nourish each in the appropriate way. At their intersection we find the mediating instruments that we grasp under the names of symbol or myth, and that translate the spirit to the flesh and the flesh to the spirit.[31]

28. See Edward Schillebeeckx, *The Eucharist*, translated by N. D. Smith (New York: Sheed and Ward, 1968).
29. C. E. M. Joad, *Decadence* (New York: Philosophical Library, 1949), pp. 108, 281.
30. Eliade, *The Myth of the Eternal Return*, p. 4.
31. Such a mediation between human beings and the Absolute is argued with a rich erudition by Henry Corbin. Starting from the Persian and Ismailian gnosis, his thesis is that the "Angel-Holy Spirit" and other angels—Michael and Gabriel for example—are the messengers of Light, announcing and interpreting divine mysteries inaccessible to human beings. The real idolatry is to insist on addressing the Deus absconditus directly. The human-divine encounter (for example that of Moses) was only with the divine face, an angel, not with the living God. See Corbin, "The Necessity of Angelology," the second part of his book *Le Paradoxe du monothéisme* (Paris: Éditions de l'Herne, 1980), p. 182.

If the rationalist trend has increased its impetus in the past two hundred years, we may attribute that in part to the church's alarm that Christianity might be overpowered by secular doctrines and that the appropriate response should be to accept the basic postulates of these doctrines at the level of secular civilization. Thus even in its alarm, the church did not wholly oppose the new trends, which would have meant the continued reaffirmation of the Gospel message and of human dependence on it. Instead another strategy was conceived and put into effect: the church accepted secularization up to what it considered a maximum tolerable level, and the excessive preoccupation with the individual human—less as a creature than as an autonomous being—now reached maturity in the church as well as in secular society.

This is the notion expressed by Hans Küng when he writes that dependence on God gives us the freedom to experiment with our projects and espouse any because we can have an absolute trust in God's law (theonomy), the only absolute in this world of relative things.[32] The Hebrew prophets understood dependence on God differently. They warned against "experimentation with projects" and threatened experimenters with God's wrath unless they submitted to God's "experiments" with them. (Consider, for example, Abraham's submission to God in his readiness to sacrifice Isaac.) The new human centeredness is at the core of modernism with its postulate that modern people are emancipated from divine law and can now take their own and the world's destiny into their own hands. God is still recognized, but more as an abstract limit than as an acting power, as a king in name alone who has abdicated his throne and delegated his authority to a race of viceroys.

This way of looking at God and humanity manifests itself triumphantly—and with the growing intolerance of a newly formulated absolute—in theology and morals, in sermons and catechisms, in research groups and postconciliar institutions, in seminaries and universities. Carried along by their commitment to a synthesis of Christianity and the world, clerical intellectuals follow the logic of their arguments and urge the church to enter the modern mainstream. It is irrelevant to our discussion just what ideology is espoused as a result. The important thing is that the church is perceived by many at the end of the twentieth century

---

32. Küng, *On Being a Christian*, p. 536.

less as the representative in this world of the supernatural than as just one among many voices—and no truer than the others—that speak out on mostly mundane matters: political, economic, diplomatic, social, or sexual.

It is no wonder that a climate reminiscent of the two previous periods of Christian-pagan conflict has been created. In the late Roman Empire it was paganism that in its agony tried to adapt itself to its rival's dynamism, faith, and charity, to its general worldview. Somewhat earlier, around the middle of the second century when the world did not know much about Christianity, the "Letter to Diognetes" was written to inform a future convert that Christians were not ordinary people like other citizens, but indeed better in their performance of their duties toward family, neighbors, and the state. Two centuries later, when people knew about Christianity, the pagan world made efforts to save itself from collapse by adopting Christian norms. It elevated its own religious standards from the level of crude polytheism, introduced a new morality, and created institutions of charity and sacred learning. Still, the copy failed to compete with the original; reformed paganism in the late empire did not succeed in acquiring the spirit and the enthusiasm of the Christian religion.

A thousand years later, however, it was Christian civilization that began making concessions to a revived paganism. Humanists, Neoplatonists, and adherents of the occult and magic prodded the church to accept its own absorption and transformation into a syncretistic pseudoreligion, a pure intellectual construct. Indeed Pico's pantheon resembles the private chapel of Emperor Alexander Severus, peopled by effigies of leading and fashionable deities and prophets. Numerous Catholic thinkers and artists drew inspiration from underlying pagan tendencies, while those who remained Christian in inspiration were often attracted to Protestant forms, in many cases rebuffed by Rome's paganistic ostentatiousness. But Christianity in general had enough spiritual resources to make a brilliant response to the pagan revival and to keep Europe busy elaborating new forms in literature, architecture, music, and speculation—note the work of Pascal, Leibniz, Kepler, Newton, Cervantes, Bossuet, Racine, Rembrandt, Milton, and Bach, among others.

In the past two centuries Christianity has lost many of these spiritual resources. The temptation to adjust to the modern penchant for rationalism and scientific norms has proved irresistible. I have emphasized throughout this chapter that the temptation was found in Christianity from the beginning, and that it follows from its essence. The elimination of myth was demanded by the historical birth of Christianity and by the ongoing, linear tradition of the Christian concept of a providential creator God. More than Jewish history, which chronicles the story of a tribe's clarification of its monotheism, Christian history lent itself to myth making since parallels were easily found between the Gospel story and primordial folklore. The virgin birth, the child, the persecution, the preaching, and the resurrection are elements known to all religions in which truth is derived from a drama of symbolic dimensions. Yet since the nonhistorical, cosmogonic element in the Christian religion was taken over from the Hebrews and clarified in the light of Greek philosophy, Christianity was spared the difficulty of dealing directly with such questions as the origin of God, of time, of the world, and of evil.[33] This too augmented the historicity of the religion and diminished its mythical or mythifiable parts.

For even more evident reasons rationality was stressed far beyond what other religions could sustain. The creation of theology and doctrine with as much discursive precision as that displayed in Greek philosophy created a climate favorable for speculation, but it was a climate in which both Christian and rationalistic, anti-Christian theories were able to thrive. When the age of reason (in reality, rationalism) took over the central areas of intellectual life in metaphysics, morals, history, and other disciplines, not only were powerful attacks launched against Christian positions in the name of Kantian agnosticism, but signs arose inside Christian speculation itself—in biblical criticism—demanding adjustments to the new criteria.

This is, in fact, one of the main points stressed by representa-

33. Paul Ricoeur, who distinguishes several cosmogonies according to how they explain the origin of evil, makes the point that where creation is regarded as good from the beginning, there is no room for a prior and continuing chaos that is evil. (See his *Symbolism of Evil*, p. 203.) Evil then makes its entrance into the world through human beings, and it does not have to be excluded ritually at certain regular periods. History is thus conceived as an original dimension of the creation, and a linear not cyclical dimension. (See chap. 4 of *The Symbolism of Evil*).

tives of neopaganism. Having desacralized the world around it, Christianity turned upon itself and desacralized, demythologized, and desymbolized religion. It profaned the cult and the mystery while it injected a kind of lukewarm semi-Christianity, a mainly moralizing discourse, into institutions and public life. Both religion and public life thus lost much of their specificity.

The adaptation to modernity and the parallel reduction of myth and symbol in the lives of Christians pose tremendous problems. On the level of statistics this is obvious in the number of those who desert the church, the liturgy, the Supper, the sacraments, and the moral and magisterial commands. One gets the impression that an ever-smaller hard core of doctrine, "the essentials," is desperately resisting an ever-growing sphere of "inessentials" that erode from it. The process is accelerating: in the past two decades many practices of the Catholic Church have been relegated to the class of inessentials—such as the use of a uniform, archaic, and thus fixed language and genuflection while receiving communion. And in both Catholic and Protestant churches new practices have entered: the presence at the altar of nonconsecrated persons, the experimentation with liturgy—to say nothing of moral experimentation—late baptism, marriage of homosexuals, and trial marriages.

Yet what many call inessential constitutes the fabric of which the sacred is made, insofar as the sacred translates transcendent truths that must remain entire in order to be credible objects of reverence. The sacred is a world of mediation consisting of objects, words, signs, and gestures, the vital core of which includes a transcendent origin, uninterrupted permanence, awe, the repetition of the archaic, the solemn, the unquestioned sameness in content and form. It is said, often derisively, that all this is constitutive of the magical; but the remark only betrays the speaker's belief that modern humans are superior to those of past ages insofar as they are more rational. That they are more rational is of course debatable; and besides, it cannot be demonstrated that "more rational" is equivalent to "superior"—perhaps the opposite is true. In every period, the sacred enables believers to put aside distraction to concentrate on what the sacred signifies, thereby allowing the transcendental pull to elevate them to a higher life, or at least to higher moments. The sacred may be called a "secondary cause" through which God acts so that his people may reach him.

Let us bear in mind the words of Charles De Koninck, "It is natural to man to grasp even the most certain principles under the dependence of the senses."[34]

The desacralized milieu in which we live today and the demand for facts and data over transcendent truth impoverish our symbolic and mythic dimension. Certain thinkers hold that this is more than an ordinary phenomenon of civilizational change. They see a permanent transformation from the sacred worldview to the scientific one, and therein the end of the Christian civilization after an existence of two millennia. We shall see in the next chapter that this conviction is an essential part of the neopagan postulate. René Guénon insists in his writings that Western civilization has by now liquidated itself in materialism, having renounced the spiritual principle. Only Oriental civilization has remained faithful to this principle, although it too must struggle valiantly in order not to succumb to Western blandishments.

What do Guénon's views imply if we follow his thesis? As a disciple of Oriental wisdom, he argues that the various civilizations of known human history form parts of what the Hindus call the Kali-Juga cycle—the fourth or so-called dark age of a Great Year (Manvantara). The Kali-Juga began 6,000 years ago, that is, at the time when our earliest documents and monuments indicate human entrance into history. The degeneracy of this fourth age is manifested in the loss of primordial truth, which came down to us through sacred traditions. Though these truths can never become wholly extinguished, they are now veiled, accessible to ever fewer people; but they will shine again for a brief moment at the end of the cycle, which is at the same time the beginning of the next cycle.

Guénon explains that the law of degeneracy and renewal is the law of being. Within a Great Year the distance from the Great Principle steadily grows: materialism spreads and inertia conquers the spirit. Though this thought is an element of Hindu specula-

---

34. Charles De Koninck, *Le scandale de la médiation* (Paris: Nouvelles Éditions Latines, 1962), p. 267. Let us add a note from a decree of the Council of Trent on the restoration of certain ceremonies to conformity with the requirements of human nature, which, "without external help, cannot easily rise to the mediation of things divine." Session 22, "Doctrina de ssmo. Missae sacrificio," cap. 5, "De solemnibus Missae sacrificii caeremoniis," in Heinrich Denziger, *Enchiridion Symbolorum*, edited by Johann-Baptist Umberg (Freiburg: Herder, 1937), p. 333, no. 943.

tion, it is not alien to our own religious and scientific discourse. Our science too knows the law of entropy (the second law of thermodynamics), the increasing degradation of matter and energy within a closed system such as the universe to an ultimate state of uniformity. We may also think of Simone Weil's book *La Pesanteur et la grâce*, in which she describes with a sure intuition the two movements of the religious soul, the journey away from God and the return toward him. It is part of the mystic's experience.

There is, however, a momentous challenge in Guénon's thesis. If he is right and Christianity coincides with the last third of the Kali-Juga's duration, then the present decadence (desacralization, the loss of the symbol, the myth turned into rationalistic systems) is final, and the next cycle will contain a new, perhaps superior, religion. In other words, if Oriental determinism interprets the world correctly, then Christianity too is subject to the Great Principle and must vanish at the end of the cycle because of flaws that inevitability developed within it. If, on the other hand, Christianity is to manifest its unique truth and so overcome the cyclical view of history (the law of Eternal Return, the law par excellence of paganism, Hindu, Greek, and other) it must recapture the sense of the sacred before total decadence sets in.

Christianity is thus rightfully perceived as a true means for measuring the tension in the contemporary situation. The decadence that it measures and that it shares is not in doubt when we examine the component elements of the situation: weakening of myth and symbol, the excess to which rationalism has been carried, and the alarming opaqueness where the sacred ought to mediate. Guénon's analysis calls forth an even more threatening specter—a predestined grandiose failure in which the dark age of the Kali-Juga indeed overwhelms the Christian thrust of opening up history. Without coming to such conclusions, let our diagnosis stop at the evident: the Christian impact on civilization has weakened because of some of its intrinsic features. This is, however, only one diagnosis. As we attempt to reverse the trend and restore Christianity, we must assert and believe that such a reversal is possible, and we must act to restore the role of symbol in Christian truth in opposition to the false ideologies of paganism.

CHAPTER 4

Neopaganism

THE CRITIQUE OF MONOTHEISM

It may seem strange to begin a chapter on the rise of the new paganism with references to biblical literature and analysis. But it does not seem so strange when we take into account that the neopagan writers of today, like the Christian writers in the second and third centuries, begin the elucidation of their theses about the emergence of a new civilization by drawing on and then taking up positions against earlier postulates. In fact, it appears that at a crucial juncture the neopagan position is given support by the developments in the study of myth and its interpretation by some Christian scholars and thinkers.

We can see this in a comparison of the pagan and the Judeo-Christian explanation of the origin of evil in the world. The pagan myth explains that the world and humanity came into being after a gigantic conflict between the gods, some of them good, others evil. We must note here that "good" and "evil" should not be taken in an ethical sense. Evil is merely the equivalent of chaotic disorder, and good the equivalent of the defeat of chaos and the establishment of order. But chaos is never completely dispelled in the theogonic myth, even though the gods who represent it are annihilated after their defeat. For example, Zeus struck down the Titans—the forces of chaos—with the fire of heaven; yet he shaped humanity from their ashes. Thus humans carry traces of disorder (evil), but also of order (good), since the Titans had eaten of the flesh of Dionysus, divine son of Zeus. This myth thus explains the origin of human good and evil in external sources. Human beings are not responsible for possessing both in their makeup because they were made that way.

A further message of the myth is that evil is of the same age as good; it remains in existence as a self-contained principle, shadowing the good and maintaining considerable power. While the myth explains the existence of evil in the world, it also makes it clear that evil continues to tempt humans, who are often nothing more than playthings of good and evil forces (gods and spirits). We recognize here the permanent pagan theme, the core of pagan religions.

The Hebrew and Christian concept is radically different. These traditions acknowledge God as the creator of all things; he is without rivals, holy and good, the absolute beginning. He did not combat and overcome an evil god in order to create the world; and he does not share power with evil forces (disorder) through a previous violence and drama. As Paul Ricoeur notes, the conflict, crimes, adultery, and trickery that abound in pagan myths are excluded from Yahweh's sphere of the divine; he is not surrounded and challenged by animal-headed gods, demigods, Titans, giants, and heroes.[1] He is all-powerful and all-good, the ethical Absolute.

The Hebrew and Christian religions do not explain the presence of evil in this good creation by reference to a war among gods, a *theomachia*. That is not how the world came into being. Rather, God spoke his word (logos) and things came into existence. Human beings were created, not out of the ashes of Titans, nor from the dismembered body of Tiamat as in the Mesopotamian myth, but out of the earth (the name Adam comes from the Hebrew word for dust or the ground), in the image of God. Evil then entered the world not through God or through the process of creation but through God's creatures, the human beings to whom he had granted the freedom to choose; and Adam chose disobedience and sin.

Two consequences of this new conception of evil now follow. One is that all people must carry the tremendous burden of evil, formerly borne by the gods; and all must enter alone into the presence of the one God, who is omnipotent and all-good. In pagan mythology as it was described by Homer, one could be a friend and an accomplice of one god who would grant protection

---

1. Paul Ricoeur, *The Symbolism of Evil*, translated by Emerson Buchanan (New York: Harper and Row, 1967), pp. 239-40.

against another god's wrath (as in the relationship between Athena and Odysseus). But in the Hebrew conception, taken over by Christianity in an attenuated form, one can no longer play the gods off against one another, and one could certainly never find in God an accomplice for evil or unjust actions against others. Rather, in this tradition, all must face a reproachful God as they are, alone and plunged in sinfulness.

The second consequence is that with this new conception of evil there also develops a new view of human freedom and power and of the distance between God and humanity. In the pagan conception, the gods, taken singly or as a group, are not all-powerful. Fate may stand above them, and they may be victims of surprise, malice, or punishment by forces whose origin is not necessarily explained by the myth. They are often bound up in rivalries that tend only to drain them of energy and to neutralize their action against one another. And even though, despite all this, the gods are much more powerful than humans, they are often defied and opposed by these weaker creatures. Human beings, in having many masters and owing complete allegiance to no single one of them are in some sense free. Note how different this is from the tradition rooted in Hebrew thought that was then attempting to overtake the world. In this tradition the ethical distance from creature to creator is infinite. God is innocent; humans are sinful. God is perfect; humans are wicked and miserable. God possesses all the powers; not only are humans sinful through their freedom of choice, but they must use this same freedom in their effort to gain God's forgiveness.

As philosophers of the German idealist school (Hegel, in particular) pointed out, the Hebrew, then the Christian, God accumulates all the positive qualities while humanity is correspondingly bereft of them. Hegel's statement "It is time to take back all that we have projected into the alien individual" gains perspective in the light of the Hebrew dialectics of all or nothing—to which the alternative seems indeed to be paganism, where the gods appear as men writ large, sharing with them some very human frailties. Thus we may understand why the German Romantics, from Hegel and Hölderlin to Nietzsche, were so infatuated with (Greek) paganism, which appears as more human and tolerant than the Hebrew and Christian religions.[2]

2. These German philosophers were often sons of Protestant ministers, as Nietzsche himself noted, with a relatively superficial knowledge of Catholi-

Neopaganism

The neopagans subscribe to this analysis and derive from it their arguments on the relative worth of religions, on ethical relativism, and on the values that various civilizations promote. To monotheistic religion, which concentrates all the positive values in God, leaving humanity in a submissive position, they oppose the pagan worldview expressed in the myths as superior because polytheism grants its adherents a greater independence, a larger area of choice, and a more serene, unruffled conscience, insofar as they serve a variety of gods with relative interests, rather than one absolute God. The amoral nature of the pagan gods permits the pagan to jettison the moral burden and, in the long run, to adopt a value-free reflection, focusing not on moral betterment, but on the improvement of intellectual, psychological, and biological qualities. The objective is to produce a nonscriptural human being, a non-Christian, a pagan.

Let us emphasize this point, the core of neopaganism. Its main philosophical charge against the Hebrew and Christian religions is that within their framework humans receive their existence and their values exclusively from an outside agent.[3] Facing the holy and good divinity who imposes, by right of perfection, alien standards of thought and behavior on his worshipers, human beings have no choice but to divest themselves of their natural instincts,

---

cism. Their concept of God was more severe, their human being more sinful, their grace harder to obtain. The mediating element that the Catholic Church developed to such an extent that it has been accused of incorporating magic and superstition is practically absent from Calvinism, for example. This attitude goes a long way toward explaining the German thinkers' preference for Greek paganism. "The Greek gods," remarks Bruno Snell, "make no curt commands, issue no arrogant threats: they insist on a willing and understanding heart rather than on blind submission. Even the culprits and the blissful play a smaller role than in Christian mythology." *The Discovery of the Mind: The Greek Origins of European Thought* (New York: Harper and Row, 1960), p. 178.

3. Although neopagans are accused of anti-Semitism, their real opposition is not to the Hebrew but to the Christian religion in which the element of transcendence receives a greater emphasis. Yahweh's religion is very much ritualistic; Christ's places the accent on faith. Hegel, in many respects a precursor of the neopagans, concentrated his attacks on the Catholic Church, not on the Protestant churches, arguing that the first removes a substantial part of human existence from the political sphere where it asserts its right of control, whereas the Protestant churches, withdrawing into the exclusive sphere of religion, leave the state free to organize society.

healthy impulses, and independent judgment, and to live a life that is not really their own and that does not follow from the basic choices they would otherwise make. In contrast, such basic choices can have normal outlets under the dispensation of pagan deities, who, as Hegel observed, are nothing but the magnified and imaginary projections of the human will and desire. When each human impulse "beyond good and evil" receives consecration through a model considered divine, life becomes freer than it can ever be under the restrictive model of the monotheistic absolute.

Does neopaganism advocate, then, the worship of animal-headed gods, Titans, and giants? Does it have a preference for the Homeric gods, with their conflicts, crimes, and adulteries? If the questions are put this way, the answer is, of course, no. Those who speak for neopaganism disclaim any intention, attributed to them by adversaries, of restoring specific forms of ancient worship. Their objective, as we shall see shortly, is the creation of a new civilization with nothing Christian in its foundation stones.

The neopagans base this desire for a new civilization on a very particular interpretation of history. Parallel to Christian history, which they see as false, distorting, and inhibiting, they believe there has been running a true history that defied, whenever possible in the course of the Dark Ages, the obscurantist speculation of Scholasticism, Then, during the Renaissance and after, this parallel history resisted attempts to suppress the scientific worldview and method. Beginning with the Enlightenment, the church felt cornered for the first time; its reaction to the threats posed by modernization and secularization was to engender counterideologies that were subtly antimodern and that were intended to prolong the church's domination. These ideologies, the neopagans argue, culminate in liberalism and socialism, through which the church has tried to remain in power with the help of new dominant classes—first the bourgeoisie, then the proletariat. Already, the neopagans say, the church had contributed to the liquidation of earlier allies—monarchy and the aristocracy.[4]

---

4. The neopagan judgment is that socialism and Marxism are outgrowths of the Christian attitude of favoring the weak and the inferior against domineering values and higher culture. This is the exact opposite of the Marxist interpretation, which sees the church's response to the modern challenge as encouraging reactionary classes and class ideologies.

Liberalism and socialism were not, as such, the inventions of the church, but the church recognized at their birth the flesh of its own flesh. Liberalism was a secularized modification of the teaching that the human person is sacred, crudely reformulated as individualism. Socialism was the secular expression of the church's concern for the poor, the downtrodden, the weak, and the suffering. Although these ideologies were born outside, even against, the church, in the neopagan perspective they are seen as essentially Christian. The socialist utopia in particular corresponded to a secularized state of beatitude, reachable through the alliance of the ecclesia with the workers, as first Hughes-Félicité de Lamennais had preached. After him, of course, came an ever-increasing number of Christian social visionaries, reformers, and revolutionists, as well as those today who call themselves Christian Marxists.[5]

In spite of such an analysis, simplified and tendentious, neopaganism has long remained ambivalent toward Christianity. It took hostile note of the Hebrew tradition, as taught by the prophets, of absolute submissiveness to and service of God, a tradition that also weaves its way through the whole of Christian history. The neopagans reject the model of Christ and St. Francis who exemplify the Suffering Servant of Yahweh, who "has borne our griefs and carried our sorrows; . . . he was wounded for our transgressions, he was bruised for our iniquities" (Isaiah 53:4-5). They also reject much in the structure of the Catholic Church, which, in contradiction to the prophetic demands to be submissive, assimilated large portions of the Roman concept of hierarchy, authority, and institutional organization. As Charles Maurras, one of the modern inspirers of neopaganism, put it in his positivistic period, over against the "four obscure Jewish evangelists," there is the luminous order of Roman statecraft, overpowering what is dangerous in the pure content of the Gospels. The Gospels continue to teach love, charity, and turning the other cheek, but the the new state of the church is ready to check their outpourings and to channel them according to higher political considerations.

Now, neopagan accusation focuses precisely on the loss of the

---

5. That Lamennais was excommunicated does not alter this neopagan overview of history. As was often the case in the history of the church, a pioneer was sacrificed for advocating a position that was later made permissible, if not official.

"Roman" element in the church and on the advocacy without reservation of the "slave morality" of the Suffering Servant. As long as the two tendencies remained parallel and simultaneous, with the Roman principle slightly but securely ahead of the servant tradition, Western civilization retained its orderliness, its progress-oriented character, and its climate of achievement. At each outburst of uncontrolled impulses, the church knew how to adopt a prudent but sure conduct—although only in the area of politics and society, because it was hopelessly backward in matters of science and speculation.

The crisis has now erupted anew. The church has succumbed to the forces it had nurtured since its remote biblical origins. After having multiplied the ideologies that were meant to serve it as monastic orders of a new type, it has yielded to these products of its own miscarried Machiavellianism. Western civilization, inseparably tied to the destinies of the church, is foundering under the weight of the new alliance between Christianity and subversion. Alain de Benoist, a leading thinker of the New Right in France, proscribes the Bible and the works of Marx as books to be placed on a new Index. He also believes that the egalitarianism of the liberal Western consumer society stems from the church's teaching.

For all these reasons, many believe that the time for the liquidation of Christianity and the rescue of civilization from its grasp has come. New ideologies—and neopaganism is no exception—are always impelled by the belief that the worldview they want to abolish is already on the point of self-liquidation. Medieval heretics justified their program by declaring that the church had descended into the lowest abyss of corruption; Marxism counted on imminent world revolution, estimating that the capitalist system was collapsing through the economic polarization of the wealthy and the poor; and neopaganism, judging by its own satisfaction at the ecclesiastical subversion of order where firmness used to prevail, also proclaims the self-induced end of Christianity and the possibility of a new civilization. It is essential to understand, however, the thesis that the enterprise of repaganization is not the equivalent of a return to the past and its gods; it is nothing less than a new way of apprehending reality, a new epistemology, a new wisdom in the pagan sense. It may best be grasped if we imagine it as a speculative return to the end of Greco-Roman times, with the intention of undoing the Augustinian conception of humanity, God, and history and replacing it with the pagan conception, as it was formulated from Celsus to Julian and as it would have evolved without the Christian interlude.

This is not a reversal of measured chronological time; it is based on the cyclical view of history. The neopagans believe that it is possible for free humans to choose a certain ideal period as a privileged point of world history and to revive it in a new form. We are very far here from the concept of tradition, which is renewal in consonance with accumulation, and from the dialectical movement of thesis, antithesis, and synthesis. The neopagans believe that a new civilization may be engendered by the will of exceptional people who make the overarching choices and bring to existence well-conducted societies with new configurations and values.[6] Through its Nietzschean, existentialist component, neopaganism asserts its project—human self-launching in history, the invention of new values and civilizations.

This does not seem to the neopagans to be a very difficult task, once there are exceptional individuals in sufficient number. Only God-centered civilizations are paralyzed before the prospect of fundamental change, since they scrutinize God's will and its impact on human destiny in order to chart their course. Such a problem does not exist in the neopagan purview since there is a continuity from humanity to the gods. The gods do not transcend the human condition; rather, they represent and express it. In consequence, the meaning of a civilization is not worked out through a permanent dialogue between human beings and God, or through a once-and-for-all fixed set of values, but by free human agents for whom past, present, and future coalesce in the privileged moment of the *now*, and then in subsequent such moments. Under these circumstances, history has no meaning because a meaning denotes, for neopagan nominalist epistemology, a superhuman giver of meaning—ultimately a unique *theos*, creator of the unchanging structure of being. Once again, this view elucidates the relationship of the neopagans to history, time, and civilization: they do not exhibit a will to return to a historical moment but

---

6. Even at this point the influence of Hegel and Nietzsche is in evidence—especially their radical anti-Christianity and their belief in world-historical figures and the *Übermensch* (Superman).

desire the possibility to recreate the pattern of the past in the present. They desire the free recourse (again, not return) to paganism in the attempt to formulate a new beginning, a new starting point, parallel to the new beginnings apparent at intervals in the past.

It is thus false to suggest that neopaganism means a nostalgic attachment to tradition, earlier values, a glorious cultural heritage, indeed to Western civilization. Only a superficial perspective, distorted by political prejudice, can place neopaganism in the category in which, politically and culturally, the Christian Right and a certain "reaction" are said to have their abode. The neopagans are nominalists who reject any concepts and entities that are not of a certified, ad hoc human invention, who consider themselves masters of concepts that they make and unmake at will, according to need, utility, or policy. They want to escape the Platonic view that there are preexisting realities in the mental and moral universe not to be transgressed and ignored. Among such pseudorealities they include history, destiny, tradition, God, fixed values, and concepts themselves.[7] Since ultimately only human beings and the material universe waiting to be shaped by them exist, the highest rank belongs to the best human, the strongest self-shaper and shaper of others. Nietzsche celebrated the victory over the self *(Selbstüberwindung)* as the most exalted power that one may possess. This includes freedom from dependence on external agents for one's being and the outstanding achievements of will.

In a conception that does not grant nature special consideration and that downgrades society as it elevates the exceptional individual, the highest achievement of the human will can only be *history* as a human invention: the shaping of the values of a new civilization. The highest act is performed when one makes history, since in neopagan phenomenalism there is nothing higher than the creation of a civilizational imprint by which history is identified and which it carries as its label.

In this respect, one of the exemplars of neopaganism is Giambattista Vico, who did for history what Spinoza had done for religion and Descartes for science: the spadework of radical secu-

---

7. In all this, one cannot overlook the similarity to the Epicurean sage. See my article "In the Shadow of Nietzsche," *Modern Age* 22 (Summer 1978): 257-64.

larization. Vico's thesis is that we understand only what we create by our own effort. God created nature, and only he can possess the true knowledge of it; humans can merely imitate and organize. But they compensate for this by being the makers of history and civilization: they make institutions and laws and shape their social (nonnatural) environment. It follows that they can also remake history, when they so desire, by reformulating some of the basic institutions—specifically religion, marriage, and burial—that others had invented in different forms and circumstances in former ages. In short, the neopagans believe that civilization is under human control. Consequently, humans are the masters, not the servants, of religion, which as always follows the cyclical rhythm of *corso* and *ricorso* (course and return) of Vico's formulation. For the neopagans, the wise ones are those who realize that all things follow an essentially identical model—the cycle of growth, maturity, and decline—and who consequently submit to the universal immanent forces and deny a personal divine intervention, revelation, and providence.[8]

With Vico's *New Science*, a dissertation on the universal principles of the development of human civilization (first published in 1725), the world of history became vaster in a sense since new disciplines were encouraged to explore its diverse aspects. But in another sense it was narrowed and impoverished because it had been entrusted to the exclusive care of humanity, although Vico also showed within what tight limits humans were able to act. At any rate, Vico's science proposes that human initiative is able to launch a new civilization, not by rebelling against the constants of the human condition as formulators of utopias propose, but by adapting to the natural rhythm of powerful, immanent forces. "Every nation goes through rise, development, maturity, decline

---

8. M. F. Sciacca locates one of the decisive shifts to modernity in philosophical speculation in Vico's *New Science*, and he argues that Hegel took his inspiration from Vico's work. The shift was from the universal to the particular as the object of philosophy; thus history (human beings and events) became philosophy's paramount subject. This was clearly contrary to classical (Aristotelian) premisses, but—and this was the essence of Vico's thesis—only in history are the knowing agent and the content of knowledge identical. See Sciacca, *Lecciones de la filosofía de la historia*, translated by Celia de Caturelli (Córdoba and Genoa: Studio Editore di Cultura, 1978).

and fall, yet the world of civil society has been made by men, its principles are thus to be found within the modifications of our mind."[9] Vico does not deny, in so many words, the workings of providence, but the term serves him only as a label for forces he cannot otherwise identify. Providence may then be just another term for nature or for the parameters of determinism.

History seen as a flux, divided into vast civilizational cycles and returns, changes the neopagan expectation from the Christian end of history (and its secularized version, the ideal society of "progressive" ideologues) to the projection of an entirely new civilization. Neopagans derive encouragement from the vast new vistas opened up in the past few decades by archaeology, ethnology, and other disciplines: we have discovered and begun to investigate not just mere collections of unrelated data but the coherent structures of many past and present civilizations. Obviously such studies show the multiformity of human civilization, and the neopagans miss no opportunity to point out that Christianity is but one form among many. In fact, they say, if the purpose of history is to allow a wide variety of ways to address human problematics, Christianity is really an antihistorical force because its messianic fanaticism has invaded other areas of culture. Indeed, this is true not only of Christianity but also of the ideologies that derive from it their mentality of expansion and conquest: Marxism, democracy, liberalism, and various egalitarian subcreeds.

Neopagans thus welcome the rehabilitation of non-Western and non-Christian religions, art forms, social structures, architecture, poetry, and legend, whether Greek, ancient Peruvian, Celtic, Viking, or Siberian shamanistic. This is not just eclecticism for its own sake. The neopagans emphasize again and again that the plurality of civilizations—and in a sense their immortality, since they can be rehabilitated and recaptured in form and meaning—permits a new awareness, a positive reevaluation, of one's own roots. They repudiate Christianity in the name of ancient, secular European civilization, which they claim forms the basis of the true religion, art, and social structure of the Western world. They profess to admire the division of early European society into three

---

9. *The New Science of Giambattista Vico*, translated from the Italian by Thomas G. Bergin and Max H. Fisch (Ithaca: Cornell University Press, 1968), pp. 79, 96.

Neopaganism

rigid classes of priest-intellectuals, warriors, and agro-artisans, an articulation we also find in Plato's *Republic*. It is difficult to tell whether this model appeals to neopagans on racial or aesthetic grounds (its symmetry and stability) or because it stresses the role of the elite as the repository of thinking and governance.[10] At any rate, it is a contrast to modern society and politics in which neopagans find Christian presuppositions embedded: the claim of integrating all citizens in an egalitarian framework, inefficient methods of leader selection, and the prosperity of the community as the main objective at the expense of "higher" values that liberate individuals and elite groups.

In Chapter 1 I examined the pagan concepts relating to the universal questions of time, the origin of the cosmos and everything in it, and the limits of human being and knowledge. The idea of the universe as a meaningless flux in need of a human but not a divine articulation, which was rehabilitated after Heraclitus by Vico, is an epistemological sine qua non of the neopagan worldview that signifies that meaning can come only from humanity. Nietzsche did not miss the point: Christianity had riveted the world to a certain meaning, and his task was to break this attachment and send the world once more on its course of flux, this time with care taken that the so-called certainties of the past would be irreversibly dissolved. These past certainties were rooted in the linear concept of history, with a creator at the beginning who determined both the course and its end, thereby reducing human beings to the humble status of executors of a foreign will. The new, freely invented meaning, such as it is, is derived from the assumption that the universe is without a beginning and an end but is an endlessly repeating cycle of possibilities. This Nietzschean—and indeed, Pythagorean and Hindu—notion found new expression in Alain de Benoist's protest against "a return to the pagan gods." Strictly speaking, this is not a return to the past but an openness to the past in the present—and also to both the past and the present in the future since everything is *corso* and *ricorso*.

The objects and events within a cycle all suffer a similar fate—

---

10. Georges Dumézil, the foremost student of Indo-European language and the political structures under which it developed, enjoys great favor in neopagan circles.

they become worn out, porous, and irrelevant, as we see in Hindu speculation. The only thing worthy of attention and effort is the enterprise of initiating a new cycle, the initiation understood both as beginning and as entrance into the sacred. "For a commencement to be repeated," Martin Heidegger writes in his *Introduction to Metaphysics*, "one should not imagine it as something given, then imitated. Commencement is more original than that, it brings with it something disconcerting, obscure, and uncertain."

The civilization that follows ours will resacralize the world that Christianity desacralized when it destroyed myth and transferred the immanent sacred to the transcendent saintly. This allows the exceptional human, who is in tune with the source of being, to assume the role of maker of worlds and civilizations, the role of a demiurge. Nietzsche wrote that the world, once purged of Platonic and Christian metaphysical illusions, is divinely free for human beings to reinterpret, since it is nothing but a bundle of psychological needs without a cause and an end external to it. Put differently, human beings are all that exists, and they are master of their own psychology. The entire post-Socratic and Christian structure of being and philosophizing is fictitious; the world is without an ontological reality, without prior concepts and values. Nihilism, Nietzsche adds, does not imply the devaluation of everything; only the Greco-Christian universe must be bracketed and denied.

With this radical denial, language as logos, as the meaning-giver par excellence of Western civilization, is also liquidated.[11] For Nietzsche, the language we use is not a transcription of reality; rather, it is a purely conventional set of propositions, an as-if arrangement. His nominalism is so thorough that he finds no causal or symbolic relationship between word and thing. The great purge of the old civilization must liberate language from the lie by which it had been put to a deceptive use: speaking of the world of transient phenomena as if they were permanent.[12]

---

11. Those who originally translated the Old Testament from Hebrew into Greek used the word *logos* for the Hebrew term referring to God's word.

12. Nietzsche finds that an unjustifiably stabilized language structure (grammar and syntax) lies behind the similarly unjustified institutionalization of our individual experiences. Compare this with what the French literary critic Roland Barthes said about language in his inaugural lecture at the

Neopaganism

For some, the lie was even bigger. It pretended that God created the word, whereas the word, as Heidegger holds, is itself the foundation of being. There is a momentous speculative point here, characterizing the philosophical basis of neopaganism. The word that founds being is the word of the philosophers; they are the absolute, the "shepherds of being," as Heidegger calls them in his *Letter on Humanism*. In a response, Hans Jonas characterizes this position accurately: For Heidegger, being is vague, undefinable, inarticulate; only the (human) answer to the call of being is clear, and this answer is the philosopher's, more exactly Heidegger's.[13] There would be no word, no meaning, without the philosopher, as Heidegger himself confirms: "Man's distinctive feature lies in this, that he, as the being who thinks, is open to Being, face to face with Being; thus man remains referred to Being and answers it. Man *is* essentially this relationship of responding to Being, and he is only this.... It is man, open toward Being, who alone lets Being arrive as presence."[14]

Obviously, this is a reversal of roles, a reverse theology. Jonas, speaking for the monotheistic concept discussed at the outset of this chapter, reaffirms the transcendence of God whose "voice comes not out of being but breaks into the kingdom of beings from without."[15] For Heidegger, as a representative of the doctrine of human absoluteness, God is an immanent being, and as such is inarticulate and undefined. Indeed, he is an idol whose will and meaning reach us through the philosopher's—or the poet's—efforts at unveiling. Heidegger wrote apropos of the German poet Hölderlin that "poetry is the foundation of being through the word." The poet is the medium through whom the future gods send their messages. "Wherein Hölderlin founded anew the essence of poetry, he first determined a new time. It is the time of the

---

Collège de France in 1976. In short, he thinks that language structure is fascist because it is ordered according to subject, predicate, and subordinate parts of speech.

13. Hans Jonas, "Heidegger and Theology," a chapter in *The Phenomenon of Life: Toward a Philosophical Biology* (New York: Harper and Row, 1966), p. 258.

14. Martin Heidegger, *Identity and Difference*, translated by Joan Stambaugh (New York: Harper and Row, 1969), p. 31.

15. Jonas, *The Phenomenon of Life*, p. 248.

gods who have fled *and* of the gods who are still to come. This is the time of *need*, because it stands amid a doubled absence and nothingness: in the no-longer of the gods who have fled and the not-yet of the gods still to come."[16] To characterize this in the language we have used earlier, we may say that the poet stands in the time of expectations, between a decrepit Christianity and a youthful repaganization.

By now we have sufficiently established the pagan-speculative credentials of neopaganism. It was in the nature of paganism—Hindu, Greek, or whatever—to conceive of its god as an immanent force, as part of the universe. Such a god cannot be a person because in human experience no "person" is found outside human beings, at least no person who thinks, as Heidegger insists. The tremendous novelty of the Hebrew and Christian view of God is that he is both personal—thus near and familiar—and transcendent, a being outside the universe that he created and maintains. Though the Hebrews did not conceive of Yahweh as incarnate, they came close to assuming this because of the mediating dialogue with him through the long line of prophets and patriarchs from Abraham all the way down to the Babylonian exile. In Christianity incarnation became a reality. While God always remained transcendent, he was also at the same time incarnate in Jesus Christ, who consecrated human history and offered salvation directly to all people. The dialogue with God, begun through the Hebrew prophets, was thereby continued. It was documented in the Gospels, God's unmediated words, and institutionalized through his presence in the church he founded.

Since we live in a civilization engraved by the Christian religion at all the decisive junctures, it hardly occurs to us to think how difficult it is for the mind to grasp God as both transcendent and personal, a concept radically excluding and contradicting his immanence. Immanence alone, without transcendence, is more readily grasped; pantheism seems better suited to the natural inclination of the mind. Indeed, all pagan religions are, with variations,

16. Heidegger, "Hölderlin und das Wesen der Dichtung," in *Erläuterungen zu Hölderlins Dichtung* (Frankfurt am Main: Vittorio Klostermann, 1951), pp. 38, 44. An English translation (by D. Scott) of this essay may be found in Heidegger, *Existence and Being* (Chicago: Henry Regnery, 1949).

pantheistic: The world-all is all that is, and since experience tells us how small a part we are of this totality, we draw the conclusion that we are playthings of hidden forces. We are their potential victims unless we learn the art of propitiating them, rendering them favorable, and maneuvering so as not to be crushed by them.

This scramble for survival is life in the pagan cult. Pagan wisdom consists in the attempt to understand this life and to properly place human beings in the order of powers. It is not the acquisition of a propitiatory art but a state of mind that recognizes the clash of tumultuous forces around and inside humanity and works out a way to live with them. The result is the tranquility of the inner life: the sage, equidistant from the tumultuous forces, internally neutral, and occupied only with the self, since the outside world is unmanageable, mostly hostile, and fundamentally meaningless.

Neopaganism capitalizes on the difficulty human beings have of conceiving of a God simultaneously external to the universe and yet personal and present. Neopaganism finds it easier to see God, humanity, and nature as a continuum. In de Benoist's words, which amount to a veritable credo, paganism assumes that the universe is alive. It *is* a divine being, and this world-soul is the sole true being—there is no other. It is imperishable, uncreated, without beginning or end. This god or world-soul accomplishes itself in and through the world; the creature is consubstantial with the creator. If there was anything that could be called a creation, it was certainly not a creation in the Christian sense of the word. Rather it was nothing more than the beginning of a new cycle in the world's history.[17]

It is logical for neopagans to put humanity in the place of the immanent being, who in any case was a unity of creator and creature, the world-all. This human is then the absolute master, the demiurge of history and civilizations, generating and rearranging things at will—the Nietzschean and Heideggerian ambition. The demiurgic enterprise reorders the human condition and revalues the moral code by which we have lived. The Superman of neopaganism is no longer content to remain a passive pagan sage—to remain in wise detachment from the world. Now he is prompted to rearrange the polarities that Christianity formulated between sin and saintliness, nature and supernature, humanity and God

---

17. Alain de Benoist, "La Religion de l'Europe," *Elements* (Fall 1980): 9.

and to replace them with a single new polarity: the herd against the exceptional heroic individual. This is an amoral division, and Nietzsche boasts that he has given it its final formulation. The old morality is abolished, and since it is replaced by no new morality, this demiurgic state is indeed "beyond good and evil."

In his own way, Heidegger expresses the same ideal: "Man struggles for a situation which permits him to become the being which gives the measure to all beings and determines [or decrees] all the norms."[18] In a more accessible style, de Benoist explains that just as he is the "creator of nature, man is also the creator of gods. He himself becomes god whenever he transcends himself, whenever he reaches the limits of what is best in himself."[19] Again, the "best in himself" has no ethical connotations; the goal is not moral purity but the Nietzschean exaltation of the self. In the words of Leo Strauss, in regard to the Platonic state, these exalted individuals, the leaders who arrest the degradation imposed by the herd,

must be philosophers, new philosophers, a new kind of philosophers and commanders, the philosophers of the future.[20] Mere Caesars, however great, will not suffice, for the new philosophers must teach man the future of man as his will, as dependent on a human will in order to put an end to the gruesome rule of nonsense and chance which was hitherto regarded as "history": the true history . . . requires the subjugation of chance, of nature . . . by men of the highest spirituality, of the greatest reason.[21]

---

18. Heidegger, *Chemins qui ne menent nulle part* (translation of the German *Holzwege* [n.p., 1950]), p. 85.

19. De Benoist, "La religion de l'Europe," p. 11.

20. Remember that Giordano Bruno, a believer in the immanent universe animated by the world-soul, claimed that he would be a *capitano* in the new civilization. Note also Hegel's claim that he actively promoted the maturation of the world-spirit. Eric Voegelin calls Hegel a "sorcerer" in "On Hegel—A Study in Sorcery," *Studium Generale* 24 (1971): 335-68, while Frances A. Yates calls Bruno a "magician."

21. Leo Strauss, "Nietzsche's Beyond Good and Evil," in Leo Strauss et al., *Studies in Platonic Political Philosophy* (Chicago: University of Chicago Press, 1984), p. 184.

Neopaganism and Modern Intellectuals

In his own time, Nietzsche, the highly original thinker and brilliant reformulator of the pagan worldview, stood alone in the academic and scholarly world. His insights ranged over the fields we now know as ethnology, anthropology, sociology of religion, and depth psychology, among others, but these disciplines were still in the initial phases of their development and were far from matching his intuitions. The new development that has lent importance to the neopagan worldview, adding prestige and intellectual dimension, is the scholarly interest in the disciplines that probe some of the same problems neopaganism has approached.

This new scholarly interest is threefold, channeled through the study of myth (by both mythologues and specialists in the human psyche), through science (especially biology and physics), and through modern literature. It would therefore be an error to underestimate the neopagan impact on our civilization, or to see it confined to the New Right movement in France and elsewhere, which lately has attracted some curiosity in the press. Modern scholarship, which as one of its achievements has rehabilitated mythical thinking and thus the idea of a common core of religiosity through the ages, finds in the god figure the representative of a basic human need. This need seems to be partly instinctual, partly derived from the symbolization of experience, and partly the natural product of basic human drives and impulses. Yet the disciplines mentioned above—mythology, science, and literature—have often deliberately ignored the reality of God as a transcendent being who, through revelation, compels human attention. Such an approach would obviously not find a place in scientific investigation. Nonetheless, it is clear that we are dealing with new methods and new conclusions in these fields.

In the scholarship of the nineteenth century, there was no room for "pagans." Scholars and writers considered the questions of religion and God as of no further interest since they were settled or would soon be settled by science. Today, however, we witness a notable transformation of the intellectual climate. Under the pressure of the above-mentioned disciplines, which have fully developed only in this century, erudition has so uncovered the subject that interest in paganism has grown to respectable proportions—and with it interest in neopaganism as well.

Myth as Model: Neopaganism in Anthropology and Psychology

Some of the recent representatives of the new scholarship in the study of myth—Mircea Eliade, C. G. Jung, René Girard, Joseph Campbell, Paul Ricoeur, and others—have even acquired the reputation of being favorable to Christianity since, unlike many nineteenth-century scholars—Sir James Frazer, Max Müller, and Émile Durkheim—they have shown interest in religion (not merely in magic or primitive thought) as a permanent and valid quest, possibly bordering on the extranatural if not the supernatural. I think, however, that it is excessive to credit them (or burden them) on this basis with partiality to monotheism in general and to the Christian religion in particular. Rather, their curiosity and scholarship merely tend to document certain permanent themes in the human spiritual makeup, as when Eliade writes that "almost all the religious attitudes man has, he has had from the most primitive times."[22] Such a conclusion does not necessarily lead one closer to the area of faith; it merely induces a more sympathetic approach to the hypothesis that there is a place in one's inner structure for religious beliefs and related manifestations.

Scientific curiosity is directed to more than just human religious structure. Recent scholarship has blazed new trails in the study of civilizations from various angles, and it inevitably draws important conclusions about their resilience or fragility, and, in general, about the conditions of their existence. The use of these studies is the more tempting for neopaganism, for they display a bent for what may be called a civilizational therapy. Through the study of the history of civilization, humankind, social structures, language, and the psyche, as well as through the study of present-day human and animal behavior in tribal and herd existence, many scholars and scientists (among them Konrad Lorenz, Mircea Eliade, Georges Dumézil, C. G. Jung, Claude Lévi-Strauss, René Girard, Edward O. Wilson, and Hans Eysenck) have come to believe that humankind may now be able to construct a new worldview more in harmony with its fundamental needs than previous worldviews were. Eliade observes, for example, that modern people have ceased being religious in the Christian sense but that this may open new vistas before them. He says, "I feel like a

---

22. Mircea Eliade, *Patterns in Comparative Religion*, translated by Rosemary Sheed (New York: Sheed and Ward, 1958), p. 463.

precursor, aware of being in the vanguard of tomorrow or of the day after tomorrow."[23] These are the words not of a strictly objective, descriptive, and interpretive erudite but of the guru, the sage with a special insight and message in whom René Guénon would have found a bridge to Oriental wisdom. Indeed, Eliade's formative years were spent in India as a student of Hinduism, a period he regards as one of intellectual delight and spiritual deepening.

Similar inclinations can be found in the writings of Lévi-Strauss and Girard. Beyond the scope of their professional interests and investigations, they contemplate and elaborate the outlines of a utopian image, of the myth of humanity's future arrival at or return to a nonhistorical stage that is at the same time both a beginning and a point of final arrival. In Lévi-Strauss's conception this is clearly Rousseauistic: a return to or the recreation of the neolithic age, when intelligence was already developed, adequate instruments were used for necessities, and there ruled a kind of precorruption ethic. To say this about the overall intent of Lévi-Strauss's work is not to engage in polemics. He and other mythologues today see this return as not only desireable but also inevitable. They see modern Western decadence as an irreversible process, which eventually will be replaced with a long period of stability—a process akin to the Hindu cycle and the Great Year.

Lévi-Strauss reveals in his comments his nostalgia for a humanity still centered in myth in all the important events of life. For example, he describes in a positive light the myth that the Cuna tribe of Panama resorts to in difficult cases of childbirth. When a woman faced difficulties, he says, a shaman would conjure up, through a kind of epic poem, mythicomagic occurrences, heroes, and evil figures, who would fight for or against an easy birth. This "battle" would last for days, and would end most of the time in victory: that is, in the safe delivery of the child. The shaman is able to involve the woman in the epic battle through her birth pangs; and she, by her participation in the collective ancestral myth, feels part of and is comforted by the living reality of the tribe.

Lévi-Strauss contrasts the epic battle in which the shaman is able to involve the mother-to-be with psychoanalysis and its very

23. Eliade, quoted in "Mircea Eliade et l'avenir de la religion," *Commentaire* 8 (1979/80): 639.

different demands on the patient. Psychoanalytic treatment organizes a personal myth in which the patient is walled up within his own, otherwise untranslatable, symbols and which leaves him as solitary as before the "cure." There is a disturbing trend here, observes Lévi-Strauss. Psychoanalysis, a body of scientific hypotheses applicable to certain precise and limited cases, is being transformed into a kind of diffuse mythology of pathologic experience. There is a danger that the group may attempt to gain security through the construction of a new universe based solely on the curative myth employed in the "conversion" of individual cases.[24]

It is clear that what we may describe vaguely as "religious expectations" are addressed nowadays not to Christianity, which is blamed for desacralizing itself and the modern world, but to the myth, pregnant with new beliefs and new adventures of a sacred nature. However, given the subject matter, the scholar who finds himself in the unusual role of narrator of the myth as well as myth-maker seems tempted to construct his own version of what his findings imply. Hence René Girard's intriguing hypothesis about the sacred, the foundation of which he finds in the community's overarching will to protect itself against internal anarchy and collapse. In this interpretation, the sacred is a prophylactic myth erected around the first violent act by which the community cemented its union in a permanent and permanently disguised complicity. The hypothesis is not very different from Freud's "primordial acts" of parricide and incest; its questionable originality consists in seeing in the sacred a political construct.

This is a somewhat troublesome hypothesis, for nowhere does Girard suggest that violence and its concentration in the primordial murder, with the beneficial consequence of the subsequent expulsion of the perpetrator from the community, are part of the human psychological or moral structure. Though Girard postulates violence and a first murder as a requirement for the founding of a political community or religious group, another mythologue is entitled to postulate a different community and religion founded without violence—a community that does not need a sacrificial victim or subsequent appeasement. In fact, Girard himself postu-

---

24. Claude Lévi-Strauss, *Structural Anthropology*, vol. 1, translated by Claire Jacobson and Brooke Grundfest Schoepf (New York: Basic Books, 1963), pp. 187-204.

lates just such a (religious) community, purged of violence, when he writes that the sacrificial character of the Christian God is now slowly erased, and, with it, historical Christianity as well. "There arises anew the Gospel text . . . as the most beautiful, true, and living thing ever witnessed."[25] In other words, communities of a new kind are possible by some magic trick, but the condition of their emergence is that the old myth vanish. We are in the presence of the *useful myth*, made by human beings, without even a trace of the transcendent. We may be justified in calling it an ideology.

What is true of the modern mythologues—namely, that they set out, armed with their method of investigation, on the uncharted land of the future (an unjustified and quasi-ideological enterprise)—is even more evident in the psychologists' investigation of the deep layers of the psyche and the mind's reliance on myth. It is well-known that Freud regarded psychoanalysis as a technique for abolishing deep-seated emotions that were related to certain human religious needs—the feeling of guilt over the Oedipus complex, the desire to murder the father in competition for the mother—and replacing them with the rational pursuit of demythologized sexuality. This, according to Freud, would be the liberation of our energies from psychoses and neuroses for the positive work civilization demands of us.[26]

Jung, though he was no longer bound by Freud's positivistic psychology and began with very different presuppositions, aimed at a similar transparency of human relationships. For example, he singled out religion among the factors helping his patients interpret their troubled inner lives because religion provides collective roots and tradition-sanctioned images and thus the beginning of a return to the archetypes of the collective unconscious. Correspondingly, he criticizes Protestantism for the suppression of "dogma, liturgy, ritual and the sacrificial role of priesthood," which opens the way for the desacralized, the strictly rational.[27]

25. René Girard, *Des Choses cachées depuis la foundation du monde* (Paris: Grasset, 1978), p. 259.
26. Hugo von Hofmannsthal reports that in a conversation with Freud in 1927 the master told him in a peremptory tone that religion has its origin in the child's and "young humanity's" anguished need of help. Cited in Ludwig Binswanger, *Discours, Parcours, et Freud* (Paris: Gallimard, 1970), p. 346.
27. C. G. Jung, *Psychology and Religion*, the Terry Lecture Series (New Haven: Yale University Press, 1938), pp. 22-23.

But all this does not amount to a rehabilitation of religion. Jung believed that human beings, torn out of the primeval matrix, perceive themselves to be incomplete beings, and that it is the task of psychology to restore their unity. The pagan element is obvious in this thought, and indeed the Swiss psychologist understood the full implication of his intuition when he discovered the affinity of his hypothesis with the secret teaching of alchemy. Alchemy too strives to reintegrate opposing elements and principles, and its ideal images are the primeval egg, the sphere, and other unitary figures, all of them symbolizing the unity of humanity with the cosmos, the synthesis of the conscious and the unconscious.

In the alchemist's work, Jung found the pattern for his own therapy and, beyond it, the pattern for the world engendered by the universally successful application of this therapy. The concordance between his own program and that of medieval alchemy is remarkable. The alchemist who wanted to further the development of consciousness remained a Christian, Jung writes, but "wanted to 'realize' the unity foreshadowed in the idea of God by struggling to unite the mind *unio mentalis* with the body. . . . Since most of the alchemists were physicians, they knew the transitoriness of human existence, and were impatient to wait till Kingdom come for more endurable conditions better in accord with the salvation message. . . . Especially they wanted to save the body from its moral weakness (original sin)."[28]

This whole passage is fascinating; it shows that Jung too was pained by the "transitoriness" of humanity's divided condition and saw his own role as a reintegrator of passions and intellect in an endeavor to bring about, earlier than Christianity promises, the ultimate *unio*. Not only does he enlist in this posthistorical enterprise the myths present in the human unconscious; he also fabricates a drama of mythical qualities and proportions, a myth of post-Christian salvation, making the work of Christ unnecessary. He shares the alchemists' impatience to accelerate the process of "integration," and when he attributes to them the "gnawing discontent" of having to endure the "unendurable dissociation" of the physical and the mental in humanity, we can be sure that he expresses his own impatience as well.

28. Jung, *Mysterium Conjunctionis: An Inquiry into the Separation and Synthesis of Psychic Opposites in Alchemy*, translated by R. F. C. Hull, Bollingen Series no. 20 (Princeton: Princeton University Press, 1970), p. 542.

The support that neopaganism obtains from these projection myths establishes the scientific respectability of its own projection of a new cycle, the chief characteristic of which is a no-longer Christian civilization. In an interview in 1976, the year of his death, Heidegger summed up the quest for the saving myth of the West: "For us there remains the sole possibility, in thinking and in poetry, of preparing a readiness for the appearance of God or for the absence of God in decline."[29] The statement carries Heidegger's customary ambiguity: is it pessimistic or hopeful? The neopagans would answer that the statement takes stock of both decline and renewal and would perhaps quote another Heideggerian proposition: that our age is situated between the gods who have fled and those who have not yet arrived. Whether we follow Eliade, Jung, or Heidegger, we see in their thoughts a myth, formulated in one way or another, that prepares for a new, post-Christian cycle and a new salvation for post-Christian humanity.

To Build a New Future: Neopaganism in Science

After the renewal of interest in myth by mythologues and psychologists, the second major channel of the renaissance of the pagan worldview is to be found among the "hard" sciences. Biologists and physicists hope to contribute to the construction of a new civilization along neopagan lines by helping to create a new, better-planned humankind. The biologists Konrad Lorenz, Edward O. Wilson, Robert Ardrey, Irenäus Eibl-Eibesfeldt, and others in the field that may be called "animal sociology" propose in their investigations a new kind of materialist reductionism, the integration of the human species in the great biological reality of the animal world. If, generally speaking, the left is fascinated by the machine-like features and potentialities of the human being, by the mechanized and calculably performing individual and group— and this has been the trend in modern times from La Mettrie, author of *L'homme machine*, to B. F. Skinner—the neopagans like to demonstrate the continuity of animal and human in instinct, behavior, and performance. Thus some of the above scientists argue that in numerous circumstances (aggressiveness and territorial defense, for example) human beings behave like animals.

29. Heidegger, quoted in an interview conducted by R. Augstein and G. Wolff, *Der Spiegel*, 23 September 1976.

Some scientists suggest that many of our nonphysical characteristics—our intelligence, or our selfishness and nonaltruism in social relationships, for example—are prefigured in our genetic makeup and our relation to lower animals. They believe that the strategy of animal breeding might then be usefully applied to the selection of more intelligent and self-reliant humans. Through a reoriented biology, biosociology—and only through that—we can prompt human beings to modify their traditional (inefficient) behavior for a more desirable one. Indeed, they believe that there already exists a biological drive that actively pursues the elimination of the paleocortex—the seat of emotions and irrational conduct—for the benefit of the neocortex—the locus of intelligence, foresight, and rational planning. Just as Jung was impatient to help the collective psyche along in what he thought was its natural direction, the biosociologist hopes to establish the appropriate conditions for the physical and intellectual improvement of the human race.

This is not preoccupation with race, nor even a clear physiological determinism. Yet the impression one cannot escape, because it is inscribed in the theses and the terminologies, is that if human beings are free, it is only because they are so programmed. They are not pulled toward the heights by any sort of transcendence but live according to some preexisting pattern and the demands of necessity. They are superior to the animals, primarily because in the absence of the anatomical tools for survival (claws, teeth, speed, strength) they have taken recourse to intelligence and inventiveness. Yet even these mental tools are restricted by a certain determinism. Human beings have created history and culture, but the nature of human action differs little from the drive of the beaver to build dams and of the bee to collect pollen. The biosociologists intimate (at least they never state otherwise) that an animal's defense of its territory is comparable to patriotism, the desire to protect not merely a certain area but also the symbols pertaining to it, the memories of past sacrifices, and the language in which poetry and songs were composed. It is quite apposite that de Benoist quotes Nietzsche's aphorism: "Only that which evolves remains related to me." Neopagan humanity is not permitted to fall back, to be purposeless, sentimental, nostalgic, happy, or sad since the law of the universe commands only firm

Neopaganism

advance. Humanity thus lives out only one-half of history: from origin to zenith. Decadence is the merited punishment of the other half.

Biology, or biosociology, is not the only scientific discipline to show the influence of neopaganism. Raymond Ruyer expresses a somewhat abstruse and rarefied version of neopagan philosophy in a recent book, *La Gnose de Princeton* (The Princeton Gnosis), that describes the new quasi-systematic wisdom formulated by a group of scientists, many of them physicists, most heavily represented at Princeton University and the Institute for Advanced Studies there.[30] Ruyer is only their mouthpiece, pulling together what are still random speculations and conclusions. He himself reminds the reader that the theories presented closely resemble Lucretius's *De rerum natura* and the classical Stoic treatises, and that they seem to be addressed to the "eternal Memmius," the Roman official for whom Lucretius had written his work in order to strengthen him in the face of inevitable death and annihilation.

The wisdom in Ruyer's book is as falsely humble as the old Roman's poem. Lucretius denied, simply by ignoring them, good and evil, the meaning of actions, beauty, freedom, and altruism. If everything is determined from all eternity and proceeds in the same way without end, then the only sensible attitude is to look on, pass, and withdraw. The "Gnostics" of Princeton, unlike Lucretius, do not deny the existence of the spirit; in fact, they attribute a consciousness to the universe. They believe in a vague intellectual pantheism, a universal linkage of all to everything.[31] But in this universe, which is self-created, everything exists by necessity; everything is part of a well-functioning and self-organizing mechanism. God is the totality of the os, assert the Princeton associates—but without the imaginativeness of Giordano Bruno and the subtlety of Nicholas of Cusa.[32]

They see religion as an ideological agitation, engendering hard-

30. Raymond Ruyer, *La Gnose de Princeton* (Paris: Fayard, 1974).
31. See below for some further characteristics and details.
32. Ruyer mentions the influence of visiting Japanese and Chinese scientists on their colleagues at Princeton. In a revealing passage, he claims that "the Princeton Gnostics are like the sages of the Hellenistic period, witnesses of the dissolution of the old city-states into empires with uncertain outlines." *La Gnose de Princeton*, p. 9.

ly anything but periodic mass-murder and catastrophe. The only reasonable attitude to the world is to ignore this turbulence, because then religions will slowly return to their natural state—a universal paganism, which will most likely be a stable state. The Princeton Gnostics lay the foundation of this steady-state paganism in the spirit of Epicurus by working out his physical postulates. As Ruyer notes, the new Gnostics are more monks than ideologues; but in this context monk means "sage," as Ruyer himself acknowledges when he adds that they intend this endeavor—a physical theory with its "religious" derivative—to suggest that they are like the sages of the schools of antiquity in its decline, the Epicurean and the Stoic.[33]

Like the Stoics and the Hindus, contemporary physicists express themselves with ambiguity when the ultimate questions about matter and spirit arise. Christianity seemed to have settled the issue and, with a very different conclusion, so did modern materialism. The work of the modern physicists Planck, Einstein, de Broglie, Heisenberg, and Bohr, among others, has cast increasing doubt on the certainties of materialism; and the new physics of space and subatomic material has prompted science to abandon its clear distinctions—first between matter and energy, then between matter and consciousness, and finally, at least at the present stage, between matter and spirit.

This was the spectacular premise and conclusion of the science colloquium at Córdoba, Spain, in October 1979.[34] Finally it was stated boldly after a series of timid, then increasingly audacious, suggestions physicists had been making for years. Stéphane Lupasco had spoken almost twenty years before of subatomic par-

33. Ibid., pp. 9-13.
34. The Córdoba colloquium shed an interesting light on the "ideology" of modern science: psychology, neurophysiology, nuclear physics, astrophysics, and other specialties. The doctrine that attracted the foremost representatives was Oriental mysticism! Its indeterminateness, based on Hindu and Buddhist materialist ontology, itself dissolved in the void, suggests to these scientists the idea that a common substance can be found for consciousness and science (a form of monism). Eastern mysticism, from Zoroastrianism to Taoism, penetrates today into Western intellectual and scientific circles much as occultism from the Middle East conquered humanist minds during the Renaissance. See *Science et conscience: Les Actes du Colloque de Cordobe* (Paris: Stock, 1980).

ticles as nonmaterial "energy events" and posited that the universe can be understood only if we grant it a "fundamental psychic dimension."[35] Fritjof Capra had discussed a "physical taoism," manifest in "universal interconnections," the last word about the world-all, beyond which there is nothing but "metaphysical anguish."[36] And Maurice Olivier had already made a return to Vedic literature and its nondistinction of objects. He defined reality as the fusion of past, present, and future, the vision one would have from a state of cosmic consciousness.[37]

What might be called "Western Hinduism" and "Neostoicism" have now penetrated the postulates of contemporary physics, from which they are challenging and interacting with chemistry, biology, and psychology. "There is not one building block of the so-called living matter which would not be listed on the Periodic Table of the elements."[38] This assumption that everything is in fusion with everything else dissolves both the categorically presented scientific conclusions and the truths of religion. Thus a new worldview springs into focus, based on the decomposition of time, space, logic, matter, spirit, and consciousness. A tabula rasa is offered on which a new civilization may sow new seeds.

The Litterateur as Sage: Neopaganism in Modern Literature

In what sense can one speak of modern writers—mainly novelists—as pagan and sage? I remarked earlier that philosophical meaninglessness leads to moral meaninglessness, and thence easily to the aesthetic pose, as if art were the last resort in an otherwise objectless world—not, of course, the great constructive art of Aeschylus, Dante, or Balzac, which takes the transcendent and contingent reality of the world as its material, but rather the literature that shrinks to focus on the subjective world of the self, dark and pessimistic, and falsely illumined by heroic resistance to the barbarians' assault. This is the pose, the gratuitous gesture per-

---

35. Stéphane Lupasco, *Les Trois Matières* (Paris: Juilliard, 1960), p. 105.
36. See two books of Fritjof Capra, *The Tao of Physics*, 2d ed. (Boulder, Col.: Shambhala Publications, 1975), and *The Turning Point: Science, Society, and the Rising Culture* (New York: Simon and Schuster, 1982).
37. See Maurice Olivier, *Physique moderne et réalité* (Paris: Éditiones du Cèdre, 1962).
38. Lupasco, *Les Trois Matières*, p. 101.

formed in a religious, political, and social vacuum, as pure self-affirmation and demonstration of self-surpassing. Such literature thrives on pessimism and decadence because it must prove its values and viability by placing its narrative at the precise moment when a historical epoch (a cycle, in the words of the neopagan) goes under and the dawn of the next becomes perceptible. At least it is perceptible to the writer-sage, who is aware that he will never cross over to the new land and must remain its herald in the old. He is Zarathustra's man with a lamp, trying to convey the message to uncomprehending bystanders, but arriving too early to profit from it himself. This literature is the third channel by which the neopagan worldview is revived today.

The literature of which I speak was not created by adherents of neopaganism exclusively, just as the scientific enterprise described before shows much more than just neopagan influence. Nonetheless, a certain science and a certain literature—a style, an approach, a tone, a worldview—display a very close ideological affinity with neopaganism. It is not a coincidence that many writers who enjoy great popularity in rightist publications and publishing houses employ certain topics, a terse tone, and a heroic romanticism that make them representatives par excellence of neopagan attitudes. They too find an intellectual and stylistic delight in the heroic stance; in membership in a valiant elite that sees itself as a remnant or rear guard, contemptuous of a denatured Christian civilization; and in the elaboration of myths, somber or solar, of a new civilization in which the elite individuals give the law to themselves.

One would expect these novels to be essentially political, as so many novels have been in this century of two world wars. Yet, society and state are almost entirely absent from them, primarily because the authors despise and execrate both—because they see them as the old framework to be liquidated and also because they see civil institutions as merely prolonging a world otherwise sentenced to death. In the new world, society will be a mere mythical background to the exploits of the elite, whose code of conduct will be the only valid and recognizable social link. Outside the elite, the masses of people will stagnate as phantoms in a penumbra; they are the dark foil for the *new human* who is sage, hero, and knight in one person.

This rightist literature is easily identified, just as Marxist literature possesses its unmistakable characteristics. In *Magister Ludi: The Glass Bead Game*, Hermann Hesse describes an elite in possession of an esoteric pattern, not recognizable by ordinary mortals, but serving as identification for the initiated.[39] In Raymond Abellio's *La Fosse de Babel*, the Western world, sunk into decadence, can be saved only by an odd elite assembled of fascists, communists, Christian reformers, and technocrats. They will eliminate the unfit and work for a "sacerdotal communism" that transcends the old religions and the old politics. The plot moves throughout the world, from Spain to McCarthy-era America. It mobilizes priests, revolutionary agents, super-businessmen, former SS soldiers, and seductive women. The central organization is known as the "absolute structure," and its objective is the promotion not merely of a "superior destiny" for the steely remnant but also of a kind of sacred knowledge of all things (gnosis).[40]

Dominique de Roux's *Fifth Empire* concretizes the theme by situating it not in a half-real, half-fanciful world but in the Angola torn by the pro-Western guerillas fighting the Marxist takeover.[41] The author's object is not to diagnose the sickness of Western decadence—the verdict about its irreversible course has been on record for some time—but to dissect the corpse of the Occident, "between the Soviet ice-age and the American infection . . . [between] the Eurocommunist mediocrity and the abjection of Atlanticism." In Angola, de Roux was watching "the end of history" transcribed into a semblance of action, a literature of "militant despair," if such a term may be coined. The neopagan essence of

39. See Hermann Hesse, *Magister Ludi: The Glass Bead Game* (New York: Bantam, 1970).

40. See Raymond Abellio, *La Fosse de Babel* (Paris: Gallimard, 1962). He also published a book with the title *La Structure absolue: Essai de phénoménologie génétique* (Paris: Gallimard, 1965). (In English this title would be rendered *The Absolute Structure*, the name of the central organization of his earlier book.) Abellio, whose real name is Georges Soulès, derives his nom de plume from the Provençal word for Apollo, the sun god. As a Provençal himself, Abellio admits an affinity with the Cathar movement of the twelfth and thirteenth centuries that taught that matter is evil and that Christ was an angelic being who never underwent human birth and death. Abellio's final volume of memoirs is entitled *Sol Invictus*, after the Mithraic god adopted by Emperor Julian in his fourth-century resistance to Christianity (Paris: Ramsey, 1980).

41. Dominique de Roux, *Fifth Empire* (n.p., n.d.).

the author's vision of Western twilight in Africa is revealed in the hope of resurrection after the death, an eminently mythical theme and image, and de Roux refers indeed to the tradition of *mahapralaya*, the Great Dissolution that introduces the Great Rebirth. As one of the characters of the novel says: "The sooner the disaster, the nearer the fifth empire. It is our hope, also the wound we bear in our side."

Jean Raspail's *Camp of the Saints* was a bestseller in both Europe and the United States.[42] While Abellio represents pure adventure, a mobile, Latin version of Hesse's quest for the secret knowledge locked in the rules of a game, and de Roux chronicles the last Western presence in the world's soft underbelly, an already doomed effort to contain the flood, Raspail in turn is a horrified yet fascinated witness to the subhuman flood as it engulfs the few remaining outposts of civilization, whether a well-set dinner table for a lonely celebrant or the last regiment loyal to the flag. The Third World is on the move, not as an army under well-named heroes, but en masse, a teeming, sore-and-pus-infected multitude. What had begun at Marathon—West repulsing East—is reversed on the beaches of Provence where the beggars' fleet drops anchor. The plot runs through a whole range of reactions, from attempted resistance to useless gestures and aesthetic posturing. The reader finally has no choice between the teeming mass of rotting flesh and the knights of total despair.

These images and contrasts are truly Nietzschean, and the authors are well aware of the inspiration. They see themselves as the last bastion of Western values—against Bolshevism, Hinduism, or an imagined barbarianism—and as the makers of myth who try to find the passage from a civilization in ruins to the rule of the Superman. In Abellio's novel, all things are possible and permitted to these Supermen, provided they lead the world to a superior destiny. In the novels and war reports of Curzio Malaparte the gloomy but lucid knights on the Russian front man a battle line in the last stages of collapse.[43] Hesse's paradigmatic story endows the esoteric glass bead game with the secret of leadership over a flawed

---

42. Jean Raspail, *The Camp of the Saints*, translated by Norman Shapiro (New York: Scribner, 1975).

43. Curzio Malaparte is the pseudonym of the Italian writer Kurt Suckert, who fashioned it after the name Buonaparte, his last Western hero.

world. Raspail depicts in his novel a handful of lucid Frenchmen who hold the line against the shapeless and filthy mass of invading Hindus. And Jean Cau, in his latest novel, *Le Chevalier, la mort et le diable*, draws from a Dürer engraving the image of the heroic figure of the West, now in its last stages, contemptuous of death and devil, riding through the forest in "prayer, war, and contemplation."

In all these visions, victory goes to the inferior, the amorphous multitude, but the loss of the cause does not hinder the small phalanx of defenders. They are captains going down with the ship, but going down in style. Action, even though inspired by despair, is the essential ingredient, the courage to say no and resist. The vocabulary of the literature faithfully expresses its basic attitudes. One must bear in mind that in Heidegger's words life as a whole is life facing death—being human is "being toward death" *(Sein zum Tode)*—and that annihilation leads to nirvana and eventually to a renewal with a different ontological structure. What remains is the aesthetic element, the noble gesture, the sole and fragile "meaning" in a meaningless world. The words themselves express the limits of meaning and of action: defiance, deadly combat, conspiracy, obsession, destiny, writing as death wish, tragedy, apocalypse—or on the other hand joy, brilliance, lucidity, comradeship unto death, loyalty, solitude, exaltation.

Ideology is a term shunned in neopagan circles, so perhaps we should use the term *affinity* in describing the relationship linking the neopagans to the mythologues and Princeton Gnostics on the one side and to the literature that chronicles defeat and renewal on the other. It is clear, I believe, that there is an visible affinity. Indeed, neopaganism has found—in the acceptance of the myth as a powerful force in human life, in the new developments in science and the new program proposed for it, and in the new literature of death and resurrection—three broad entrances into modern Western society.

The neopagan temptation did not arise in a cultural vacuum; it never does. Among the shocks that led to its development and strength (the complete list would be longer) are bourgeois decadence, the rise of Marxism, Western impotence in meeting external challenges, and internal anarchy. The last impulse, and perhaps the most powerful, was the surrender of the Christian churches to nihilism and the forces of decomposition. Nietzsche and Oswald Spengler put the matter in a philosophical and historicocultural perspective. René Guénon and Julius Evola detected the sources of renewal in Oriental or esoteric doctrines. Novelists absorbed this impetus, which was aggravated by the equation of decadence and liberal democracy; and many writers from very different backgrounds—from André Malraux to Ernst Jünger, from T. S. Eliot to Yukio Mishima—found in permissive society not only the roots of disintegration but also ugliness and shallowness: the wasteland. Henceforth, the ideal was projected into a semihistoric *beyond*, which was called "the fifth empire" (de Roux), "Aurora" (Nietzsche), or the "unveiling of new gods" (Heidegger). It could not be an absolutely new beginning since the century's scientific bent does not allow the possibility of a projection and foundation of a new cycle by the will alone. Yet the idea could be dramatized and rendered as a myth of a defeat and renewal, in the manner of the pagan myths, but integrated of course with the style and form of Western novel and justified by scholarship and science.

I have described the defeat, the first part of the myth, in the brief narration of stories and plots. Literature can only hint at the second part, the renewal, because its utopian element is never explicit—for the same reason that Marxist novels are never explicit about the happily renewed, postrevolutionary world. Such works, attempted in the framework of "socialist realism," inevitably sink into boredom since the narrative is removed from the context of the human condition: its heroes become programmed robots. The novels of the right also take the story to the threshold of the new civilization, that is, to the point at which an elite emerges. It is this elite that will undertake the task of building a new, luminous world—but the authors must abandon the enterprise before the first stone is laid. Otherwise there would be no myth. Hence the enigmatic and symbolic references to the elite that suffers defeat only to steel itself for the remote renewal.

The elite is part pagan sage when science and speculation are emphasized and part Superman when the myth is recounted in fictional form. The Princeton Gnostics embody the first type: a withdrawn elite, content in the certitude that the universe functions without a creator and without a destination. This postulate establishes a nearly perfect similarity between the "Gnostics" of

Neopaganism

Princeton, the Epicurean and Stoic sages, and the Paduan professors, all of whom worked out a model of the self-created universe. The Princeton credo, if one were formulated, would also be similar to what we read in the neopagan *Morning of the Magicians:* "Nor are we proposing some form of religion. We believe only in human intelligence, and we believe that, at a certain level, intelligence itself is a kind of secret society. We believe that its powers are unlimited."[44] This is essentially the same theme as that in the novels previously mentioned, but there we read not of intelligence, secret society, and its power, but of absolute structure, superior destiny, self-transcendence, decadence, mission, noble gesture, lucidity, history's end, and so on. Is this, in turn, not summed up by Nietzsche, who sought the perfection of humanity and for whom humanity's genuine salvation and worth were to be found only in the "highest" types?

It is no coincidence that the neopagans, in updating Nietzsche's vision with the help of contemporary science, resort to biology. The biosociologist Edward O. Wilson studies the possibility of redirecting the "genetic bias" so that "passions may be averted and ethics altered."[45] The anthropologist Lionel Tiger speaks of redirecting "evolutionary history" and advocates the "veterinarian view of the [human] species in order to prevent man from overpopulating himself to death and from jeopardizing the survival of the human group."[46] Louis Pauwels, coauthor of *The Morning of the Magicians*, speaks of "an imminent mutation in humanity" and assumes that "there are already among us the products of this mutation," that is, beings biologically and intellectually ahead of us on the evolutionary scale.[47] They are advancing on the road that we shall one day take. When Pauwels does not speak of mutants, he refers to the "white and bearded" beings from other planets, creators of the superhuman works of our prehistory (in Peru, the

---

44. Louis Pauwels and Jacques Bergier, *The Morning of the Magicians*, translated from the French by Rollo Myers (New York: Stein and Day, 1964), p. 61.

45. Edward O. Wilson, "Human Decency Is Animal," *The New York Times Magazine*, 12 October 1975, 48.

46. Lionel Tiger, quoted in an interview with Dom Moraes, published in *Voices for Life: Reflections on the Human Condition*, edited by Moraes (New York: Praeger, 1975).

47. Pauwels and Bergier, *The Morning of the Magicians*, p. 28.

Easter Islands, Egypt) which even today we do not know how to imitate.[48]

Throughout the pages of *La Gnose de Princeton* and *The Morning of the Magicians*, there runs the theme of radical discontent with the present human condition and the related theme of radical change, to be achieved by utilizing the "nine-tenths of the brain still lying fallow," by new drug-induced perceptions, by the secret society of the mutants who hide in our midst fearing ridicule and persecution. One is reminded of Pico della Mirandola's *Oration on the Dignity of Man* (1487), the prelude to his 900 theses, in which he planned the synthesis of religion and the occult doctrines: "Oh, Fathers, let us be driven by those Socratic frenzies which lift us to such an ecstasy that our intellects and our very selves are united to God. And we shall be moved by them in this way if previously we have done all that lies in us to do. . . . At last, smitten by the ineffable love . . . and borne outside ourselves . . . we shall be no longer ourselves but the very One who made us."[49]

Surveying what I have said in this chapter about the varieties of the neopagan approach and ideology, one may be puzzled by the impression that these various directions do not seem to converge and to meet in a single unified worldview. Not only do the representatives of neopaganism, whose number we divided into four groups—philosophers, mythologues, scientists, and litterateurs—seem to work in independent disciplines, but their moods and conclusions also appear to diverge. Yet I believe that two observations on their true unity are in order.

First of all, though those we have considered as neopagans do represent a diversity of focus, they are in fact unified in their diagnosis of the state of contemporary Western society and in their hopes and prescriptions for the new world that they believe is still to come. They are not mere workers in their fields; rather they all may be considered prophets or gurus or sages intent on introducing and shaping a new humanity, a new civilization, or a new arrangement of the data of the universe. Not only are Jung, Heidegger, Eliade, Wilson, Hesse, Abellio, Pauwels, and the

---

48. Ibid., pp. 113-17.
49. Giovanni Pico della Mirandola, *Oration on the Dignity of Man*, translated by A. Robert Caponigri (Chicago: Gateway, 1956), pp. 26-27.

Neopaganism

Princeton Gnostics, among many others, savants, writers, and thinkers; they are united both in the conviction that civilization, humanity, and the earth have reached an impasse and in the belief that the search for a new civilization and a new cycle of human history has already begun.

Second, I would also observe that the apparent diversity of approach does not imply an equal thematic diversity. There is indeed a common theme in the cosmic pessimism of Nietzsche, the presuppositions of Jungian therapy, the scientific optimism of Wilson, the somber mood of Raspail and de Roux, and the updated Gnosticism of the physicists in Princeton and Córdoba. Furthermore, that common theme is not difficult to locate: it is implicit in the first observation. Whether they see in the world the process of decay or the imprint of progress, or whether they see decay and progress alternating in some great cycle, the prophets or sages mentioned in this chapter all divide the world (humankind, history, civilization, and human explorations of the worlds within and without themselves) into two phases: the Christian and the post-Christian. Some may regret the passing of the first and others may merely be resigned, but the majority of them welcome the new potentials and promises and prepare the explorations along the lines of fact, fancy, or hypothesis. Yet this forward thrust, this project, resembles strangely a *return* to ancient pagan positions, both Greek and Hindu. And, perhaps not so strangely, the return is most emphatically sought by those whom one would expect to see in the forefront of novelty, the astrophysicists. Costa de Beauregard, one of the prominent participants in the Córdoba colloquium, puts his resignation and hope in a "spiritual mutation." After rejecting "politics, morals, the Christian religion and Western civilization," he wants to explore the road to Calcutta.[50] Oriental cosmic mysticism is the last word of postmodern humanity.

---

50. Costa de Beauregard, writing in *Science et conscience*, the record of the acts of the Córdoba conference, pp. 57-77.

CHAPTER 5

The New Occult

Throughout this book, particularly in Chapter 3, I have emphasized that the rise of the occult parallels the rise of neopaganism. Such a combined appearance is in the nature of things and can be explained by the ebbing of Christianity, which opens the door to the permanent temptation of the two countermovements. Reason yields to pagan superrationalism, the ultimate consequence of which is the urge to remake the human condition, to produce a new, elite humanity, an exceptional and superior race of heroes and gods. And faith yields to a superspirituality, easily copied from Oriental creeds, that seeks fusion with the divine substance instead of preserving the orthodox Christian doctrine of creation and its provision for human freedom and contingency. Toward the end of the previous chapter I discussed the close relationship between neopaganism and the occult and their joint search for a different "human" race, both superintelligent and empowered with the operation of a new kind of magic, "scientific" or mythical. This new supermagic, despite being called scientific, is no less aimed at a fantastic reorientation of our condition, in the spirit of a Gnostic dissociation from the created world. I also noted the similarity of the inspiration and impulse of the pagan-occult enterprise in the fifteenth century and in the present.

In periods such as these, scientists, artists, philosophers, litterateurs, and churchmen confess to a vague feeling that they are facing more than just a decline of their civilization and culture. They seem to perceive the enveloping presence of a vast and deep worldview, taking its position opposite the Christian one. Earlier I quoted René Guénon's discussion of the Great Year and the Kali-

Juga, which situate us in a certain stretch of time within another, more-encompassing, time so that we are carried, unaware and unasked, by a time beyond time, immeasurable and impossible to conceptualize. Our position in time is analogous to our position in the spatial universe: we are within a solar system, itself part of a galaxy, which in turn is part of a system of galaxies beyond comprehension, speeding into unfathomable space. Yet to accept as true the cyclical view of history and all its implications is much more disconcerting than to accept what scientists tell us about the physical universe. Our physical lives are and always have been bound within physical space, and we can easily accommodate ourselves to its necessary limitations and can even exert some control over it. What is beyond our physical reach is able to affect us little. Mentally, however, we are free to roam throughout time. Yet this freedom is blocked at every step by our lack of comprehension and our inability to articulate and enforce our own conception of time. We are not the masters of time.

This disconcerting sensation is, however, growing into a philosophical argument as the feeling spreads that our historical and civilizational age is coming to an end and that a larger spiritual awareness is overwhelming our "provincial" religiosity. At the end of the fifteenth century, Giovanni Pico della Mirandola must have been reacting to a similar malaise when he tried to bring about a synthesis of religion, science, and the occult, presumably in order to remain abreast of the rush of time and cosmic events. More particularly, he wanted to reconcile Christianity with the reputedly much older, vaster, and, in his view, perhaps truer religion of Hermetism. There is no convincing reason to suppose that Pico intended to renounce the religion into which he was born, as Giordano Bruno would do three generations later. Yet even as he kept the old, he yielded to the temptation of the occult, thinking either that Christianity might be strengthened if rerooted in a more profound, cosmic "religion of mankind," or that it must be dissolved into that more enveloping system.

In 1486 Pico proposed to defend 900 theses that he had culled from his knowledge of diverse Greek, Arabic, Hebrew, and Latin writings, but the commission of prelates and theologians to whom he addressed them saw the incompatibility of the elements that the young humanist-magician wanted to bring together. That same incompatibility exists today in the pagan-occult revival in Christian civilization, but it comes much less to the fore because desacralized Christianity cannot muster the kind of resistance it could five centuries ago. As a mark of this desacralization, observe the penetration into Western thinking of occult doctrines and Asian creeds. These bring to our faltering contemplative and active values not an increased spirituality, as is superficially assumed, but a call to pantheism and nihilism. Early in the nineteenth century, Schopenhauer made what then seemed to be a far-fetched observation. Our religions, he wrote, make no impression on India—the general wisdom of humanity will not allow itself to be deflected from its course by an adventure that took place in Galilee. Hindu wisdom will swell to a tidal wave in Europe and will radically transform our thinking and knowledge. Schopenhauer and his disciple Nietzsche were among those who felt that the "Galilean adventure" was no more than a sidetrack, a somewhat long but by now exhausted effort to block humanity's natural religion. The course of the latter was winding but clear: it had spread from India to Alexandria, then to the Pythagorean sect, Stoic philosophy, and the system of Plotinus, and finally it came to lay claim to the modern West.

This feeling is widespread today and is buried in the depths of Western consciousness. This is evident from the rapid success of neopagan ideologies—among them the new occult—and it is demonstrated in science, scholarship, art, and literature. It takes little insight to say that the Western curiosity with myth and symbol, though it enriches our knowledge in various directions, is symptomatic of our discontent with a desymbolized and demythologized Christianity and civilization. Joseph Campbell notes that when a civilization begins to reinterpret its mythology, the life goes out of it and temples become museums.[1] This is happening in our civilization and also in our religion as some scholars (among them Friedrich Gogarten, Rudolf Bultmann, Hans Küng, and Edward Schillebeeckx) strive to demythologize the gospel and as the church turns its interest from spiritual to social issues. Temples and churches have become not only museums—still a face-saving solution—but even "social-action centers" from which the

---

1. Joseph Campbell, *The Hero with a Thousand Faces*, 2d ed., Bollingen Series no. 17 (Princeton: Princeton University Press, 1968), p. 249.

The New Occult

call goes out for the implementation of various political programs in the name of pastoral care.[2]

Because of such calls and the consequent neglect of the spiritual and the symbolic, Christian religion and civilization fade rapidly in the sensibilities of those who seek to fulfill their need for the sacred from other sources. These sources, which begin to exercise their influence first at the perimeter of Christian civilization, are often none other than Asian creeds and the occult tradition, whose origin is also largely in Asia. When I speak of Asian creeds that are a primary source of occult influence in Christian civilization, I refer chiefly to Brahmanism (orthodox Hinduism) and Buddhism, the latter being a kind of miscarried reform of the former in India but vastly influential in other countries (among them China, Japan, Thailand, and Burma). Buddhism came into existence as an effort to internalize what in the Hindu religion seemed to have become too sensuous, too filled with gods and spirits in a pantheon teeming with millions of deities. In its native India, Buddhism had to make numerous concessions to the original creed with which it practically fused. Thus Siddhartha Gautama, the ascetic sage who taught that gods do not exist, himself became a god, and his idols

---

2. An interesting example of desacralization is the treatment of the crown of Hungary by that country's communist authorities. The crown, which represented legitimate sovereignty in precommunist law and tradition, was returned to Hungary in 1978 by the United States government. At first, it was surrounded by official respect; then it was exhibited in a museum—that is, removed from the political sphere. Later, scholars published articles about its component parts, each from a different period, attempting to show that it could not be *the* crown given by Pope Sylvester to St. Stephen, king of Hungary. Subsequently other texts appeared proving that the crown was not as ancient as had been believed, that it dates from the thirteenth century. The various press operations serve to desacralize the crown; they refute and dismantle the data that in the eyes of the public were signs of the crown's venerable origin—it was not as old as was thought, it was an agglomeration of units put together and tampered with at various times, and it did not play the role in Hungarian royal history that many had thought. So far, public opinion has stymied government plans to take the crown apart to examine each section by scientific means. What "science" would gain, sacredness would lose. Compare this procedure with New Testament exegesis as practiced in the work of Hans Küng, for example (see Chapter 3).

today are indistinguishable in their gaudy colors and vulgar shapes from those of the other gods of the subcontinent.

René Guénon spoke of a kind of pulsating universe in which succeeding time cycles alternately assert then deny the "principle of existence"—the assertion signifying good, the denial evil.[3] Since these assertions and denials of the principle (the pulsation) take place entirely beyond human control, they produce a state of universal resignation and the sage's attitude of self-suspension. I have noted that this is also the Heideggerian attitude, adopted in the time between "the gods who have fled and the gods who are still to come." But the new revelation—the periodic "unveiling of being"—is not the divine message of a personal God in his wisdom and providence; its only significance is in the response it draws from us to the cosmic rhythm of the Great Year, governed by forever unfathomable, mysterious "principles." German existentialism has drawn from some of these themes and prompts us gently to return to epochs of astral determinism.

According to Hindu wisdom, creation itself, *that there is being*, is a flaw in the cosmic principle. Before creation, in the substance of the uncreated principle (in Hindu, *Prakriti*), there was a perfect equilibrium between upward and downward tendencies. Creation broke this perfect state of primordial balance and brought victory to the downward trend *(tamas)* over the upward *(sattva)*. Thus creation, according to the Hindu sage, means separation, a downward pull away from the cosmic principle.[4]

Western philosophy and monotheistic religion were also confronted with the problems of time, periodicity, decadence, and renewal. The best efforts of thinkers, prophets, and theologians were expended on justifying a meaningful existence on all levels: of the person, the community, history, and salvation. In Chapter 1 we saw that even the birth of science was an achievement of mono-

---

3. In the teaching of the Jain, the most ancient Hindu sect, there is an endless round, illustrated by a wheel with twelve spokes. The turning of the wheel symbolizes the eternally repeated upward and downward movement of history.

4. Whatever the still-debated origin of Gnosticism, the Hindu element in it is unmistakable. "God" represents the upward tendency, hidden as the *pneuma* of the elect, and the demiurge-creator represents the downward pull, compelling the bearer of the *pneuma* (the *pneumatikos*) to lock up the spirit in the body.

theism. All the other major cosmic doctrines—whether Chinese, Mayan, Hindu, Egyptian, or Chaldean—were mesmerized by the notion of Eternal Return, and thus, ultimately, by a cosmos inaccessible to human reason.[5] But while the Christian worldview posits a meaningful and explorable universe, the occult worldview suffered no real defeat. When the *meaning* of Christianity weakens as a result of the rationalization of its sacred components, its critics suddenly see it in a double and contradictory light. One group finds that it contains and relies on too much myth and irrationality, which bars its favorable reception in intellectual and scientific circles; and the other group argues that it is too rationalistic, that it neglects the mythical, earthly element and thus alienates the masses of worshipers who seek the solace of faith and ritual.

The occult view, on the other hand, is acceptable to both groups of critics. As I showed in the preceding chapter, neopagan rationalists use the occult to explore alternatives to Christianity, myths more deeply rooted in nature and in the human response to nature's manifestations. The irrationalists latch onto the occult in the expectation of gaining a more intimate contact with the divine—in fact, in the expectation of fusion with it. But the occult cuts deeper than either of the two groups: it is not just a means of correcting inadequacies in the Christian worldview; it does not merely place Christianity in a more general perspective. Much more than that, the occult is the exact *opposite* of the Christian worldview.

This is obvious when one realizes that the occult mind regards creation, and therefore being, as a flaw in the universal principle, a flaw that must be abolished in order that perfect equilibrium may again be restored. Thus the occult is a flight from action—not only from evil acts but from acting as such—because with every action human beings become more strongly tied to the world of mere appearances and consequently retard the purification of their souls.

---

5. "While the Greeks found nothing revulsive in the idea that Socrates was going to drink the hemlock an infinite number of times in infinitely many successive aeons, a Christian could not bring himself to seeing Christ betrayed by Judas time and again if redemption in him had any meaning at all." Stanley L. Jaki, *The Origin of Science and the Science of Its Origin* (Chicago: Regnery-Gateway, 1979), p. 94.

This conflict between being and the desired state can be seen, though to different degrees, in the thought of Plato and Plotinus. Plato concluded that the world of sense perception is a copy of the world of ideas and that the soul has fallen into the body as a punishment. Yet this does not prevent his advocacy of participation in the world, notably in the affairs of the state. In the *Republic*, which deals with the essence of politics, the philosopher is not an aloof sage. He becomes eligible in his mature years for the supreme reward (and at the same time the highest duty) of society—the leadership of the state. Plotinus, on the other hand, cannot accept so great an emphasis on action in the world. The Plotinian mystic holds the world to be an ensemble of revocable emanations in which human action possesses value only insofar as it is in harmony with the ephemeral nature of the world-all, itself evanescent. The difference between the two Greek thinkers cannot be explained by pointing out, as is usually done, that in Plato's time political life was vigorous, while in the time of Plotinus Roman gigantism discouraged civic action. A better explanation is that during his student years in Alexandria in the third century A.D. Plotinus absorbed large doses of Asian creeds of which he was unable to rid himself despite his subsequent condemnation of Gnosticism.

Indeed, by this time, Eastern creeds had almost completely squeezed out the Roman pantheon and official worship, for many of the same reasons that people today find the occult more intriguing and more satisfying emotionally than Christianity. In fact, contemporary descriptions of the ceremonies, rituals, and processions of the cults of Isis, Magna Mater, and Mithra read like accounts of scenes on a twentieth-century street—processions of white-robed priests with shaved heads marching to the sound of chants and music (this in the Egyptian Isis cult that conquered the big cities of the empire) or frenzied cult participants, their hair dripping with blood, cutting themselves on the shoulders and chest while thousands accompany them with chants (this in the cult of Magna Mater from Asia Minor).

If creation is actually a fall from perfection, and if through action human beings only prolong their own and the world's suffering, then liberation must be an escape from the world and action. In the pagan view, it is to be obtained only through the enlightenment of real knowledge, which reveals and opposes worldly illusion.[6] But where is this real knowledge to be found, and how can one recognize and acquire it?

The real knowledge of the escape from the world cannot be acquired through intellectual means, with the help of words and discursive processes. In fact, it can be likened less to our usual idea of knowledge than to a practice acquired through training, a long habituation of one's self to a nonmundane state. Though this is usually called asceticism and is confused with the practice of the Christian mystic and saint, the difference between the two is nonetheless enormous. Christian mystics (and the Hebrew and Moslem as well) first become learned in their faith: books, tradition, and the teaching of the church become part of their life before the desire seizes them for a more intimate encounter with God. And this God is known; his features have been enlightened through revelation and Scripture. Although mystics may at times blur the distinction between themselves and God, a firm grasp of the faith as taught by the church will bring them back to the clear realization of their separate identity. Christian mystics always return from their approach to God—in fact, this is what God prescribes—so that strengthened with his divine presence, but never by even a temporary fusion, they may now fulfill their task of encouraging their fellows in their own intimate relationship with God. These mystics are mediators par excellence; they are transformed so that others too, with their imperfect human imagination, may grasp the truth.[7]

---

6. "The craving which . . . is at the bottom of human misery is ultimately due to ignorance—a sort of cosmic ignorance which leads to the delusion of selfhood. The ignorance primarily concerns the fundamental nature of the universe, which has three salient characteristics—it is full of sorrow *(dukkha)*, it is transient *(anicca)*, and it is soulless *(anatta)*." Arthur L. Basham, *The Wonder That Was India: A Survey of the Culture of the Indian Sub-Continent Before the Coming of the Muslims* (New York: Grove, 1959), p. 270.

7. Gustav E. von Grunebaum makes the point that Mohammed was just one such mediating mystic. "Throughout his career Mohammed had been careful to emphasize his human nature. By the undeserved and unaccountable grace of God he has been selected as his messenger, but beyond this distinction there is nothing to set him apart from his fellow-men." See von Grunebaum, *Medieval Islam: A Study in Cultural Orientation* (Chicago: University of Chicago Press, 1947), p. 91.

Compare these Christian mystics with the Buddhist "saints," the bodhisattvas. They are not mystics destined to return among people, enriched from an encounter with God; they are not like Paul, Francis, John, or Teresa. Instead they are sages moving upward *(sattvas)* who have overcome the gravitational turn of the wheel of existence and seek to escape the world. They are "potential Buddhas" on their way to the primal Buddha, and in the meantime they are the latter's manifested power in this world. How did he rise to this exalted position? Arthur Basham tells us that

> to attain bliss the hermit must, so to speak, restore the state of things before creation. The normal values of the world, sacrifice, benevolence, and even asceticism, are only good insofar as they lead the soul upwards. . . . "He who knows [the mystery of Brahman] becomes calm, restrained, satisfied, patient and confident, and he sees himself in the Self, sees all things as the Self. . . . Evil does not overcome him, but he overcomes evil. . . . Free from evil, free from decay, free from hatred, free from thirst, he becomes a brāhman."[8]

The Christian combines in every order of existence and without any internal contradiction the spiritual and the temporal, the transcendent and the incarnate, the active and the obedient, the prophetic and the historical, the worshiper and the citizen. This is because the Christian God is the creator of separate beings and things outside himself, which are thus endowed with selfhood, individuality, and freedom. All creation is contingent; it came into being by divine decision and it can be abolished in the same manner. But the Christian God was not compelled to create or to release emanations; nor did he defect and allow another to create. Rather God *chose* to create. And whatever he created, both beings and objects, are distinct from his own being. Human beings are not part of the substance of God, nor do they contain divine "sparks" in their souls. Only by distinguishing between humanity and divinity can we give full credit and respect to reason and its exploration of God and nature; to history, which is human action always lovingly watched by God; and to faith, which is not a

---

8. Basham, *The Wonder That Was India*, p. 255.

reabsorption in the divine but a state of trust in the good will of the Father.

It is in this distinctness of God, humanity, and nature that we recognize the high point of Christian ontology, which seems inadmissible to certain generations. We all have met people who resent it as an affront and insist, with arguments or emotions, that the human and the divine are one substance, though there may be more of this substance (or the substance may be in a more refined state) in the latter than in the former. Their arguments do not resort to reason; they more often are prompted by subjective feeling and self-will. They "feel" that their view of things is more correct and true.

The Asian creed puts forward its claim in much the same manner as Western pantheism and thus appeals to those who profess to feel a continuity with the divine. In the Orient, writes Maurus Heinrichs, "man is defined, not by reason, but by the heart. The intellectual faculties are situated on the periphery of the human being, and man expresses his essential self on the ethical mode alone."[9] For this reason, the Oriental is far more ready than the Westerner to find mystery and symbol in things. But, remarks Heinrichs, this aptitude is often carried to extremes, and things tend to lose their being as things. Their symbolic aspect alone is considered, which then authorizes the most extravagant imagination, as is evident in the differences between the sobriety of Greek and Egyptian art, its reasoned proportions and juxtapositions, and the luxuriance of Hindu art—and mythology—in which the fantastic seems to admit no limits and the materials, color, and narrative refuse to submit to the reasonable and measured.

The consequences of the Eastern tendency are many. To seek knowledge in the escape from the being of things is to accept the systematic extinction of the human state in the self of the contemplator. The Asian creeds prize this as "knowledge," the passage through the stages of self-domination ending in self-extinction. These stages are described by Niamatiloka Mahathera as the rejection—or, better, the denial—of tradition, history, self, action, and substance. There is nothing permanent on which to grasp, only an endless flux of physical states, sensations, and states

---

9. Maurus Heinrichs, *Théologie catholique et pensée asiatique* (Tournai: Casterman, 1965), p. 21.

of consciousness. Everything is essenceless, pure phenomenon. Existence is pain—the theme of Buddha's programmatic discourse at Benares—and pain is engendered by the long chain of births and rebirths. In the Tantras, later Hindu and Buddhist scriptures, virtues are defined not as positive qualities but as means of avoidance of the world: abstinence, concentration, internal knowledge, nirvana (self-extinction).[10] Buddhism, Zen Buddhism, and Tantra Hinduism all concentrate on the struggle to rid the self of individuality, to cast off the burden of logical thought, and to annihilate the life-force that prompts the self to action. "The doctrine of the *anatta* (the ego as pure phenomenality) is the characteristic teaching of Buddhism, which sums it up and without which it collapses."[11]

To the rational mind it comes as a shock that the Oriental doctrines generally describe this loss of self as "finding oneself." This is not so much an intellectual process as physical training and moral discipline—by "moral" meaning not love, charity, and good actions but a mastery over a hardly distinguished physical and mental energy in concentrated form. Since action and movement are condemned as both illusory and the cause of suffering, to discover knowledge is to find oneself as unchanging, the atman, the spirit, the inner self, the immobile core. But atman is Brahman, the eternal principle, "unchanging and unchanged, undivided and without parts," as the Hindu sage Sankara taught.[12]

---

10. This self-extinction was the highest virtue. In "going 'from darkness to darkness deeper yet' [the ascetic] solved the mystery beyond all mysteries; he understood, fully and finally, the nature of the universe and of himself, and he reached a realm of truth and bliss, beyond birth and death, joy and sorrow, good and evil." Basham, *The Wonder That Was India*, p. 245.

11. Alfred le Renard says that "in Buddha's doctrine, there are sensations, facts of consciousness, pain, etc., but no subject which sees, hears, suffers. Being is a process which unceasingly becomes and abolishes itself." See le Renard, *L'Orient et sa tradition* (Paris: Dervy, 1952), p. 117.

12. The quote is from Rudolf Otto, *Mysticism, East and West* (New York: Macmillan, 1932), p. 19. The sage Sankara emphasized throughout his teaching that the individual soul (atman) is a mere part, a reflection, of the world-soul (Brahman) that will rejoin the whole even as the air in a bottle will rejoin the air outside if it is broken. Sankara's *Six Strophes on Nirvana* illustrate, in the negative style of the Upanishads, the nature of the atman: "I am neither spirit nor intellect nor the thought nor the sense of the self / I feel no aversion, no

Thus knowledge as identification with the inner spirit, atman, is the same as identification with the world-spirit, Brahman. (Brahman is the traditional word for the totality of the universe or its nothingness; Brahma or Brahmo is a nineteenth-century name for a kind of Christianized amalgam of Hinduism.)

After this, it is not surprising to read in René Guénon's works that human existence is only one aspect of being and that reason does not help us reach other aspects—only acts, symbols, and forms can help us reach the inexpressible. This is what he calls metaphysics. He means by this that those processes that we in the West consider intellectual are, in the Oriental perspective, considered beyond intellect and reason.[13] The two worlds could not be farther apart. While classical Greek thought focused on the maximal development of the logos (creative and reasoned speech) in order to explain the world, the cosmos, and the place of humanity in them, Hindu speculation focused on seeking ways to recover the spirit, the same in Brahman and atman. Again, while Greek philosophers tended to incorporate their metaphysics into other disciplines, Hindu sages remained interested in spirituality alone. They attributed supreme importance to the soul's immediate seizure of the Absolute, but this, however, is a capture of itself. In a climate that placed such emphasis on the spirit, neither science and philosophy nor reasoned public life could develop. The divisions of the caste system—like the rigid separations within the Gnostic system—are the consequence of the Hindu view of the universe: they divide society according to perceived differences in a group's grasp of the eternal void.

Oriental speculation never leaves this magic circle; its encounters with Western metaphysics, science, and technology do not change its essentially spiritual view of the world but result only in an enhanced grasp of the phenomenal and pragmatic. Thus Orientals who have encountered and accepted some of Western thought must henceforth divide their personality between absolutely spiritual pursuits and the exclusively practical order. Westerners who

---

attraction, no greed, no confusion / For me neither good actions, nor moral stain, nor pleasure, nor suffering has any existence / I am without determination, without form."

13. This is the thesis of Guénon's *La Crise du Monde Moderne* (Paris: Gallimard, 1946); see esp. p. 99.

have adopted some of Oriental thought are perhaps even more damaged. The Western mind is too metaphysical and ethical to engraft on itself a totally different way of thought—to live with a divided mentality. Induced to underrate their rationality, their sense of measure, Westerners under the influence of Eastern thought tend to absolutize themselves and turn into extramoral *Übermenschen*.[14] They replay in caricature the mystical union, except that instead of meeting God they meet their own emptied husks and do not return from their "trip."[15] If the spiritual encounter is not crowned by a more complete assumption of natural and human reality, it produces only a rarefied atmosphere, a spirituality so pure that it denies the lower levels of reality and the human part in them.

The core of Oriental teaching is a maximal isolation from the world by the bodhisattva or the yogi. The atman must also float like Brahman, suspended in the void.[16] The extreme radicalism of Eastern mystics is far from the detachment of Western pagan sages. The latter, no matter how superior their pose, never cease drawing on the world outside: knowledge, learning, observation, the shapes and colors of a multiform cosmos. The self-unification of the former, on the other hand, strives for the annihilation of the self, nirvana, the point "where the wheel of rebirth is not turning," the center, "absolute nothingness," the "primoridal vacuum," the source of the universe.

14. For example, Mircea Eliade speaks of Yoga as an "experimental method to achieve the status of man-god." *Techniques du Yoga* (Paris: Gallimard, 1948), p. 224. Olivier Lacombe, an authority on India, writes of the Vedas, the collections of writings that comprise the Hindu sacred scriptures, and the Upanishads, a class of Vedic treatises that deal with philosophical problems, that Hindu spirituality permits the passage from the human condition to that of the man-god, the Superman. See Lacombe, quoted in Joseph de Sainte-Marie, "Intériorité chrétienne et intériorité 'orientale,'" *La Pensée Catholique: Cahiers de Synthèse* 177 (November-December 1978): 39.

15. Note the similarity of this trip to the "trip" of the drug user under the influence of drugs. Whatever the trippers meet, they do not return to an increased sense of self-enrichment and moral worth.

16. Under the influence of Christianity, modern Hinduism recognizes the mythic god Brahma as a personal God (Brahma, the nineteenth-century name for a kind of Christianized Hindu god, is not to be confused with Brahman, the Absolute Indeterminate). But his worshipers are a small sect, and Hinduism as such does not prescribe belief in him.

Henri de Lubac reports the observation of a seventeenth-century Jesuit priest, Louis Frois, that one hundred times a year the Japanese bonzes, Buddhist monks, devote an hour and a half to meditation on the axiom "There is nothing." From a similar, contemporary description of Chinese Buddhists, de Lubac reports the observation of the Dominican Noël Alexandre that "'the doctrine . . . is pure atheism. Emptiness *[le vide]* which they consider the principle of all things is . . . without beginning or end, without movement, without knowledge, without desire. . . . [They sink] in a non-reflective contemplation.'"[17] The Tibetan monks, writes Alfred le Renard, concentrate on the idea that all substance is unreal, false, and impermanent. They purpose to dispel all belief in the reality of phenomena. If traces of belief in reality survive, the meditation must nonetheless be directed to the ethereal nature of everything, its emptiness, its existence without beginning or end.[18]

The remarkable thing is that all the meditation on nothingness and all the focusing on the central emptiness and self-extinction should nevertheless erupt in so many striking metaphors and, in fact, in the desire to name and describe the nameless and the ineffable. Even those who wish to abolish the self cannot help but speak about the stages on the way to nirvana.[19] Self-dissolution does remain the final objective, however, and the techniques of reaching it converge in Sankara's formula: "Brahman is atman and atman is Brahman." This original and ultimate identity is the

17. Noël Alexandre, quoted in Henri de Lubac, *La Rencontre du Bouddhisme et de l'Occident* (Paris: Aubier, 1952); see pp. 85-87.

18. See le Renard, *L'Orient et sa tradition*, p. 128.

19. There are manifestations of this paradox—the desire for unknowable nothingness juxtaposed with the desire to describe and explore it—in Christian churches as well, both East and West. The writings of Pseudo-Dionysius the Areopagite and the Rhineland mystics—Meister Eckhart in particular—are fine examples. In the *Divine Names* Pseudo-Dionysius puts forth the thesis that God cannot be named; yet he demonstrates this richly and with pious poetry. Eckhart studs his sermons with such statements as "The Soul is troubled so long as it perceives created things in their separateness. All that is created is nought." From Plotinus to Fichte, Western philosophical literature has tried to express the nature of the Godhead, but the concepts of creation, reason, and the delight in reality—and mainly, perhaps, the doctrine of the Incarnation—have set clear limits.

principle that governs the world but which must be achieved, again and again, in individual existence for the escape to be completed. I mentioned earlier the fusion of opposites that is so central to alchemy, to Taoism (the principles of yin and yang), and to the cabala, and that finds expression in the androgynous figure and in other symbols of completeness. Nirvana itself is complete when the distinction of eternity and time is overcome, after the occult follower receives the illumination that the two are aspects of the same total experience. Reconciliation is also manifest through the awareness that self and universe are in a state of interpenetration, and that the ego must be absorbed in the wholeness in order to escape the evil of personhood (separateness).

It is easy to point out how different the presuppositions, mental processes, and objectives are in the Christian worldview. Christianity postulates a world of distinction, differentiation, analysis, and conceptualization. Even Epicurus, whose phenomenism relates him to the Brahmanic and Buddhist view of the world, is unwilling merely to flee from the torrent of things as the Oriental sage does. He stretches beyond pure phenomenalism and founds the theory of the *clinamen*, which proposes that the order of the world is due to the random arrangement and rearrangement of atoms into numerous varieties of composition. Explanation and systematization, the organization of experience and knowledge, are part of the Western intellectual arsenal; what we so find and make is not only rational science, it is at the same time artistic composition in which we delight.

Why then does the occult tempt the modern West? Since the eighteenth century, Western Christian civilization has admitted the validity, then the superiority, and finally the exclusivity, of the scientific worldview and of the ideology built on it. These admissions were not made by the church as such, but the church did little outside of preaching to reverse the trend, as if it too shared in the change and had a stake in secularization. In many respects, the church has contributed to the triumph of rationalism and has accepted humanistic values in a precarious attempt to bridge the gap originating in the secularization of the Renaissance between the world of faith and the rest of life. Although the mass of the faithful did not recognize it, critical minds began to detect the decadence threatening the increasingly rationalistic and narrowly based (industrial, technical, egalitarian) civilization, and they became intellectually prepared to link the fate of the church to what they saw as a darkening future for Western civilization.

Let us bear in mind that the pagan revival of the fifteenth century followed upon the church's catastrophic crises in the fourteenth—the papal schism and the Avignon papacy, the battles of religious orders, the ideological separation of the secular and spiritual realms, and the theological and political challenges of William of Ockham, Marsilio of Padua, and John Wycliffe. One could draw up another list of the challenges since the eighteenth century.

The sudden prestige of Buddhism in the 1700s was facilitated by the philosophes and their colleagues, who welcomed the Oriental creed as a demonstration that religion is possible without God and that it can be contemplative, virtuous, *and* materialist, all in one. But even more formidable challenges followed: revolutions, class antagonisms, the rise of social sciences theorizing about society without the divine, and the development of a psychology that claimed to cure the soul without reference to God. To all these, the response of pure Christianity in itself would have been adequate; yet the church appeared increasingly committed to the civilization it had helped to shape and which now found no place in its self-satisfied agnosticism for Christianity.

The church did not find the firmness, or perhaps even the faith, to reassert in more than just books and pious warnings those truths that are the equivalent of the myths and the sacred for pagans. The supernatural remained surrounded by doctrine, of course, but it became more and more rare to hear it discussed affirmatively in Catholic universities or to see it translated through inspired means into art and literature and architecture. Where today are the conditions that led Suger of Saint-Denis to construct his abbey church to reflect and symbolize the reality of faith in magnificent combinations of stone, glass, and light? "Starting with the entrance," according to Georges Duby, this building "is an orthodox apologetics, defying the heretical deviations." He then adds these words, which reveal a notion absolutely foreign to the modern mind: "By rehabilitating matter, Catholic theology demolished the basis of Catharism."[20] Where today is the Christian apologist,

---

20. The Catharist dualism was based on the belief that matter was evil, in opposition to the good world of the spirit. Orthodox Christian theology of course rejects any such dualism. See Georges Duby, *Les Temps des cathédrales: L'Art et la société, 980–1420* (Paris: Gallimard, 1978), pp. 131, 178.

prelate, doctor, or artist who would feel at home with these intentions and would state them and struggle to fulfill them in response to modern heresies and deviations?[21]

Just as we have lost the drive to incorporate the truth of our religion in our worldly life, we have also lost our conception of original sin. The doctrine of original sin is a myth in a way, insofar as it lays bare an overarching truth in dramatic form, a truth that is impossible to state otherwise. The doctrine is a magnificent explanation for human evil, the only explanation compatible with the concept of an absolute beginning in the creative act of God, the only one compatible with the belief in God as absolute goodness. Pascal, certainly not an obscurantist, found in original sin the solution to all the questions about evil that his libertine friends could think of. I can conclude only that original sin is a paradigmatic truth that so overwhelmingly impresses itself on the human mind that people have long spontaneously understood and believed it, saying that it cannot be and cannot have happened otherwise. Yet the past hundred years or so have almost completely undermined and dissolved the belief in this doctrine. Kierkegaard was perhaps the last great creative thinker and Dostoyevski the last great writer to reaffirm the prevalence and originality of sin, though in this century Martin Buber and Georges Bernanos speak in similarly prophetic accents. Today, the reality of sin is usually whitewashed, so to speak. Sin was replaced first by guilt, then by the mere "sense of guilt," which transfers the onus from the individual to others who are ultimately responsible: to those who induce this "sense of guilt in others." (Oddly, it occurs to no one that if this is the case, then sin is not abolished but is merely transferred to those who induce the sense of guilt in others.)

Despite this sophistry, sin and evil do exist. The grave thing is that we moderns have squeezed them out of the myths in which we

---

21. Suger was by no means attempting to incarnate and control the sacred in the physical, in the church structure; yet neither was he hesitant in his belief that the physical can stand in the service of the sacred. On the occasion of the celebration of the magnificent church at Saint-Denis, he stated, "To those who criticize us, objecting that in this celebration a saintly soul, a pure mind, and a faithful intention suffice, we admit that, indeed, these are the most important. But we declare also that one must use ornate sacred cups and other beautiful things in the service of the sacred sacrifice: with a pure heart and a noble exterior." Quoted in *Les Temps des cathédrales*, p. 122.

The New Occult

believe—progress, perfectibility, and science—so that no corresponding word and symbol exist in our internal life or in public discourse. Thus gigantic realities—the supernatural, evil, sin, and redemption—have no translations in the modern psyche, or rather they are falsely translated, thereby creating confusion, ignorance, and false consciousness. The sacred—the symbolization of immensely important realities—is relinquished by oversight and by plan, without the church's doing anything but politely lamenting its passing. In this, the church meekly follows the strongest modern ideology, the ideology of industrial society in which efficiency depends on making humans similar to machines.

In this situation, the Asian creeds and the occult appear as a seductive beacon. Their immobility, to be explained by their pantheism, is interpreted as a solid tradition; their symbols, which reflect the escape from reality, are admired as the translations of the "immensely important realities" just mentioned; and their denial of the legitimacy of reason is perceived as the ideal of the serene soul tending toward more genuine values.

Christian men and women are thus caught between two pressures. On one side is the church, which no longer seems committed to a Christian civilization and appears to have settled its doctrinal differences with the secular way of life; and on the other side are modernist ideologies—among them liberalism, Marxism, scientism, technology, and mass democracy—which strive to eliminate the last remnant of the sacred, and do so with only token protest from modern Christianity. The ground thus prepared is ready to be permeated even more fully by ever-escalating rationalist premises. The scene in any city in the Western world, and increasingly in the countryside as well, persuades us that religion has been thoroughly and systematically excluded from the active life of the citizenry. Old churches look like museums, new ones like factories. Priests and nuns look like busy bureaucrats, particularly since they hardly ever display signs of their sacred calling. Sermons, like newspaper editorials, deal with political, social, and economic issues. Christian schools imitate secular ones in inspiration and curriculum. Public life itself is consecrated to the idols of ideology. In no sector of government, law, economic life, or the media—or even literature and art—can one find even traces of civilization's Christian component. Sociologically and perhaps psychologically the church has become irrelevant, as paganism was irrelevant in the last two centuries of the Roman Empire.

The spiritual vacuum that prevails in modern society with the complicity of the church makes it quite natural for people to turn to pagan religions and the occult, even as two thousand years ago people turned from paganism to more emotion-laden creeds and to Christianity.[22] As I have amply documented, Asian creeds give the all-important reassurance that one is an organic part of the world-all. In the general climate of atomized individuals and anonymous public pressures, this is a tremendous positivum. Underlining it is a further assurance: that the myriad routine acts of daily life, meaningless and mechanical, are not what the world-all wants of humanity. On the contrary, the Asian creeds deny the authenticity of these acts and state that the world-all wants all human beings to find themselves beyond the turmoil of their busy existence, at the "center of the wheel" where things come to a halt. The extinction of the karma (the élan vital), which industrial life has in any case reduced to a force of social productivity, is not a frightening prospect to modern mass humanity. Moderns can still meditate—and perhaps many do, while watching the torrent of things on television—on the theme of the Japanese bonzes: "There is nothing."

The occult itself, which reappeared in Christian civilization about the time of the First World War then grew rapidly in influence some two decades ago, is inseparable from the Asian creeds. Many of the occult practices we know in the West are derived from Oriental religions. In their native habitat they serve a purpose that is too potent for Western individualism, whereas in the West many take them as mental and spiritual gymnastics. Yet adherence to the practices provokes a corresponding state of mind; the creed originates and the practice ends in the vague but profound feeling of emptiness, now so widespread.

22. Arthur Darby Nock gives some of the reasons why citizens of the Roman Empire turned to Christianity: The Savior was not merely a figure of unique attraction nor a mythical personage, but a historical figure invested with deity. Christianity freed its adherents from fate, the daemons, and death. It rejected all but a certain prescribed form of worship, showing a sure knowledge of its own truth. Its monarchic episcopate gave it a unity and a purpose. And finally, it asserted the value of each individual. All these factors worked together to give Christianity both a perceived and a real power—the Christian God could defeat the other gods. See Nock, *Early Gentile Christianity and Its Hellenistic Background* (New York: Harper and Row, 1964), pp. 102-4.

The New Occult

The occult is based on the belief that the world is alive with forces both within and without humanity and that these forces communicate with one another in a never-ending interaction. The occultists—shamans, astrologers, yogis, alchemists, magicians, or simple adherents—are those who are able to concentrate these forces upon themselves and to bring them into harmonious cooperation, thereby freeing the self from oppressive states, but also provoking changes in the extrahuman milieu. The overall objective is to reintegrate individuals and the dispersed forces within them—dispersed because they are individuated—with the archetypal realm in which these powers, and hence the individuals who are their locus, again find unity with the whole.

The restoration of unity is not social adjustment but an act of healing, a return to the transcendent without boundaries of time and space. The occultist as healer is the mediating agent between the esoteric realm and the "patient." This healing consists in the establishment of a link between the community and superior forces, a link that may find expression as narrative (myth), collective ritual, or psychophysical therapy (as illustrated in the case described by Lévi-Strauss of the shaman's treatment of difficult cases of childbirth among Cuna Indian women in Panama). The myths, rituals, and therapies vary over time and place, but all are related to universal archetypes. There is a curative magic, writes Stephen Larsen, in finding one's meaningful place in the cosmic order.[23]

Those who have fallen to the lure of paganism reject orthodox religion as of no help in the quest for healing. It is widely believed today that religion is merely an ethical and legal system that favors cold consciousness at the expense of the rich undergrowth of the unconscious, and the ego at the expense of group experience. In addition, so the charge goes, Christianity does not situate its worshipers in the "cosmic order" but does the opposite. It lifts them out of the pagan cosmic order rejected and demythified by Christianity from the start and situates them within creation, an order held together by providence and divinely ordered laws of nature rather than occult forces manipulated by secretive initiates.

The occult intends to transform a fractured state of existence, marked by diverse senses and an overabundance of preoccupa-

---

23. Stephen Larsen, *The Shaman's Doorway* (New York: Harper and Row, 1976), p. 65 and the epilogue.

tions, into a severely concentrated and trained unity. But what the occultist regards pejoratively—diversity and multiplicity—is in fact mental and sensory nourishment, the dulling of which adversely affects our intelligence. The unity achieved by occult therapy is really emptiness, endurable by an athlete of asceticism but not by one who desires to live in the harmony of the faculties. Indeed, while shamans and other occult mediators are trained to stand guard at "the doors of perception" (the title of a book by Aldous Huxley), the ritual drama of their initiation and the re-enactment of the community's integrative myth clearly show the need for people to receive their impressions from the collaborations of ideas, images, and symbols—that is, from the translation of the purely spiritual into the mixed language of human representation. This is why Christianity so wisely makes room for sense experience in liturgy, ceremony, and art, proclaiming through visual and musical means the content of the faith. In contrast, occultists do little more than tolerate the material world. They believe in no worldly renewal and so withdraw from sense experience and focus on spiritual powers of a suprahuman kind.[24]

While all these processes are reputed to be cosmic, it is easy to see that they take place within the psyche of the subjective self. Neopagans and occultists fail to realize that the psyche cannot be removed from the physical being, the world, and the civilization that surround and shape it. The attempt to live as a soul or psyche alone—even though unsuccessful—causes the fading of the supernatural and leaves the soul in a dissatisfied state. As Titus Burckhardt notes, "In every collectivity unfaithful to its own traditional form, to the sacred framework of its life, there ensues a collapse, a mummification of the symbols it had received, and this process will be reflected in the psychic life of every individual."[25]

Today, the occult penetrates the lowered defenses of the Christian tradition, and those whom it persuades are the masses of

---

24. These powers may indeed be qualified as suprahuman because they have no contact with the material world and interact with the body only insofar as their integration with the human spirit occurs through the disciplining—that is the dissolution—of the human being's physical component.

25. Titus Burckhardt, "Cosmology and Modern Science," in *The Sword of Gnosis: Metaphysics, Cosmology, Tradition, Symbolism* edited by Jacob Needleman (Baltimore: Penguin, 1974), p. 173.

men and women who miss the sacred symbols that used to be present everywhere as identifying signs of their civilization. They feel malaise at the apparent absence and unreality of the supernatural, which through many centuries translated itself into the language of symbols. The Christian symbols are now worn out; they are represented and recognized as mere routine and convention, if at all. The entire symbology of Christianity yields to other, sometimes older, symbologies with their underlying creeds and doctrines. The others have, better than Christianity, maintained their freshness and intrigue and their power to heal.

I have noted several times that healing, in the sense in which Asian and occult creeds understand it, is the equivalent of the disintegration of the individual self and integration with the world-all. Our increasingly paganized civilization views this as a positive development, and if one starts from pagan premises this is certainly correct. C. G. Jung speaks of the Original Man as a "sphere" produced by the combination of all four elements by means of a circular movement.[26] He is partially correct in this view because he refers to the symbolic expression of the totality humanity would *like* to become. The Middle Ages, the Renaissance, the age of Romanticism in artistic pursuits—they each had their ideals: the saint, the virtuoso, the suffering young hero as locus of contradictory passions. The image of the ideal individual is well embedded in all times. Certainly it is foreign to no one today to speak of the "well-integrated person" as an ideal, although thus formulated it may be only an insignificant contemporary ideal. But if we look deeper and take this ideal seriously, and there are many who do so, we can see that for some it is by no means the Christian ideal. Rather, it is the ideal of Oriental and esoteric doctrines for which such an integrated totality is the bodhisattva or the androgyne, the man-god. Such an integrated being recognizes no transcendent being above: the human individual becomes the terminal point, the answer to the riddle of the universe.

The struggle to achieve this integration requires techniques that have nothing to do with prayer, good works, repentance, divine understanding, grace, or mercy. Occult literature abounds with

---

26. Jung, *Mysterium Conjunctionis: An Inquiry into the Separation and Synthesis of Psychic Opposites in Alchemy*, translated by R. F. C. Hull, Bollingen Series no. 20 (Princeton: Princeton University Press, 1970), p. 7.

the description of the techniques available to the would-be adherent who needs only sufficient will power to engage upon and persist in practicing them. When alchemists strived for the "chymical marriage" between elements in a vessel (which Jung saw as proof that they suspected a hidden godliness in humanity),[27] they were seeking nothing other than integration. The ambition of their life and work was more than Promethean. According to Jung they wanted to heal the wound caused by Christ, who "split the spiritual and the physical." They sought to produce a fifth element, *caelum*, the pure and incorrupt physical equivalent of heaven and the original substance of the world. The residues of their alchemical experiments, those elements that could not be integrated and unified, they called the *terra damnata*, the damned earth, equivalent to the residues of humanity who are damned for their inability to achieve integration.

Such beliefs are not the exclusive domain of the alchemists. Many people throughout history have believed that through integration, often with the help of certain mechanical and chemical aids such as bodily and respiratory exercises or personality-changing drugs, one can become divine. Even if the result is contemplation and concentration (the opposite of dispersion and distraction), reason is excluded, played down, and regarded as the essence of alienation. It is this sort of integration that is patently anti-Christian. It is nothing more than self-induced stultification and the extinction of interest in the world.

The alchemical replay of creation, this time according to a different, "improved" scenario, suggests that occult healing tends to impoverish the adherent and that the cost of integration to human nature and aspiration is very high. The product of the occult is the sage, not the Hellenistic sage but the Oriental variety. With reason and emotions extinguished, only will remains in the midst of an otherwise devastated landscape. Whether shaman, guru, or bodhisattva, the "integrated" person is a monument of will, a fact that leaves open the question of which direction the will may take.

This particular kind of religious practice, with its mingling of religious gymnastics and renunciation, has had such a hold on the Hindus, and its observances have been so conspicuous in all their activities, that outsiders

---

27. Ibid., p. 109.

have been led by the spectacle to attribute a deep, comprehensive, and esoteric religiosity to them. And this religiosity has been mistakenly associated with the Western conception of spirituality. . . . But in no form of Hindu renunciation is there any trace of the religio-moral idea that man's nature is innately sinful. . . . Hindu renunciation and asceticism . . . constitute the method of obtaining more and ever more power over men and nature by showing for some time how little one cared for the prizes and enjoyments offered by the world.[28]

28. Nirad C. Chaudhuri, "The Paradox of Hindu Spirituality: Reflections on 'a Religion to Live By,'" *Encounter* 52 (March 1979): 27-28. Compare what Arthur Basham has to say about the Hindu ascetics. These Hindu solitaries "would indulge in fantastic self-torture, sitting near blazing fires in the hot sun, lying on beds of thorns or spikes, hanging for hours head downwards from the branches of trees, or holding their arms motionless above their heads until they atrophied. . . . The original motive of Indian asceticism was the acquisition of magical power." Basham, *The Wonder That Was India*, p. 244.

CHAPTER 6

From Christianity to Paganism

Voluminous historical, political, and philosophical studies—veritable summas—predicting Western decadence and diagnosing it in detail have not been lacking in the last half-century. Among these the best known are the works of Oswald Spengler and Arnold Toynbee, who conclude that the history of a civilization can be divided into periods of origin and rise, then growth and maturity, and finally degeneration and eclipse. It is often overlooked, but surely significant, that such works are usually written in what the author considers the third period, not only when past events may be seen in review, but also when a resigned wisdom is able to draw conclusions. Thus the testimonies of Spengler and Toynbee (and of Romano Guardini, Alexander Rüstow, Amaury de Riencourt, among others) are valuable not only in themselves but also as symptoms of the thesis they wish to demonstrate: that civilizations are mortal and that the perception of twilight is an ongoing human characteristic.

More attention has been paid to the historians than to the philosophers, whose more complex reasoning may keep their similar—in fact, more radical—views hidden from the public. René Guénon and his school regard Western civilization merely as one span of time within one of the endlessly recurring cycles conceived by the Hindus and other pagans. As I mentioned in a previous chapter, this cycle can be considered an alternation of movement toward or nearness to some Absolute Principle and movement away from or distance from it. As a section, so to speak, of this immeasurably vaster stretch, our age too is subject to the laws of movement toward and away from the principle. Heidegger, who also was fascinated by Oriental wisdom, described the rise and decline of civilization as a symptom of the presence and absence of the gods, the veiling and unveiling of Being itself, which manifests itself to the appropriate philosopher, the "shepherd of Being."

All these formulations—whether on the part of the Christian Toynbee, the Oriental-minded Guénon, the neopagan Heidegger, or the Stoic Spengler—suggest that many outstanding thinkers of this age feel intellectually and spiritually uncomfortable with Christian civilization, in part because they find it narrow and in part because they interpret its submission to the temptation of secularization as a sign of weakness. They believe that this weakness is an indication that history (or the god, or the Great Cycle) has abandoned our civilization. Whatever the cause, it is evident in the minds of these scholars that Christianity is less and less able to meet the challenge posed by new ideologies and mass movements in our century, and that it is unable to provide fresh answers to the questions posed by metaphysics, psychology, and ethics. One could express dissatisfaction with the Christian response to contemporary problems without taking a radical and anti-Christian stance. Yet when we consider the researches of the new mythologues—Mircea Eliade, Claude Lévi-Strauss, René Girard, and Joseph Campbell, scholars much more favorable to religion as such than many in the previous generation—we are struck by the fact that they too bypass the postulates of Christian thinking as if they were irrelevant.

For example, Eliade writes in the preface to his book *The Quest* that the "sacred" is an element in the structure of consciousness, not a stage in the history of consciousness.[1] Thus the sacred is an internal not an external element in human life and thought; it does not act of itself or through another agent in human history. Eliade seems to comment on his statement in another of his books in which he gives this lapidary formula: "We must do what the gods did in the beginning."[2] That is, humanity is in control and can re-

1. Mircea Eliade, preface to *The Quest, History and Meaning in Religion* (Chicago: University of Chicago Press, 1969).

2. Eliade, *Patterns in Comparative Religion*, translated by Rosemary Sheed (New York: Sheed and Ward, 1958), p. 417. He is here quoting from the

create history and the sacred. As for Girard, he finds the sacred inscribed not in the structure of consciousness but in the structure of the community, whose orderly survival it guarantees. The act of violence that served as the founding act of the community is henceforth defined as sacred and is to be ritually imitated periodically—hence violence is expelled (reduced to that one act). It seems that both theories place the sacred inside the human being or the community and pay no attention to the view that the sacred may be a channel for divine intervention in human life.

The phenomenological premises of Eliade and Girard deal with human behavior admittedly more richly and generously than the positivist scholars who preceded them. Yet modern students of myth still take it for granted that everything has been said about the sacred when we enclose it in the human psychological and symbol-seeking economy. They thus present myth making and symbol seeking as therapies for treating a civilizational sickness—but no more than therapies. It matters little to most scholars today that this therapeutic view of the sacred reduces religion to a phenomenon strictly inside human beings without real links to the transcendent. We should not be astonished to find in the works of so many writers on religion the more or less open statement that God is a human product. This much is intimated by Jung, who regarded religious belief as a potent means of therapy but as hardly privileged over other means such as sexual fantasy, ideology, or the recollection of childhood events. Alain de Benoist is more blunt. In early European religions, he writes, humanity was the measure of God. The community of the gods was conceived on the model of human society and was its ideal representation. And human beings were the creators of the gods, the givers of meaning.[3]

We are justified in regarding the historical theories of Spengler and the others as symptomatic of a general attempt to move out of the framework of a Christian civilization whose God is no longer "sacred," that is, no longer believed in. Neopaganism and the new occult, which I have explored as two principal examples of the

---

Satapatha-Brahmana (7.2.1.4), a Vedic treatise and the oldest Indo-European text from India.

3. Alain de Benoist, *Comment peut-on être païen?* (Paris: Albin Michel, 1981), p. 212.

From Christianity to Paganism

attempt to break out of the Christian framework, may be labeled ideological movements, although such a label may be judged too narrow to cover the multitude of theories, hypotheses, and academic areas that show a neopagan or occult infiltration. The scientific disciplines and the quasi-religious phenomena linked to neopaganism and the occult enlarge their general significance and give evidence of a new civilizational direction.

Gilles Quispel observes that human beings always need a time center or a temporal frame of reference that can serve as a guidepost for the recognition of past and future. "Our historical marking of the years tacitly presupposes a caesura between the era before the birth of Christ and the era which came after it. Our history is oriented toward a center."[4] I thought of Quispel's remark as I read the diary of the Hungarian Orientalist, G. Germanus, which he wrote and published in the 1960s. Germanus used the time references of neither Christianity (which have become the most common references in the modern Western world) nor Islam (to which he was a convert). That is, he does not write in terms of anno Domini, or before Christ, or in the year of the Hejira. Rather he refers to events and times as either "before our time" or "after our time." The communist state publishing house obviously shied away from the Christian notation, just as many at the time of the French Revolution insisted on counting time from the present—which they considered the beginning of a new era in history. Not until Napoleon's presence on the imperial throne was this practice reversed.[5]

A much more radical way of abolishing the birth of Jesus as the time center of our civilization is the attempt to rehabilitate the idea of the Great Year and its subcycles. Although such attempts have

---

4. Gilles Quispel, "Time and History in Patristic Christianity," translated by Ralph Mannheim, in *Man and Time*, vol. 3 of *Papers from the Eranos Yearbooks*, edited by Joseph Campbell, Bollingen Series no. 30 (New York: Pantheon, 1957), p. 85.

5. This style of dating has made inroads into American scholarly practice as well. Whether in deference to nonbelievers and believers of religions other than Christianity or in an attempt to rid their work of references to sacred time, many scholars now use the abbreviations B.C.E. and C.E. to refer to the time "before the common era" and "of the common era." But in this attempt they fail, for the first year of the common era is by definition the first year of our Lord.

so far been limited to high intellectual circles, their influence should not be underestimated in a general scrutiny of our cultural reorientation. Karl Jaspers proposed the theory of "axial years," periods of about 2,500 of our years that begin with an exceptional accumulation of great spiritual leaders and great religious and philosophical systems. Jaspers saw the beginning of an axial year about 600 B.C. with the origin of Buddhism and Confucianism, the apogee of the Hebrew prophets, and the birth of Greek philosophy. But with this scheme one is hard put to explain Jesus Christ and the birth of Christianity and its increasing influence in religious life and philosophy from Paul to Augustine, to say nothing of the later rise of Islam. To begin a new axial year at least some six hundred years before all this is to completely ignore the importance of these developments; yet the attempt to articulate history from a different temporal point of view is worth noting.

There are of course numerous ways of attempting to create a new ordering of time, some more and some less sophisticated than that of Jaspers or Germanus. They are all indicative, however, of the impatient attempt to leave the Christian framework behind. Futurological and prospectivist methods of research, for example, have recently become fashionable. In this respect, several authors follow the line suggested by Jaspers, although they have different ways of dividing up the historical continuum. A vaster division than "axial years" measures eras in terms of a cultural way of life. First of all a culture may follow a nomadic way of life, then a sedentary-agricultural one, then it may enter an industrial age, and finally move into the imminent electronic age. Not only do these four periods, cutting across other subdivisions, indicate a distinctive way of life; according to these scholars they identify similarities in economic production, ethical beliefs, attitudes toward the divine, and patterns of social and family life. The serious scholars heading such projects claim not that they intend to realize utopia but that the availability of data and the rapidity of the calculation of probabilities prompt them to chart the future. They speak of computers, the precision achieved in statistics, and the data accumulated by planetary research to justify their new sciences. For my part, I believe that mechanical inventions do not so much prompt new directions of research as they are the result of research already undertaken in the attempt to satisfy the new mental and moral desires of humanity.

Are these speculations the last traces of positivist theorizing? Are these the divisions of history so eagerly sought in the last two centuries by Hegel, Marx, Spengler, Auguste Comte, Marquis de Condorcet, Nikolay Danilevsky, and others? Or are they anticipations, partly unconscious, of a new sectioning of time, a new history, a new civilization?

Indications favor the second interpretation. The Princeton Gnostics shuffle the various elements of philosophical and other pursuits and combine them in new combinations—and certainly not along positivist lines. They do not hesitate to draw together into one overarching conception elements from myth, mystery, mathematics, and even theories on the concept of human freedom. One may speak of this as a *scientific deism* since it declines the crude anti-Christian vituperation of Voltaire and the scientific anti-religious stance of the materialists (such as Eduard Buchner, Thomas Huxley, Bertrand Russell, and Ernst Mach) and it finds systematized knowledge once more compatible with the existence of a universal force, a scientific supermind.

In truth, however, only the mood behind this reformulation of the relationship between God and world, faith and science, may be said to be new. The enigmas recently revealed in the depth of the psyche, in the behavior of tribes, in the heart of new scientific theories such as the big bang theory of the origin of the universe—all these prompt a reexploration of old ways of thinking rather than a truly original way of looking at the world. Under the new formulas one detects the old animism, pantheism, and monism. Matter, already endowed by Epicurus with the ability to explain the qualities of life, and considered by the Stoics to be the origin of all things in the "fire of Zeus," remains, after all, the matter we always knew. In spite of probability theories, matter is subject to a strict causality. Statistics do not contradict it; they merely indicate our human inability to track it down. The novelty is that now we make matter assume even more functions than the ancients ever did. They could only theorize about the atom while today scientists "see" the atom and its subdivisions—the new *atomos* (indivisible) matter—in their cyclotrons and their equations on the blackboard. Yet the new knowledge that they claim is but a return to the old monism reasserted again and again, the monism of Lucretius or Giordano Bruno. They have turned full circle to say that matter is the only stuff in the universe, but, they add, it is so porous, so unpredictable, so full of tricks that we might call it "spirit" and thus satisfy our religious cravings at the same time.[6] Whether in the mode of the ancients or of the moderns, God is still defined as the totality of the cosmos.[7]

My thesis is not that Christianity carries the burden of guilt for these various and converging efforts to break away from its hold but that it renders itself vulnerable to them. Christianity has opened itself at certain points to a critique that subsequently widens into a counter-Christian worldview, the search for a new civilization founded on other than Christian premises. This in itself is not a demerit. Even the critic Nietzsche hailed the Christian centuries for having compelled human beings to live in a culturally fertile tension, and while laboring for the demise and replacement of Christianity, he regretfully observed that this tension had come to an end. Nietzsche saw the Christianity of his time as yielding to one of its temptations: the encouragement of bourgeois vulgarity and socialist equalization, both of which would eventually lead to the exhaustion and decadence of Christian civilization. Because the *Übermensch* was supposed to live and could live most fruitfully as a being-in-tension, it was part of Nietzsche's endeavor to restore the tensions to civilization, but on a more secure base than Christianity.[8]

---

6. Note the words of James K. Feibleman on this subject. "The new atom is complex, and its indefinitely analyzable levels and properties make it possible for it to sustain not only the physical properties such as mass, density, and dimension, but also all of the qualities that were once carried only by spiritual values, or according to idealism, by the consciousness of human subjects." Feibleman, *The New Materialism* (The Hague: Nijhoff, 1970), p. 42.

7. If God is not identified as the totality of the cosmos he may be identified with chance. "If x never rises to existence, and cannot grasp itself as an object, it is because x is God." Raymond Ruyer, *La Gnose de Princeton* (Paris: Fayard, 1974). Pierre Teilhard de Chardin identifies God as the Supreme Programmer. This God created matter and so programmed it that it gradually spiritualizes itself until mankind matures to the point of becoming a "supermankind" and encounters Christ, who meanwhile has become "super-Christ."

8. Today, about a century after Nietzsche, the neopagan New Right in Europe proposes again the same, Nietzschean, program: the restoration of the tension that Christianity and its ideological residues intend to abolish, level, equalize, and eliminate.

From Christianity to Paganism

In earlier chapters I examined the vulnerable points of Christianity as a religion and as a civilizational order. In Chapters 1 and 3 I argued that Christianity's insistence on the rationality of the universe and history (which resulted in the demythologization of the universe and the refutation of the cyclical view of history) has led to its excessive reliance on rationalism. This is not to say that such a thing happened only within Christianity: rationalist excess is always a potential trap of the mind. But in the case of Christianity its essential truthfulness excludes the possibility of modifying its tenets. Christians simply cannot hold that the universe is a product of a drama among the gods, that human beings are little besides the battlefield of good and evil spirits, and that history is a gigantic game of cosmic forces. One who would assert these things would have to oppose dogma, doctrine, the teaching of the church, theology, and philosophy. These are all bound tightly together in a single bundle from which nothing can be extracted without risking the collapse of the whole. The extremely close link between the spiritual and the intellectual in Christianity blocks the kind of inconsistency that other religions tolerate—not because they are more permissive than Christianity (in fact they are usually more strict on the demands of practice and ritual) but because they lack the theological rigor that necessitates and produces consistency.[9]

In all this, when I say that Christianity is vulnerable to excesses of rationalism, I mean not just the church but also the civilization that it helped to found and guided along the way. Even so, more lines than one can be distinguished; the rationalists and demythologizers took more than one path. It may be debated, for example, whether the demythologization of the pagan heaven led of necessity to the systems of Vico, Hegel, and Marx, or to the systems of

---

9. As if aware of its vulnerability from the side of myth—or, on the contrary, confident in its force—Christian practice tacitly allows the persistence of the (pagan) mythic element beneath its Christianized surface. Not only outside the Western world, but in Europe as well, pagan mythology has survived to this day and has been translated into practice, though the Christian believers may not know the source of these practices and may have invested them with Christian meaning. For some interesting illustrations, see Gerald Brenan, *South from Granada* (New York: Farrar, Straus and Cudahy, 1957), who notes that in parts of Spain some villagers have preserved pre-Hellenic, perhaps Iberic, myths on which Moorish practices were later grafted, and now accept the whole as "Christian."

Augustine and Bossuet, in a completely different direction. At any rate, the Christian concept of history is so challenging—since we are free to develop its particular form within the very broad outlines provided by Christian revelation—that the many problems raised often resulted in false adaptations, vast counterconcepts, and new gods sponsoring other historical interpretations.

As a concrete illustration, it seems obvious that though Christianity was not founded with a ready made philosophy of history, Christian thinkers soon formulated one, from Paul to Augustine and others since then. Yet Christian philosophies of history are by no means all the same—some in fact are quite unlike each other. In contrast, Buddhism, Hinduism, and Islam, and the cultures heavily influenced by these religions, have no elaborate philosophy of history since they lack also the rational basis to demand it of them. In consequence, the non-Christian world was never rent by the clash of opposing philosophies of history the way the Christian world was, particularly in our own time when the Hegelian-Marxist system is confronting the Augustinian one. Yet nobody would deny that even though Marx and Hegel were great adversaries of Christianity, their philosophies of history belong to Christian civilization and that their views would not exist without the doctrine and doctrine-based conceptualizations of Paul and Augustine.[10] The rationalism of Marx and Hegel, with its excesses, can be regarded as an outgrowth of Christianity itself, which also attempted much earlier to formulate within the bounds of reason an overview of history's meaning.[11]

We reach similar conclusions when we turn our attention from reason to faith, the other foundation of Christian religion and philosophy. In other religions, especially pagan ones, faith has no role beyond what we would call belief, in some cases not even that.

---

10. In his history of Western philosophy, Bertrand Russell has a passage in which he compares, in parallel columns, the most important dogmas of Christianity and Marxism. The parallel shows how Marxism is patterned on Christianity. See *A History of Western Philosophy* (New York: Simon and Schuster, 1945), p. 364.

11. Greek historiography, with its peak achievement in Thucydides and Polybius, never rose to the level where it could have formulated such an overview. It was prevented from doing so not by the relative narrowness of an outlook based on the polis but by the lack of concepts with which to break out of the cyclical view of history.

The Greek mysteries, Orphic and Eleusian, consisted in initiation, ritual, and the sense of belonging to a community linked by a "secret" that was not to be disclosed to the profane. The secret may have been the story of the god's or the goddess's descent to the underworld, the eventual reemergence, and the symbolic meaning derived from this passage through death and resurrection. The story itself was a symbol, particularly in Orphism, of the soul and its passage (punishment) in the body. We should not consider this so much *belief* (certainly not belief in the Christian sense) as an exalted and refined *interpretation* of what takes place in nature—the death and renewal of the seed, the disappearance and reappearance of the sun and of the celestial bodies, and the changes of the seasons.[12]

It is true, as E. R. Dodds writes, that the Orphics made the discovery that human beings were not simply mortal beings but possessors of "an occult self of divine origin."[13] Yet this interpretation still demanded no faith in a divine being and in redemption through it. Instead, it demanded only a reinforced cult to which the Pythagoreans were to add theories of Hindu origin, the migration of souls. The whole system had at its center the travels and travails—and finally the escape—of the soul, but not faith in a ruling and saving God whose redeeming act is final. Thus we can say that faith in the Christian sense is the hope of redemption; belief, even when it extends beyond mere membership in the cult, is the acceptance of natural events in a sacralized version, that is, interpreted with the help of symbols.

Socrates, Plato, Plotinus, and Greek speculators in general reached astounding heights, but they did not worship. They were unable, within the limits of their worldviews, to do more than

12. In contrast, Christ's death and resurrection has a very different meaning from that of such doomed and revived deities as Osiris or Adonis. Arthur Darby Nock points out that whereas in pagan myths death means defeat, the death of Jesus is triumph: *Dominus regnat de ligno* (the Lord reigns from the wood [cross]) is the keynote of Christian resurrection. The entire soteriological work of Jesus is concentrated in the sacrifice of the cross. See Nock, "A Note on the Resurrection," in *Early Gentile Christianity and Its Hellenistic Background* (New York: Harper and Row, 1976), pp. 106-7.

13. E. R. Dodds, *The Greeks and the Irrational*, Sather Classical Lectures no. 25 (Berkeley and Los Angeles: University of California Press, 1951), pp. 139-49.

contemplate with an attitude of intellectual marvel the adumbrated rationality of the cosmos. The state religion, in Hellas and in Rome, was a dry cult, a quest for protection addressed to national deities that were virtually held in bondage to the state through the appropriate ceremonies and sacrifices. Among archaic tribes in all parts of the world, religion is a fantastic and almost always sophisticated myth that explains in great detail everything that happens in nature and in human society. All of life is imbued with the signs of the sacred: the gods can be seen everywhere. But oddly, these gods are almost as impotent as humans. In no pagan religion are they as powerful as the God of monotheistic religions. The pagans do not have even the concept of a good, just, forgiving, and yet powerful creator God, and they cannot even begin to comprehend the God who came to human beings in Christ.

Yet at this point we meet the "vulnerability" of the Christian faith: it is an internal affair, between God and one of his people. To be sure, it is supported by the story of Christ (the "myth") and by the rich ritual centered on the worship of the liturgy and the celebration of the Mass (the "sacred symbols"). And of course Christianity does have an undeniable corporate element since any member always belongs to a body of believers who together participate in the sacraments and welcome new members into their midst. But the contents of the sacraments are internalized as if the myth and the symbols, the sacred and the cult, unrolled only in the soul, in intimate solitude.

This internalization results in part from Christianity's exalted view of individuals, their responsibility, salvation, and struggle between good and evil. But with the exception of the fervent, who turn their inner life into a temple to God, worshipers are unable to escape the world and Christian culture, which are both organized around the exercise of reason. Faith for many consists more and more of rational understanding (through catechism, credo, prayers, and readings) and a series of acts of consent and will. They cannot "let themselves go" and cannot weave new images and experiences into the fabric of their religion's "mythical" component, since that component is not myth but true history, certified and taught as such. Their mythical imagination is radically curtailed by the very truth of their religion. Great religious educators such as Ignatius instructed the members of their orders to focus in their meditations on the sufferings of Christ, making it vivid to their mind's eye. The willed concentration in such exercises shows how little the average Christian can achieve in the dimension of myth, which presents an abundant field for the pagan imagination, including wars within the pantheon, heroic deeds, trickery of spirits, and, most important, the application of all these to events in daily life.

This is why depth psychology, the exploration of myth, the use of mind-transporting drugs, and the penetration of Asian creeds have, in various combinations, worked together to offer an alternative to Christian civilization. The offer is all the more tempting for people in the West since they no longer live in a fully Christian civilization in which myth, symbol, the cult, and the sacred have a powerful presence embedded in doctrine. Instead, we live today in a residual Christian civilization from which these vivifying components have all but been eliminated. We saw the nostalgic cultural diagnoses made by Lévi-Strauss, Gilbert Durand, Eliade, Jung, Paul Tillich, and others, and we explained the inrush of the Asian creeds and of the occult by the incredible desiccation of our civilization under the aegis of the industrial-technological formula, the culmination of rationalism. Both Tillich and Jung observe that Protestantism has proceeded in the last two centuries with a dedogmatization of major proportions. Tillich speaks of liberal Protestantism for which he expected in his youth to substitute the morality of a socialist Protestantism.[14] But the latter then chose new gods, those of social service and, often, of Marxism. This long process of desacralization, in which our industrial society replaces theology with science and the sacraments with technological services, issues in no greater understanding of God and the world but only in a greater emphasis on efficiency.

The vacuum that the vanishing sacred leaves behind is filled by the new gods of the new civilization. In the case of the modern West, we characterized this new religion as neopagan, that is, variously Greco-Roman, Oriental, and occult. The Oriental and the occult influence is an old temptation to which the Western world periodically succumbs, including now and in Hellenistic times. E. R. Dodds puts forth the intriguing thesis that Plato filled the spiritual vacuum in Greece by effecting a combination of the

---

14. Paul Tillich, introduction to *The Religious Situation* (New York: Meridian, 1956).

rationalist tradition native to Greece and magicoreligious notions derived from shamanistic Nordic culture. Earlier Greek writers may have worked on the Nordic myths themselves, looking for allegories they might interpret, says Dodds, but it was Plato who transposed the revelation theme of these myths to the plane of rational argumentation.[15]

It certainly never hurt the pagan cause that the new creeds seemed to offer a quick release from the ails that the old religion could fully heal only in the next world. Hans Leisegang observes that the Gnostic prophets dismissed their Greek origin and preferred to clothe their ideas in Oriental garb, either authentic or false.[16] This procedure seemed more credible to their audience, which aspired to divine status or at least wanted to be initiated into techniques of union with the eternal substance. Henri de Lubac locates the beginning of the major thrust of the Buddhist penetration of the West in the eighteenth century, coinciding with the beginning of Christianity's eclipse. And today, after the torments of our century's wars and revolutions, the Asian creeds appear in a peaceful light. Appropriately, the manifesto of T'ai-su, published in 1918, states that "Buddhism alone teaches and practices the doctrine of human brotherhood and universal peace, taking as its basis the affirmation that all men participate in Buddhahood."[17]

Despite all this evidence, a good case can be made for the proposition that what attracts members of a weakened Christian civilization to Oriental creeds and occult doctrines is not Buddhism, the Tantra, the Tao, the Zen, Brahmanism, or shamanism. Much

15. Dodds, *Greeks and the Irrational*, p. 209.
16. Hans Leisegang, *Die Gnose* (Leipzig: A. Kröner, 1924).
17. Quoted in Henri de Lubac, *La rencontre du Bouddhisme et de l'Occident* (Paris: Aubier, 1952), p. 239. In contrast to this manifesto, one has good reason to doubt the peace-loving and brotherly nature of the Oriental creeds. From the earliest Moslem observers in occupied India to present-day Hindu writers, there is unanimity in describing the Hindu hatred of foreigners and of fellow Hindus who mix with foreigners, wear their garb, or eat their food. Brahmins so fear the loss of their position in this highest caste that Brahmin nurses refuse to touch the body of a patient from another caste. Nirad Chaudhuri mentions that Rabindranath Tagore, the Nobel Prize-winning poet, was regarded as only a semi-Brahmin because centuries before a member of his family ate of the Moslem pilaf. No Brahmin would marry a member of the Tagore family.

more important, it seems to me, is the presence in each of these new religions of the pantheistic worldview and the hope of self-divinization, or at least self-elevation above the status of mere creature. I have referred several times to the intellectual difficulty of grasping a God extraneous to the universe; it is perhaps even more difficult to grasp him so spiritually, since the dialogue we conduct with God in our soul produces the conviction that he is located within us. It takes certain temperaments only a moment of distraction to persuade themselves—and to translate this persuasion into a text or a sermon—that God resides in the inner self, that he is the "inner spark," or that the soul itself soars to the Godhead, fusing with it.

The occult and the Oriental creeds offer an easier solution than Christianity does to the tormenting dilemma of God and soul, psyche and nature, and the person and the universe. Jung's psychology, like the investigations of Eliade and others into religion, myth, and the sacred, reveals a new type of person, beyond the objectivity expected of scholarship and the scientific method. I observed before that, by a certain aspect of their activity, these men emerge as prophet-scholars, prophet-philosophers, prophet-novelists, even prophet-scientists. This pattern, this type, is evident in Nietzsche, Heidegger, Raymond Abellio, Hermann Hesse, and the Gnostics of Princeton. Not only are they scholars, writers, and scientific researchers; they also propose a teaching, a worldview, a way of mastering the problems of life. These new prophets take their places alongside Christian thinkers, humanists, and various ideologues. But unlike these last three, the new prophets are no longer within the orbit of Christian discourse. The attraction they offer the West is the Oriental-pagan ideal of the completed human being, produced by the fusion of elements that Christianity had always held in distinction and that rationalism had finally rent wholly asunder. As the alternative to Christian salvation, immortality, and beatific vision, Jung suggests the alchemical-psychological fusion of the soul's bipolarity—an obvious replacement of the vertical elevation of the soul to its creator with a horizontal conjunction of opposites.

Jung's proposal aims at a quasi-divine state, the same state of equilibrium and fusion sought by the Hellenistic-Roman sage and the Oriental bodhisattva. How deeply modern people respond to this alternative to Christianity, to the offer of salvation without moral demands, was illustrated, though at a fairly crude level, by the success of Herbert Marcuse's *One-Dimensional Man*. The one-dimensional man is a product of industrial processes transformed into a way of life, which in turn is a product of rationalism. We noted that Christian civilization only half-opposed the explosion of rationalism, several proponents of which were members of the clergy (Nicholas de Malebranche, for example). To be sure, Marcuse sought the "complete man" in the wrong places: Freudianism and Marxism, hedonism, and the permissive society. Yet the book's glowing popularity and the basic intuition that suggested its title are obvious reflections of the modern quest for internal completion and fusion with a new absolute. Paganism and the occult seem to satisfy this need on all social and intellectual levels: of the sophisticate, the philosopher, or the drifting individual who feels marginalized. For the discontented of Christian civilization, for those who cannot live with the Christian tension, the pagan worldview and all its promises (albeit false) have become an acceptable option.

CHAPTER 7

The Desacralization of Christianity

I gave the title "The Christian Desacralization" to Chapter 3, wishing to describe not the desacralization of Christianity, as here, but Christianity's desacralization of culture, the involuntarily but intrinsically rationalistic influence of Christianity on the civilization it has fashioned and nurtured. The historically rooted origin of Christianity, I tried to show, together with a Christology that demanded belief in a being both divine and human at the same time, introduced a strong rational element into the religious discourse of the next two millennia. Reason, thus inherent in Christianity, was exposed to the risk of degenerating into rationalism when it was not carefully balanced by faith and mythical/symbolic elements.[1] I mentioned several examples from the history of Western thought of just such a degeneration: the "two verities" propounded by Averroës and his followers, the "Latin Averroists" of Padua; the eagerness with which humanists from the fourteenth to the eighteenth centuries tried to interpret the Christian religion as a subclass of a primordial "natural" wisdom; and the alchemists' efforts to accelerate the redemption of humankind through the interplay and "maturation" of the chemical elements.

  1. "In proportion as religion becomes the religion of the Good Tidings, its center of gravity shifts toward what can be expressed with words; the magical material, the mythical spectacles, and the cult's play element disappear from it." Eugen Fink, *Le Jeu comme symbole du monde*, translated by Hans Hildenbrand and Alex Lindenberg (Paris: Éditions de Minuit, 1966), p. 184.

From our perspective, these occurrences suggest a gradual desacralization of Christian civilization through the use of reason as the preponderant faculty of understanding and interpretation. Yet we saw that others—including René Guénon, C. G. Jung, Mircea Eliade, René Girard, Claude Lévi-Strauss, and Gilbert Durand—speak not of a gradual process but of a "catastrophic rupture," a "metaphysical catastrophe." Indeed, Durand locates in Averroism the beginning of the Western conversion to "empirico-rationalism," which was to result, according to him, in today's "idolatry of history."[2] The Iranian Moslem philosopher Daryush Shayegan holds that this same Averroist influence made explicit the inherent antagonism in Christian thought between Greek science and the traditional Christian worldview. Shayegan says that even though Averroës himself never asserted that the conclusion of faith may be different from the conclusion of reason, Latin Averroism, the speculation formulated in Padua, did arrive at such a dichotomy, and it later led to the Cartesian dualism of mind and body. In other words, what in the conception of the medieval Arab thinker was merely a kind of pedagogy—the teaching of the same truth on two levels, exoteric *(zahin)* and esoteric *(batin)*—was seized upon in Christian speculation as a description of a radical cleavage of the mind in which the intellect clearly predominates.[3]

In the Renaissance period, the Paduan Averroist teaching spread to only a few other university faculties; in the seventeenth and eighteenth centuries, however, it became the mainstream thought under the label "classical rationalism": Descartes, Bacon, Spinoza, Malebranche, Hume, and Kant were all adherents. There were only a few voices expressing alarm, and some of them—Schelling, Schopenhauer, and Kierkegaard in the nineteenth century—elaborated irrationalistic theories in opposition. Also in the nineteenth century, Franz von Baader was among the few who recognized that the break from the traditional Christian worldview occurred during the time of Reformation and the growth of humanism. He assessed the significance of the break as a "Western catastrophe" and saw it as the split between faith and

---

2. Gilbert Durand, *Science de l'homme et tradition; Le nouvel esprit anthropologique* (Paris: Berg International, 1979), p. 93.
3. Ibid.

knowledge, leading in one direction to natural science with atheistic postulates and in the other to antiscientific theology (that of Schleiermacher, for example). Now in the twentieth century rationalism is victorious—at least many would like to live as if that were so. As Giuseppe Tucci, an Italian specialist on Hindu and Tibetan thought, writes, "In India the intellect has never prevailed to the extent of obtaining mastery over the faculties of the soul, of separating itself therefrom and thus of provoking that dangerous scission between the intellect and the psyche which is the cause of the distress from which the Western world suffers. The West, indeed, as though to designate its present inclinations, has coined a new word, unwonted in the history of human thought, the word "intellectual"—as though it were possible to have a type of man reduced to pure intellect."[4]

Such was my conclusion in Chapter 3, here further documented. In subsequent chapters I suggested that the desacralization did not stop with Western Christian civilization but has turned against the Christian religion itself. Desacralization focused especially on the great stumbling block of Christianity: the Incarnation. This is not to say that the very idea of the divine entering human form was alien to the pagans. In fact, paganism often proceeded in a similar way: it conceived of heroes whose metamorphoses allowed them changes of status. But this process was copied from nature and embroidered upon by imagination. Such divine heroes were acceptable because they were products of fancy that required only marginal intellectual assent and understanding. In Judaism, the truly divine God remained transcendent; neither Moses nor the prophets nor the expected Messiah laid claim to divinity or were considered divine by others. The acts of God in history were understood as sovereign interventions that clearly delineated the sphere of the divine from the sphere of human action and dependence.

Christianity marked a great change from this pattern, however. The God made man, the absolute relativized, the infinite made finite, the transcendent as personal and human was asserted as true and factual—it required much more than the exercise of the fancy

---

4. Giuseppe Tucci, *The Theory and Practice of the Mandala: With Special Reference to the Modern Psychology of the Subconscious*, translated by Alan Houghton Brodrick (London: Rider, 1961), p. 1.

for assent. Christianity then surrounded the figure of the incarnate God with the testimony of history and subtle, systematic, theological and philosophical reasoning, precisely formulated by doctors and councils. They distinguished and debated such concepts as God's triune nature, his personhood, his creativeness, his participation in history, his moral demands, and the consubstantiality of Father and Son. In short, they built around the God made man a formidable scientific system that both encouraged scientific reasoning in general but at the same time also seemed to deny the validity and truth of its object. This placed a tremendous burden on the believer's faith, which had to be reconciled at every step with the evidence brought up by reason.

Under such intellectual pressure, there has always been a great temptation in Christian speculation to resolve the God-man tension—which also lay at the root of further tensions—in favor of one of its terms. Intellectually one could not accept both; one had to choose either Father or Son, the eternal God or the created Jesus, the aloof and disengaged God or the concretely involved manlike historical personage. Arianism and its later versions up till our time were attempts to resolve the conflict in this way. The Arians chose in favor of common sense and discarded the mystery: Jesus for them was the first and most exalted among creatures, but a creature nonetheless. This view has allowed the personalization of Christ in human terms and at various times in history has permitted and allowed his absorption as a mundane protagonist. In our century, it has also promoted his politicization.[5]

5. This was, in fact, the serious charge of Henry Corbin, one of this century's great students of Arabic and Persian thought. Like Ernesto Buonaiuti, Corbin held that the immediate postapostolic church was eschatological, as was apocalyptic Judaism. This position was "Christoangelological"; it saw in Christ a "superior angel," not a God. "In proportion as Christianity ceased to be eschatological, it settled down in history" and promoted "the humanization and politization of the esoteric mystery." In contrast, the Islamic gnosis rejected incarnation, thus preventing secularization.

Corbin points to the precariousness of the equilibrium between human and divine nature in Christian dogmatics. Each of these natures tends, he writes, to absorb the other. He sees as a consequence of the declaration of Christ's absolute divinity the inevitable (with the decline of faith) absolutization of the human, the social, and the totalitarian political. Corbin—and some Christian mystics, including Meister Eckhart and Jakob Böhme—was protected against such a development by placing between the Absolute and man, between

All this entails the descending movement of Christ the God, while modern, self-exalting humanity see their own course ascending. It is no wonder that the contemporary imagination—and certain theological trends—seize upon Jesus as humanly manipulable, as detached from God and consequently a mere symbol, a representative, a guide for earthly aspirations. This preference for Christ separated from God is clearly reflected in the recent book of Father Jean Milet, *Dieu ou le Christ?* (God or Christ?).[6] His thesis is that we—modern human beings, the twentieth century, and post-Christian civilization—are moving away from theocentrism in the direction of Christocentrism. The former represented order and a sense of measure; the latter, in keeping with the "revolutionary spirit" of the New Testament, favors the spirit of protest, of pagan humanism, and of humanistic atheism. The author obviously ignores the central point of the Christian creed, the consubstantiality of God and Christ from all eternity to all eternity, which explicitly prevents such a separation. But in any case, he claims that he speaks less as a priest than as a sociologist, and that he merely draws conclusions from the attitudes of Christian revolutionaries, correlating them with other observable phenomena—including the decline of faith (the death of God) and the easier self-identification of revolutionaries (often atheists) with the figure of Christ. This new "Christocentric revolutionary spirit" is revealed in the ever more common attitude, "I do not believe in God, but I can find in Jesus a friend or model."

It is easy to recognize in Milet's thesis a neo-Arian conviction, which may even be unconscious, shaped by fashion. It is clearly a rationalistic thesis, as Arianism was in the fourth century. It is equally clear that this rationalism has at all times been encouraged by the dogma of Christ's humanity, which was magnified at the expense of his divinity in the hopes of easing the tension between the two. It was the philosopher Eric Weil who spelled out this central problematic of Christianity with sufficient clarity. According to him, believers in a personal (human) Christ are philosophically obliged to dismiss God's transcendence.[7] If God is an existing being among other existing beings, his status as a totality is

---

heaven and earth, the angels as intermediaries. See his *Le Paradoxe du monothéisme* (Paris: Éditions de l'Herne, 1980).

6. Jean Milet, *Dieu ou le Christ?* (Paris: Éditions Trévise, 1980).

7. Eric Weil, *Logique de la philosophie* (Paris: Vrin, 1950), p. 192.

compromised; he then exists, said Paul Tillich, the way an object or a stone exists.⁸ Both Weil and Tillich thus conclude that Thomistic "rational theology" reduces God to the status of an object.

Now if Milet strayed toward the Arian heresy, Weil and Tillich tend toward the existentialist error. They hold that God's transcendent status is altered or diminished when he is spoken of as an object of our thought, and that Thomism is rationalistic when it points to the (God-created) ability of the intellect to think about and to know God. Heidegger had a similar view: if he had a conception *(Vorstellung)* of God then he would be citing the divine before the court of his human judgment. This view, and that of Weil, leads to agnosticism. Furthermore, these speculations suggest that the humanized Jesus tempts the Western mind to open a cleavage in the Christian God-concept that allows the humanity of Christ to prevail over his divinity. If this is the case, then Christ is little different from other human beings, who can then do as he did. Weil puts it this way: "With Christ, God really came down to earth; he truly became man. If God not only is God but descends to earth, then man ascends to heaven. . . ."⁹ In the line of Lessing, Kant, Hegel, and Feuerbach, Weil states that the development of the human personality in Western Christendom is actually the instruction of how to be divine, given by God to the human race; in the process God renders himself superfluous. Thus we should see Christianity as humanity's faith in itself as its own creator. He concludes that "the human personality is . . . the end product of the secularization of the Christian idea."¹⁰

Whatever we think of this argument, it seems that, at least in the mind of vast segments of the West, the Christian God has died and that this death is simultaneous with the assumed ascent of humanity to divine status. Since human beings now understand themselves to be absolute—and this is the recurrent message of modern science and ideology—they need no symbols, myths, or the sacred that used to mediate their understanding of a transcendent being. The humanized Christ with whom human beings are able to iden-

---

8. Paul Tillich, cited in Raymond Vancourt, "Quelques remarques sur le problème de Dieu dans la philosophie d'Eric Weil," *Archives de Philosophie*, Les Fontaines Chantilly 33 (July/September 1970): 485.

9. Weil, *Logique de la philosophie*, p. 315.

10. Ibid., p. 317.

tify—inasmuch as the relationship between God and Christ is severed—becomes the guarantor of a religionless, rationalistic world system. In other words, the emphasis on Christ's humanity at the expense of his divinity justifies a symbolless, desacralized conception of the world. The traditional God used to be opaque; humanity needed a means of mediation in order to comprehend him and follow his will. But now humans are transparent to themselves; they require only reason (science) to grasp their own absolute essence.

It is sufficient to focus on the new conception of the sacraments as a measure of Christianity's rapid loss of symbol and the sacred, brought about by the emphasis on Christ's humanity and the connected rationalistic frame of mind.[11] The Council of Trent emphasized that the Reformers were in error when they saw in the sacraments "purely external signs of grace received by faith."[12] The council asserted that the sacraments are not mere signs but confer grace by themselves—in other words, they repeatedly bring Christ to the worshipers. The modern view, which is essentially that we can know only signs, not being, shifts interest to the sign itself, which is basically a subjective thing that varies according to person, place, and time. In the modern view, if a particular sign is able to call forth my response, if it reminds me of an event, then my commemoration of that event with the help of the self-chosen sign has at least as genuine a validity as the sacrament administered by the corporate church.[13] My subjective celebration has an existential value; the church's celebration is impersonal, reified, and alienating.

The symbol, contrary to the sign, is a pact in which members of a corporate body recognize their common participation in a being that transcends them singly and collectively. The symbol unravels in a myth, subsequently acted out in rites, but not just any myth.

11. "The sacred appears as superfluous and mendacious as soon as people begin to doubt the existence of its foundation." J.-J. Wunenburger, *Le Sacré* (Paris: Presses Universitaires de France, 1981), p. 101.

12. Council of Trent, Session 7, "Canones de sacramentis in genere." Canon 6 in Denziger, *Enchiridion Symbolorum*, edited by Johann-Baptist Umberg (Freiburg: Herder, 1937), p. 300, no. 849.

13. This change from being to sign has been effected in contemporary philosophy by phenomenology: a thing *is* its perception by a perceiver.

We speak of a story with a truth value since it tells us about the world's origin, the meaning of life, and the end of the world and of ourselves. The rite permits the participant to experience once again the paradigmatic events told in the myth: the performer and the participant communicate with the mythical-yet-true event through symbols, the keys that open the analogies, and are thus able to transcend their temporal and spatial limitedness. This is the significant difference: the sign is a *remembrance* in the present of a past event. The symbol incorporates that but goes beyond it: it is the *renewal* of a past act in the present in which past and present are unified and made continuous. Through symbol Christians are able to participate in God's history. As Joseph de Sainte-Marie explains, the symbol calls forth images and, through them, emotional and other responses made to be joined—joined in religious acts when God is worshiped and in magic when the objective is merely to capture and secure the services of preternatural forces.[14] Thus in method alone religion is not hostile to magic since both recognize the existence of forces external to humanity, though not always divine. In both, too, the symbol mediates between two orders, two worlds.

What we witness today is the transformation—the degradation—of the symbol into the sign. That is, the instrument that participates in the reality of being is ever more transformed into a simple reference, a reminder, as the green and red traffic lights remind motorists of their duties on the road. And the process does not stop even there. The new interpretation displaces the religious emphasis itself. Many modern religious authors (even some priests) and various analysts of the religious situation speak of the sacred as located now in human contingency, in human dignity, in cosmic symbolism—in other words, in humanity's assessment of themselves as the only conscious reality in the world. Outside of humanity nothing really is, nothing has being. Behind the sign there is nothing; they are merely convenient guideposts for human communication.

It is no wonder that alongside traditional religious rites—the celebration of the liturgy, confession, and communion—new rites are invented that receive official endorsement. For example, peni-

---

14. Joseph de Sainte-Marie, "La liturgie, mystère, symbole et sacrement," *La Pensée Catholique: Cahiers de Synthèse* 191 (March/April 1981): 44-45.

tents now sometimes bring a stone to the ceremony, apparently to represent the weight of sin; the worship service may begin with the recital of a tale from Andersen or with concentration on the stars. Whatever has meaning in the eyes of this or that individual or group may be assimilated into the celebration since what counts is no longer the sacramental reality but the commemoration by whatever signs the group agrees upon. For example, from the Roman Catholic point of view, the Eucharist has been degraded from the belief in Christ's real presence in the host to the view that the Mass is a mere commemoration of an event in the past that will always remain in the past.

As Gilbert Durand remarks, modern Western thought rediscovers the symbol in psychoanalysis and ethnology, but the only social importance of the symbol is now for the sick patient or the primitive tribe.[15] The symbols that do manage to retain their power become generalized—they are judged to be applicable to all of Western civilization, including religion. Christians are not distinguished from the rest; they are told to participate in the universal myths and symbols, with the implication that these others are equal in value to their own. In this manner they are lifted from the limits traced by their own religion, and they gratefully join the much larger symbolization that awaits them.

The meaning of the symbol is thus misunderstood; it becomes an arbitrary sign, a gesture, an act. The true grasp of the nature of symbol implies the conviction and faith that there is a reality behind it. Then to grasp the symbol in practice implies a repeated return to the primordial event founded in that reality. But this return is not a commemoration in which a single past occasion remains forever in the past; much more than that it is an immersion into the origins of that reality that are also an eternal part of the present. The proper exercise of symbol is a renewal of the past event rather than a mere remembrance of it. For this reason the return and the immersion lend destiny its explanation and justification, its safety against destruction by chaotic powers. Repetition authenticates the symbolic object, as do the weight of time, the participation in unique events, and sacralization by similarly laden significances. Henry Corbin puts clearly the ongoing significance

---

15. Durand, *L'imagination symbolique*, 2d ed. (Paris: Presses Universitaires de France, 1968), p. 38.

of symbol when he says that "the symbol . . . is never explained once and for all; it must be deciphered again and again, just as a musical score invites new performances."[16]

In Christianity, not only does the incarnate Word assume the central symbolization; it also mediates between the divine and the human orders, which is the function par excellence of symbol in religion. In instituting the symbolic sacraments, Christ made provision for the continual renewal of the mediating function. And indeed, in the Incarnation itself, Christ himself becomes the most potent symbol of all. Obviously, if Christ were merely an ordinary human being the Mass could be a sign of his sacrifice, but it could not symbolize the transcendent. If, on the other hand, we grant the divinity of Christ and yet state that he is forever present in the host, then the sacrament itself gains the power of mediation and the human person of Christ—the Incarnation—becomes superfluous. There are some who would argue along this line that the sacraments instituted by Christ are incomparably more potent than any symbol could be. In fact they are not symbols, they say, but they offer grace by themselves. These people have strayed too far in the direction of the divinity of Christ and in the process have lost sight of the balance provided by his humanity. It is this balance—and there must always be some tension here—that makes of him and of the sacraments symbols. Here the divinity of Christ enters and grants to the sacramental acts the power of renewing, not just remembering, the original acts.

Yet now in the twentieth century a much more common fault results from desacralization. Instead of seeing the Incarnation as the establishment of Christ, and the sacraments as eternal symbols, we see only Christ pulled down to his humanity. For many people in their interpretation of the Incarnation, the gains in Christ's humanity are matched by corresponding losses to his divinity—not in truth, of course, but psychologically, from our point of view. This is what causes great confusion in our symbolic imagination. The wholly human Christ lacks the potency to imbue the sacraments with the power of renewing the original acts. Both Christ and sacrament become powerless objects. A Christ tilted toward humanness becomes an object of reason, and the sacraments he instituted turn into empty gestures.

16. Corbin, quoted in ibid., p. 12n.2.

In this perspective, resacralization can occur only through a new emphasis on Christ's divinity and on God's transcendence. This would be a reversal of the trend of many centuries, a return to the point of rupture characterized by the various thinkers previously discussed. A return to certain forms of the past and a new beginning are just what some thinkers are proposing today. The return for them would involve a reabsorption of Christ into Hebrew monotheism, thus terminating the scandal of the Incarnation and the Trinity. I think there is hardly any need to argue why this would be an impossibility. Nor would it solve the problem of desacralization, for certain concepts of the Reformation, which was a kind of return to Old Testament concepts, contributed more than any other factors to the weakening of symbols and sacral elements.

The new beginning is most vigorously attempted through the existentialism of Heidegger and the theology most strongly influenced by him. But Heidegger does not want to strengthen monotheism or religion as such; rather he teaches a return to being, a pre-Socratic and premetaphysical position. By separating being and God, he thus cancels God's reality and effectiveness (from the point of view of being at least). God is then no longer the author of being but becomes a voice from inside being, a voice that is not even that of revelation but merely an inarticulate appeal that obtains meaning only from the philosopher's response. Thus there are as many gods as there are new beginnings and towering sages who shape the new cycles. (And we know from our earlier discussion how much neopaganism owes to Heidegger.)

Contemplating today's religious panorama, we may make a cautious generalization. The process of desacralization cannot be halted unless we restore the equilibrium between Christ's divinity and humanity, and with it the sense of metaphysics as the study of being. Even though we might desire to restore culture, we cannot on the strength of will and desire alone plan and direct and carry such a program to completion, for it requires a complete civilizational turnabout. In the meantime we are not even holding our own against desacralization. Various forms of secularized Christianity feed Western culture with continuing desacralization, and so the process still goes on in the other direction.

On the other hand, while Christianity cannot seem to provide the impetus for renewal, the civilizational turnabout is written on the flags of several modern ideologies, none of which proposes to restore the sacred to culture—to restore the state of Christian equilibrium. On the contrary, their objective is to construct a post-Christian civilization. From today's fin de siècle vantage point, we distinguish two main ideological currents: the one grouped around the search and struggle for the Ideal City, the other centered around the hope provided by the Superman. The first is a Christian heresy that I would characterize as utopianism; the second is a return to pre-Christian paganism. The first has practically exhausted itself as a collective myth; the second does not seem to have the breath to stretch beyond the individual to become a collective myth. The first floats in an indiscernible future; the second looks back to an indistinct past. The first is gradually being rejected as it compromises with totalitarian causes; the second cannot be adhered to because its myths lack transcendental foundations. The first has killed God; the second can produce only the sage with nothing to teach humanity. Nonetheless, neither ideology has exhausted all its energy to agitate. Indeed, the second is yet on the rise. But neither is capable of transcendence; neither can replace the transcendent; and neither can meet the needs of the human soul.[17]

---

17. The impotence of going beyond God or of remaining this side of him is well illustrated in Hubert Reeves's statement: "The cosmos is the matrix of the anthropos who recreates it with his logos." Quoted (from Reeves's forthcoming book, *L'évolution cosmique ou Patience dans l'azur*) by Pierre Solié, "Physique et psychanalyse," *Contrepoint* (Paris), no. 36 (April 1981): 13. More simply put, the universe is indeterminate; humanity supplies it with meaning. Except for the new vocabulary, we have not surpassed Feuerbach.

Index of Names

Abel 10
Abellio, Raymond 139, 144, 183
Abraham 33, 104, 124
Adonis 10, 179
Aeschylus 137
Agni 81
Albert of Saxony 51
Alberti, Leon Battista 54
Alcuin 51
Alexander the Great 28
Alexandre, Noël 159
Ambrose, St. 14
Anaxagoras 44
Apollo 11, 16, 139
Apollonius of Tyana 21, 33
Ardrey, Robert 133
Aristotle 19, 20, 21, 24, 26, 50, 52, 54, 64, 68, 83, 91
Arnobius 27, 34
Ashtarte 7, 10, 93
Athena 112
Augustine, St. 13, 23, 29, 37, 46, 47, 48, 53, 174, 178, 179
Augustus 47
Averroës 61, 77, 185, 186

Baader, Franz von 186
Baal 42
Bach, Johann Sebastian 105
Bacon, Francis 186
Bacon, Roger 68
Balzac, Honoré de 137
Barthes, Roland 122
Basham, Arthur 153, 154, 156, 169
Basilides 34
Bayle, Pierre 94

Beauregard, Costa de 145
Benedict, St. 52
Benoist, Alain de 94, 99, 100, 116, 121, 125, 126, 134, 172
Bergier, Jacques 143
Bergson, Henri 42
Bernanos, Georges 162
Binswanger, Ludwig 131
Bodin, Jean 57, 66, 67, 68
Boehme, Jakob 188
Boethius 51
Bohr, Nils 136
Bonaventure, St. 20, 54
Bossuet, Jacques-Benigne 105, 178
Brenan, Gerald 177
Broglie, Louis de 136
Bruno, Giordano 63, 64, 65, 67, 68, 74, 99, 126, 135, 175
Buber, Martin 39, 40, 162
Büchner, Eduard 175
Buddha 41, 82, 86, 102, 149, 154
Bultmann, Rudolf 88, 89, 148
Buonaiuti, Ernesto 39, 92, 188
Burckhardt, Titus 44, 166
Buridan, Jean 51
Busson, Henri 63
Butterfield, Herbert 52

Cabiri 10
Cain 10
Campanella, Tommaso 68, 69
Campbell, Joseph 10, 11, 37, 39, 84, 87, 99, 128, 148, 171, 173
Capra, Fritjof 137
Cardanus 63
Cassirer, Ernst 74

197

Index of Names

Cau, Jean 141
Celsus 32, 45, 67, 117
Cervantes 105
Charlemagne 52
Chateaubriand, Francois-René de 84
Chaudhuri, Nirad 169, 182
Cicero, Marcus Tullius 19, 20, 24
Cleanthes 48
Cochrane, Charles Norris 47
Comte, Auguste 175
Condorcet, Marquis de 175
Constantine 52
Corbin, Henry 9, 103, 188, 193, 194
Cusa, Nicholas of 51, 70, 71, 72, 73, 74, 75, 76, 80, 135
Cusanus. *See* Cusa, Nicholas of

Dales, Richard 45
Danilevsky, Nikolay 175
Dante 7, 51, 54, 91, 137
De Corte, Marcel 35, 36
De Koninck, Charles 108
De Lubac, Henri 159, 182
Demeter 7, 9
Democritus 57
Denziger, Heinrich 108, 191
Descartes, René 21, 25, 50, 186
Des Périers, Bonaventure 62
Detienne, Marcel 12
Dill, Samuel 26, 32, 61
Dionysius the Areopagite (Pseudo-Dionysius) 52, 70, 72, 74, 159
Dionysus 11, 16, 110
Dodds, E.R. 12, 13, 179, 181, 182
Dolet, Etienne 63
Dostoyevski, Fyodor 162
Duby, Georges 161
Duhem, Pierre 44
Dumézil, Georges 121, 128
Duns Scotus 20
Durand, Gilbert 91, 92, 181, 186, 193
Dürer, Albrecht 141
Durkheim, Émile 128

Eckhart, Meister 70, 74, 75, 159, 188
Eibl-Eibesfeld, Iranäus 133
Einstein, Albert 136
Eliade, Mircea 9, 13, 40, 42, 66, 90, 100-103, 128, 129, 133, 144, 158, 171, 172, 181, 186
Eliot, T.S. 142
Empedocles 26, 57

Epictetus 33
Epicurus 24, 25, 44, 136, 160, 175
Erasmus, Desiderius 57
Eriugena, John Scotus 70
Evola, Julius 142
Eysenck, Hans 128

Faust 86
Feibleman, K. 176
Ferguson, Wallace 56
Festugière, A.J. 25
Feuerbach, Ludwig 190, 196
Fichte, Johann G. 159
Fink, Eugen 185
Francis, St. 30, 115, 154
Frazer, James 11, 128
Freud, Sigmund 38, 92, 130, 131
Frois, Louis 159

Galileo 21, 51, 68, 91
Gandillac, Maurice de 36, 74, 75
Gassendi, Pierre 21, 76
Gay, Peter 94
Germanus, Gyula 173, 174
Gerson, Jean 70, 71
Gilgamesh 10, 86
Gilmore, Myron 54, 55
Giorgi, Francesco 69
Girard, René 11, 17, 128, 129, 130, 171, 172
Goethe, J.W. 10, 13
Gogarten, Friedrich 148
Gordian, Emperor 35
Grunebaum, Gustav E. von 153
Guardini, Romano 170
Guénon, René 43, 80, 101, 102, 108, 109, 129, 142, 146, 150, 157, 170, 171, 186
Guillebaud, Jean-Claude 15

Hazard, Paul 94
Hegel, G.W.F. 112, 117, 126, 175, 177, 178, 190
Heidegger, Martin 122, 123, 124, 126, 133, 141, 142, 144, 171, 183, 190, 195
Heinrichs, Maurus 155
Heisenberg, Werner 136
Henry, Paul 36
Heraclitus 121
Hercules 86
Herder, Johann Gottfried 53
Hesiod 59, 95

Index of Names

Hesse, Hermann 139, 140, 144, 183
Hobbes, Thomas 76
Hoffmansthal, Hugo von 131
Hölderlin, Friedrich 112, 123, 124
Homer 59, 95
Hume, David 186
Huxley, Aldous 166
Huxley, Thomas 175

Indra 81
Iranaeus 33
Isaac 104
Isaiah 115
Isis 7, 93, 152

Jaki, Stanley 50, 151
Jason 86
Jaspers, Karl 88, 89, 174
Joachim of Fiore 54
Joad, C.E.M. 103
John of the Cross 30, 154
Jonas, Hans 123
Judas 151
Julian, Emperor 10, 32, 53, 117, 139
Jung, C.G. 12, 13, 17, 38-42, 84, 89, 90, 102, 128, 131-134, 144, 166, 167, 172, 181, 183, 186
Jünger, Ernst 142
Justinian, Emperor 52
Juvenal 22

Kant, Immanuel 72, 186, 190
Katz, Joseph 35
Kepler, Johannes 51, 66, 91, 105
Kerényi, Karl 9, 10, 11, 17
Kern, Otto 9
Kierkegaard, Søren 162, 186
Klibansky, Raymond 52
Koyré, Alexandre 21
Küng, Hans 96-100, 104, 148, 149

Lacombe, Olivier 158
Lamb, Ursula 14, 15
Lamennais, Hughes-Félicité de 115
La Mettrie, Julien de 76, 133
Larsen, Stephen 165
Lawrence, D.H. 16
Leeuw, Gerardus van der 9
Leibniz, G.W. 105
Leisegang, Hans 9, 182
Lessing, G.E. 94, 190
Lévi-Strauss, Claude 128, 129, 130, 165, 171, 181, 186

Lévy-Bruhl, Lucien 11, 12
Lewis, C.S. 16
Locchi, Giorgio 82
Lorenz, Konrad 128, 133
Lucretius 19, 20, 21, 46, 76, 135, 175
Lupasco, Stephane 136, 137
Luther, Martin 57

Mach, Ernst 175
Machiavelli, Nicolo 68
Magna Mater 53, 93, 152
Mahathera 155
Malaparte, Curzio 140
Malebranche, Nicolas de 186
Malinowski, Bronislaw 17
Malraux, André 142
Marcion 39
Marcus Aurelius 20, 21, 24, 26, 33, 61, 71
Marcuse, Herbert 184
Marra, William A. 93
Marsilio Ficino 56, 57, 65, 66
Marsilio of Padua 80, 161
Marx, Karl 116, 175, 177, 178
Maurras, Charles 115
Maximus of Tyre 33
Medici, Cosimo de' 56, 65, 66
Milet, Jean 189, 190
Milton, John 105
Mishima, Yukio 142
Mithra 10, 31, 33, 53, 152
Mohammed 153
Momigliano, Arnaldo 48, 49
Montaigne, Michel de 21, 63
Moses 57, 64, 103, 187
Müller, Max 128

Napoleon 173
Needleman, Jacob 44, 166
Nero 26, 61
Newton, Isaac 105
Nietzsche, Friedrich 11, 112, 117, 118, 122, 126, 127, 134, 142, 143, 145, 148, 176, 183
Nock, A.D. 164, 179
Numenius 57

Ockham, William of 20, 50, 161
Odysseus 7, 86, 112
O'Keefe, Cyril B. 94
Olivier, Maurice 137
Oresme, Nicole d' 51, 71
Orpheus 7, 33

Osiris 10, 179
Otto, Rudolf 156
Otto, Walter 9, 12, 16

Panovsky, Erwin 56
Paolini, Fabio 69, 70
Pascal, Blaise 105, 162
Paul, St. 7, 48, 78, 154, 174, 179
Pauwels, Louis 143, 144
Pericles 44
Persephone 9
Philo Judaeus 41
Pico della Mirandola 57, 66, 67, 74, 97, 105, 144, 147
Planck, Max 136
Plato 13, 19, 20, 22, 24, 25, 26, 28, 30, 32, 34, 47, 52, 57, 59, 60, 65, 67, 68, 121, 152, 179, 181, 182
Pliny 24
Plotinus 22, 24, 27, 29, 30, 32-37, 44, 47, 48, 72, 74, 83, 148, 152, 159, 179
Plutarch 24, 33
Pluto 9
Polybius 12
Pompey 5
Pomponazzi, Pietro 63, 73
Porphyry 27
Puech, Henri-Charles 9, 28
Purusha 81, 82
Pyrrho 59
Pythagoras 19, 23, 26, 28, 30, 32, 57, 64, 67, 68

Quispel 173

Racine, Jean 105
Rahner, Hugo 37
Raspail, Jean 140, 141, 145
Rembrandt 105
Reeves, Hubert 196
Remus 10
Renan, Ernest 86
Renard, A. de 156, 159
Reuchlin, Johannes 57
Rhea Sylvia 41
Ricoeur, Paul 102, 106, 111, 128
Riencourt, Amaury de 170
Robinson, J.A.T. 41
Rohde, Erwin 9
Romulus 10, 41
Roux, Dominique de 139, 140, 142, 145

Rudolf, Emperor 66
Russell, Bertrand 175, 178
Rüstow, Alexander 170
Ruyer, Raymond 135, 136, 176

Saccas, Ammonius 33
Sainte-Marie, Joseph de 158, 192
Sankara 156, 159
Schelling, F.W.J. 186
Schillebeeckx, Edward 103, 148
Schleiermacher, F.E.D. 187
Schmitt, Paul 9
Schopenhauer, Arthur 148, 186
Sciacca, M.F. 119
Seneca 19, 20, 21, 22, 31, 33
Serapis 31, 53
Severus, Alexander, Emperor 33, 57, 105
Seznec, Jean 70
Shayegan, Daryush 186
Siger of Brabant 54
Skinner, B.F. 133
Snell, Bruno 113
Socrates 23, 179
Solié, Pierre 196
Spengler, Oswald 93, 142, 170, 171, 175
Spinoza 21, 66, 118, 186
Stephen, St. 149
Strauss, Leo 126
Strayer, Joseph 52
Suckert, Kurt (Curzio Malaparte) 140
Suetonius 22
Suger of Saint-Denis 54, 91, 161, 162
Symmachus 14
Sylvester, Pope 149

Tacitus 22
Tagore, Rabindranath 182
Tauler, Johannes 74, 75
Teilhard de Chardin, Pierre 76, 176
Tempier, Etienne 45
Teresa of Avila 30, 154
Theodosius, Emperor 14
Theseus 86
Thomas à Kempis 70, 71
Thomas Aquinas 20, 54, 55, 59, 64
Thot 65
Thucydides 178
Tiamat 111, 170
Tiger, Lionel 143
Tillich, Paul 181, 190

Index of Names

Titans 10, 18, 111, 114
Toynbee, Arnold 93
Tresmontant, Claude 29
Trismegistus, Hermes 57, 65, 67, 68, 86
Tucci, Giuseppe 187

Ullmann, Walter 52

Vade, Yves 15
Valentinus 34
Vancourt, Raymond 190
Vernant, Jean-Paul 12
Vico, Giambattista 75, 93, 118, 119, 120, 121, 177
Voegelin, Eric 126
Voltaire 76, 94

Wade, I.O. 95
Walker, D.P. 69, 70
Weil, Eric 189, 190
Weil, Simone 109
Wili, Walter 9, 22
Wilson, E.O. 128, 133, 143, 144, 145
Wind, Edgar 74
Wunenburger, J.-J. 191
Wycliffe 161

Yates, Frances 57, 64
Ymir 81

Zeus 10, 18, 27, 48, 110, 175
Zimmer, Heinrich 93
Zoroaster 57, 67, 68